the
voice of hope

the
voice of hope

Aung San Suu Kyi

conversations with

Alan Clements

Seven Stories Press/New York

A Seven Stories Press First Edition

Published by Seven Stories Press
632 Broadway, 7th Floor
New York, NY 10012

In Canada:
Hushion House, 36 Northline Road, Toronto, Ontario M4B 3E2, Canada

First published in France under the title La voix du défi: Conversations Alan
Clements by Stock, Paris, 1996.

Library of Congress Cataloging-in-Publication Data

Aung San Suu Kyi.
[Voix du défi. English]
The Voice of hope / Aung San Suu Kyi; with Alan Clements
p.   cm...
ISBN 1-888363-50-9
1. Aung San Suu Kyi. 2. Democracy—Burma. 3. Pacifism—
Religious aspects—Buddhism. 4. Burma—Politics and
government—1988-   I. Clements, Alan, 1951-   . II. Title.
DS530.A8613 1997
959.105′092—dc21   97-23640
CIP

Book design by Adam Simon.
Printed in the U.S.A.

10 9 8 7 6 5 4 3 2 1

CONTENTS

AUNG SAN SUU KYI is the leader of the struggle for human rights and democracy in Burma. Born in 1945 as the daughter of Burma's national hero Aung San, she was two years old when he was assassinated, just before Burma gained the independence to which he had dedicated his life. After receiving her education in Rangoon, Delhi, and at Oxford University, Aung San Suu Kyi then worked for the United Nations in New York and Bhutan. For most of the following twenty years she was occupied raising a family in England (her husband is British), before returning to Burma in 1988 to care for her dying mother. Her return coincided with the outbreak of a spontaneous revolt against twenty-six years of political repression and economic decline. Aung San Suu Kyi ("Suu" to her friends and family) quickly emerged as the most effective and articulate leader of the movement, and the party she founded went on to win a colossal electoral victory in May 1990. In July 1989 she was put under house arrest and the military junta that now rules Burma refused for six years either to free her or to transfer power to a civilian government as it had promised. Upon her release in July 1995 she immediately resumed the struggle for political freedom in her country.

Aung San Suu Kyi is an honorary fellow of St. Hugh's College, Oxford. In 1990 she was awarded the Thorolf Rafto Prize for Human Rights in Norway and the Sakharov Prize for Freedom of Thought by the European Parliament. In 1991 she was awarded the Nobel Peace Prize. In its citation, the Norwegian Nobel Committee stated that in awarding the Prize to Aung San Suu Kyi, it wished to "honour this woman for her unflagging efforts and to show its support for the many people throughout the world who are striving to attain democracy, human rights and ethnic conciliation by peaceful means."

Aung San Suu Kyi is the author of several books, including *Freedom from Fear*, which was edited by her husband, Dr. Michael Aris; *Letters from Burma;* and *The Voice of Hope*.

ALAN CLEMENTS is a journalist, a writer and a worldwide lecturer on Buddhist psychology, human rights and spiritual-social activism. He is the founder and co-director of the Burma Project USA, a human rights organization based in Mill Valley, California. He is the author of *Burma: The Next Killing Fields?* (1991) and co-author of the photographic book, *Burma's Struggle for Democratic Freedom and Dignity* (1994). He lived in Burma for nearly eight years, five of which were spent living as a Buddhist monk in Rangoon. He has returned numerous times to witness and document human rights abuses in that country. In addition, he was an advisor and script revisionist for *Beyond Rangoon* (1995), a feature film depicting Burma's struggle for democracy. Clements has been interviewed for ABC (*Nightline*), CBS (*Evening News*), *Newsweek*, *Time* and scores of other media throughout the world.

INTRODUCTION

This book claims nothing more than its basic intention: to set down an exceptional series of conversations with a unique woman, currently, the world's most famous political dissident, Aung San Suu Kyi—recipient of the Nobel Peace Prize and numerous other prestigious international awards for her courageous leadership in a non-violent struggle to bring justice, freedom and democracy to the people of Burma. Aung San Suu Kyi is, in the words of Václav Havel, one of the most outstanding examples of the power of the powerless.

Aung San Suu Kyi tells her own story in conversations compiled over the course of nine months—from October 1995 to June 1996—at her home in Rangoon. A rare glimpse into this extraordinary woman's values and philosophy is thus provided through her own words. She explains why she has chosen to risk everything in order to join, and ultimately lead, the struggle waged by the Burmese people, "large numbers of men and women who daily risk their lives for the sake of principles and rights that will guarantee...a...dignified existence." This book is a journey into the soul of that struggle set in the volatile context of present-day Burma, a South-East Asian nation of 45 million people, many of whom, at this very moment, may be risking their lives to win the right to choose their destiny.

I should like to mention why the book is arranged as it is— a series of conversations transcribed in their integrity just as they actually took place. Originally my plan was to conduct them following a strict chronological and thematic order. However, once in Burma, I had to abandon this outline. I had no idea how uncertain the situation was to become, despite Aung San Suu Kyi's release. It should be understood that she faced and continues to face the possibility of rearrest at any moment. In addition, I risked being deported from the country at any time. (Actually I have now been blacklisted from Burma permanently, as I was informed when I recently applied for a visa at the Paris embassy.) Each of our conversations took place with the full knowledge that it might be the last. With that in mind I chose to cover a range of topics in each session rather than concentrate on any single topic. So what you read is what occurred. Only slight editorial modifications, approved by Aung San Suu Kyi herself, have been made to the transcript of our interviews.

The story of how this book came into being is complex and warrants some explanation, which may also help towards an understanding of how the crisis in Burma has developed.

My involvement with Burma goes back to 1977 when I first arrived on a visa which allowed me a maximum stay of just seven days to explore the possibility of receiving ordination as a Buddhist monk and residing in a monastery to practice the dhamma—the teachings of the Buddha. All that I knew of Burma was that it preserved an ancient Buddhist culture, with approximately 1,000,000 monks and nuns living within the 5,000 or so monasteries scattered throughout the country. I was surprised to discover that the country was also a totalitarian "terror state" ruled by General Ne Win—a xenophobic, eccentric and ruthless dictator.

In March 1962, after seizing power in a military coup, General Ne Win's new Revolutionary Council had suspended the constitution and immediately sealed off the country from all outside scrutiny. Promoting an isolationist policy which he called the Burmese Way to Socialism, he expelled foreign journalists, nationalized most industrial and economic institutions, throttled the press, and established a police state based on fear, repression and torture.

At the expiration of my visa I left Burma determined to return to fulfill my wish of practicing Buddhism under the guidance of monks in this 2,500-year-old tradition. In 1979 I was granted a long-term "monastic" visa and so was allowed to become a monk. I resided in a monastery in Rangoon for the best part of the next eight years. Over these years I could feel the national tension mounting. Individuals who came to the monastery frequently spoke of their hopelessness and desperation, the corruption and deprivations they were suffering. Twice during this period certain bank notes were withdrawn, rendering worthless nearly 70 percent of the currency. With the monasteries dependent on the people's support, we felt the impact of these devaluations directly—our food supplies were drastically reduced. Shortly afterwards I was refused an extension of my visa, so I left the monastery and returned to the United States.

In March 1988, small groups of Burmese students took to the streets of Rangoon demanding radical political change. To defy Ne Win's dictatorship was unprecedented, and the results of this courageous confrontation were predictable. In one incident alone forty-one wounded students suffocated to death in a police van. These cruelties served only to invigorate the determination and commitment of the students' movement, which progressively gained momentum.

At the end of March, Aung San Suu Kyi, who was residing in Oxford with her husband Dr. Michael Aris, a British scholar, and their sons Alexander and Kim, received a fateful telephone call telling her that her mother had suffered a severe stroke. Within days Aung San Suu Kyi, who had made regular visits home to Burma during her twenty-three-year residence abroad, was back again in Rangoon at the bedside of her dying mother. Aung San Suu Kyi was the daughter of Burma's most famous and revered leader, Aung San, who had led his country to national independence in 1947 after nearly 150 years of colonial domination.

On 23 July 1988, to the astonishment and jubilation of the entire nation, Ne Win, in a televised address, announced his resignation from his party, the BSPP (Burma Socialist Program Party) and called for a referendum on Burma's political future. After almost three decades of his iron-fisted rule the people were electrified by his unimaginable decision. But hopes of a quick transfer of power from a dictatorship to an authentic democracy were thwarted, as Ne Win's party members immediately opposed his request. Outraged, and in a magnificent display of defiance, millions of citizens marched peacefully in every city and town throughout the country, calling for an interim civilian government, a democratic multi-party system with free and fair elections and a restoration of basic civil liberties. As these demonstrations gathered momentum, military commanders loyal to Ne Win responded by sending out thousands of crack infantry troops with orders to kill.

"Many thousands of us knelt down in front of the soldiers," a female student demonstrator later reported. "We sang to them: 'We love you; you are our brothers; all we want is freedom; you are the people's army; come to our side.'" The results of what became known as "The Massacre of 8-8-88" were tragic, surpassing even the carnage a year later in China's Tienanmen Square. During the bloodbath, several thousand unarmed demonstrators were killed and hundreds more injured. In the aftermath thousands more were imprisoned.

But from this suffocating darkness came a glimmer of hope, as a new leader emerged. On 26 August 1988 Aung San Suu Kyi announced her decision to enter the struggle for democracy at a rally attended by an estimated 500,000 people, who had gathered on the grounds near the Shwedagon Pagoda in Rangoon. "This great struggle has arisen from the intense and deep desire of the people for a fully democratic parliamentary system," she explained. "I could not, as my father's daughter, remain indifferent to all that was going on."

The movement began to gather enormous support. In her inspired campaign, Aung San Suu Kyi advanced in the footsteps of Mahatma Gandhi and Martin Luther King, employing tactics of non-violence and civil disobedience in pursuit of democracy. Her essential message of self-responsibility, rooted in Buddhism, developed into a high-minded political ideology that she calls Burma's "revolution of the spirit."

On 18 September 1988, as democratic changes seemed imminent, the "retired" dictator Ne Win manipulated the army from behind the scenes to take over the country in a staged coup. He turned over the rule of Burma to a twenty-one-member group of military commanders known as the State Law and Order Restoration Council (SLORC). SLORC reinstated martial law: gatherings of more than four people were punishable by imprisonment; a night curfew was imposed and military tribunals replaced the civil courts. Fanning the flames of dissent in a nation already embittered by the August massacres, many thousands were arrested by the SLORC.

The SLORC held out a hope to appease the outrage by announcing "free and fair multi-party elections" in the spring of 1990. Within three months, over 200 parties had registered with the SLORC election committee. By far the strongest and most popular of these was the National League for Democracy (NLD), co-founded by Aung San Suu Kyi and several of her closest colleagues.

Observers and democratic leaders soon realized that the SLORC olive branch was simply a feint, as the military viciously harassed supporters of democratic parties. In 1989 and 1990 the *New York Times* reported that over 500,000 Burmese citizens were being forcibly herded from major urban centers into disease-ridden "satellite towns." The areas evacuated by the SLORC were known to be strongholds of the democracy movement and home to supporters of Aung San Suu Kyi.

Meanwhile on 20 July 1989 Aung San Suu Kyi was put under house arrest and other party leaders were incarcerated.

On 27 May 1990 elections were held and Aung San Suu Kyi's NLD party won a landslide victory, taking 392 of the 485 seats contested—more than 80 percent of the constituencies. Instead of transferring power to the elected representatives as promised, SLORC instigated a nationwide crackdown, imprisoning many elected MPs. Some fled the country into exile, others were silenced in different ways.

From those turbulent days onward many events have taken place within Burma, far too many to recount here. One fact stands out. Despite her release on 11 July 1995, following six years under arrest, Aung San Suu Kyi told me quite frankly in our first conversation four months after her release: "Nothing has changed since my release.... Let the world know that we are still prisoners within our own country."

This is the setting of our story, within the oppressive and maniacal atmosphere of the SLORC's Burma, a totalitarian prison, a nation held hostage; and from within that prison comes the voice of defiance and hope, waiting to be heard.

I entered Burma in October 1995 never having met or spoken to Aung San Suu Kyi. Yet she was not unknown to me. During the preceding seven years I had written a book about the crisis in her country, entitled *Burma: The Next Killing Fields?**; and I had compiled and co-authored a second one, a photographic documentation titled *Burma's Revolution of the Spirit.*** I had also served as an advisor and script re-writer for *Beyond Rangoon*, a feature film directed by John Boorman that depicts Burma's struggle. Furthermore, I had watched many hours of videotapes smuggled out of Burma. I read many of Aung San Suu Kyi's speeches and asked questions about her of anyone I could meet who either knew her or had met her. I lectured extensively on Burma's democracy movement, especially on how it interrelates with Buddhism. And from everything I had learned, I was fascinated by Aung San Suu Kyi, as were so many others. She offered me, as she does to all, a great vision that places self-respect, human dignity, compassion and love above material and economic considerations.

I knew nothing about her of a personal nature, and apart from some brief, basic historical facts pertaining to her past which are recorded in this book, both in her words and mine, Aung San Suu Kyi's private life remains locked away from the glare of public scrutiny. Placed under house arrest, separated from her family for years at a time, she kept silent, and so grew into a living legend. Finally released and, once again, speaking defiantly and acting boldly to unlock the prison doors of SLORC's totalitarianism, she will not be stopped.

This is the Aung San Suu Kyi that I came to know—a dynamic woman with an unshakable conviction, inseparable from her principles and sustained by a sense of justice and duty. She abhors hypocrisy, while admitting to her own shortcomings. Her compassion is tangible. The one quality that I feel best defines her is sincerity. At the core of that quality lies the conviction in self-improvement. Aung San Suu Kyi is a seeker—a soul pilgrim—one who makes her life a vehicle for an awakening to deeper and greater truths. She wears her spirituality quietly, unpretentiously, and with subtlety. But this casualness makes it all the more delightful. She laughs easily and freely.

Aung San Suu Kyi is like fine porcelain, a beauty whose features are as classical as a Japanese haiku; nothing is out of place, neither the flowers in her hair, nor the perfectly pressed traditional

---

* *Burma: The Next Killing Fields?* by Alan Clements, Foreword by the Dalai Lama. Odonian Press: Tucson, Arizona, 1992.
** *Burma's Revolution of the Spirit* by Alan Clements and Leslie Kean. Aperture: New York, 1994.

Burmese dress she wears with such elegance. Her voice is harmonious and sweet, tonally punctuated with the skill of a musician. Her words are simple, so simple at times as to take you by surprise, yet spoken without equivocation. She is straight and direct.

Does she have faults? She would be the first to admit to having some. Was I satisfied with my conversations with her? Ultimately, I wanted more than she was willing to give. Aung San Suu Kyi is a fiercely private woman, secret about her personal life and any aspect of her inner world that she deems private. I found her to be like a sealed vault in some areas and an open universe in others. Slowly, I came to realize that my desire for more was of my making, not hers. As she stated in our first conversation, "Please ask what you want to, but I hope that you'll expect me to answer in the way I would like to answer." Aung San Suu Kyi is her own person in every sense and it was this aspect of our time together that I most appreciated: a woman enjoying her sovereignty and happiness while fighting for the independence of others.

This book concludes with two conversations with Aung San Suu Kyi's main colleagues, U Tin U and U Kyi Maung. Both share a commanding role in the National League for Democracy (NLD), the party that Aung San Suu Kyi co-founded with them in September 1988. Their inclusion in the book was the sole condition placed upon me by Aung San Suu Kyi.

Indeed, their contributions help to define Aung San Suu Kyi herself more clearly, as well as providing a dynamic dimension to their shared involvement in the struggle for democracy.

So, how did we begin?

It was early December 1995 and for six weeks I had been holed up in a hotel room in Rangoon waiting for a telephone call from Aung San Suu Kyi's office to give me an appointment to proceed with our first taped conversation. Back in early October, when we initially discussed the project, she explained: "Our situation is unpredictable under the SLORC, so please be patient. And of course there are no guarantees about how far we'll get, but let's try." As she walked me to the door she stopped and said: "My father used to say, 'Hope for the best and prepare for the worst.' I think this is always the best approach."

Day by day, the political crisis was intensifying. By late November, after the NLD party delegates had withdrawn from the SLORC's internationally condemned National Convention, Aung San Suu Kyi and her two main colleagues, U Tin U and U Kyi Maung, came under increasing attack in Burma's only English-language newspaper, the SLORC's *New Light of Myanmar*. Twelve pages of military slogans, racist and xenophobic propaganda and almost daily half-page editorials denounced Aung San Suu Kyi and her colleagues in violent terms. The military promised to "annihilate" those "destructionists" who disrupted the "tranquillity of the nation."

On Thursday 30 November, I was walking along dark lanes for my appointment with the NLD Deputy Chairman, U Tin U, a dear old friend. We had been Buddhist monks together after his release from prison in 1980. From a nearby monastery the sound of monks chanting reverberated through the stillness: "*Annica vatta sankara upadavio dhammino*"—"All things are impermanent in this world." I slowed my pace and as the chanting faded, I abruptly stopped in front of U Tin U's home. Eight armed military police looked me coldly in the eyes.

I walked past the police, opened the large gate and hurried up to the front door. U Tin U's wife greeted me with a determined stare and said, "He's upstairs gathering his medicines and a few belongings. I'll get him for you."

Minutes later U Tin U came down. "Don't worry," he said smiling. He took me gently by the hand and escorted me back to the door. "You shouldn't be here. Daw Aung San Suu Kyi is preparing to be re-arrested too. She's preparing papers for the transfer of party leadership and directions on what to do. Go on, you shouldn't get yourself in trouble too."

Once back at my hotel, I fired off a short fax to my publisher stating that "the book is very likely off," packed my bags and went to sleep planning to leave Burma the next afternoon.

But, the following day, the telephone rang early in the morning, and the voice of Aung San Suu Kyi's foreign media coordinator, U Aye Win (arrested by SLORC on 21 May 1996 and still in prison), informed me, "Your appointment and first conversation with Daw Aung San Suu Kyi will take place on Monday at 3:30."

At 3:20 p.m. sharp, I knocked on the large iron gate of 54 University Avenue. I was quickly ushered in by several NLD youth members—a dedicated group of young men who live within Aung San Suu Kyi's compound and act as her unarmed security guards (some were arrested in May 1996). They escorted me over to SLORC's Military Intelligence checkpoint—a small wooden structure just inside the gate. The MI chief asked me to sign in and list my particulars, while another man stepped out of the hut and photographed me. Then they nodded me on and immediately returned to playing chess and reading their books.

The large white stucco colonial-style villa, situated at the end of a long palm-tree lined driveway on the banks of Inya Lake, was a bit run-down with peeling paint and large water-stains from the torrential monsoon rains. But I liked it that the house was in disrepair. It somehow added stature to the structure. Also, there was a tangible serenity to the place, like an oasis, a calm island within the totalitarian repression outside the compound.

As I was waiting under the large porch near the front door, U Aye Win peeked his head out and said, "Please come in." He took me through the foyer and ushered me into a spacious high-ceilinged living room. "Daw Aung San Suu Kyi will be with you shortly."

I stood there gazing at history. A large batik portrait of her father *Bogyoke* Aung San dominates one wall. Several old framed photographs of Aung San Suu Kyi as a young girl with her family are hung on the other ones. Otherwise the room is empty except for a wooden chair, a small round iron table with a vase of flowers in the middle next to a Japanese teapot with two cups, and a long straight-backed sofa that contours to the wall beneath a large curtained bow-window.

I went outside on to the veranda. The lake was tranquil, while a gentle breeze was a cool relief from the heat and the echoing silence of the room.

Precisely at 3:30 the door opened and Aung San Suu Kyi entered the room. She looked radiant and energetic yet balanced with a calm confidence—a graceful determination that highlighted the sprigs of tiny white orchids in her jet black hair. But it was her warmth and sense of immediacy that set me at ease. She sat down on the edge of the sofa and said with a smile, "Well, let's get on with this book." I pressed "Record" and the story began.

> *Any achievement that is based on widespread fear can hardly be a desirable one, and an 'order' that has for its basis the coercive apparatus of the State, and cannot exist without it, is more like a military occupation than civil rule... it was the duty of the ...State to preserve...dharma and abhaya — righteousness and absence of fear. Law was something more than mere law, and order was the fearlessness of the people.*

One of the many scrolls Aung San Suu Kyi wrote and posted on the walls of her downstairs foyer during her house arrest. The passage is a quotation from the writings of Jawaharlal Nehru.
LESLIE KEAN/THE BURMA PROJECT USA

Chapter 1

"We are still prisoners in our own country"

ALAN CLEMENTS: Your father—Aung San—is perhaps the most famous man in Burma's long history. His name today, over fifty years after his death, still evokes awe in the people. He was a spiritual seeker, a heroic freedom fighter and a great statesman. And when you entered your nation's struggle for democracy on 26 August 1988, you announced in your speech, delivered at the Shwedagon Pagoda and attended by more than half a million people, that you were "participating in this struggle for freedom...in the footsteps and traditions of my father." You have also said, "When I honor my father, I honor all those who stand for political integrity in Burma." Daw Suu, it is here that I would like to begin to explore your story and try to understand what moves you to struggle for your people's freedom. What does political integrity mean to you?

AUNG SAN SUU KYI: Political integrity means just plain honesty in politics. One of the most important things is never to deceive the people. Any politician who deceives the people either for the sake of his party or because he imagines it's for the sake of the people, is lacking in political integrity.

<u>AC:</u> What about SLORC's "political integrity"?

<u>ASSK:</u> Well... (*laughs*) sometimes one wonders whether they actually know what political integrity means, because they've deceived the people repeatedly. They've made promises which have not been kept.

<u>AC:</u> Like not honoring the results of their "free and fair" elections in 1990 in which your party, the NLD [National League for Democracy], won a landslide victory? What has been the SLORC's official

explanation of why they have not honored the results?

ASSK: There has not been a real explanation. But you can see SLORC has not let the elected representatives play any meaningful role in the drawing up of the new constitution. In the National Convention nobody is allowed to speak freely. The NLD has not even been allowed to protest against undemocratic working procedures. That is why we decided to stay away from the convention until a meaningful dialogue has been successfully initiated.

AC: In examining the crisis in Burma it is so easy to focus on the vast divisions between those struggling for democracy—the NLD—and the ones oppressing democracy—SLORC. Perhaps it's a premature question, but are there actual places of goodwill and trust between both sides—areas where you find some sense of genuine connection?

ASSK: I would like to think there are but we have not been given an opportunity to find out. This is why we say that dialogue is so important. How can we find out if there are places where we can meet, issues on which we can work together, unless we talk to each other? But I heard a rather shocking report about an interview of one of the SLORC ministers by a foreign journalist. The minister said, "You can do anything with money. If you hold a ten dollar note above a grave, a hand will come out and reach for it. And if you held out a hundred dollar note, the whole body would come out." That seems to indicate that they have no principles whatsoever. If they think that everyone can be purchased with money, that's a shocking revelation.

AC: Sounds like a sociopathic fantasy...

ASSK: Well...one wonders, why? Why are they like that? I do not think they're interested in the why. There is a phrase the authorities like to use: "We don't want to hear about a leaking water bottle. We only want the water." That means, just do what we tell you, with no excuses. All we want are results. That's a very strange attitude.

AC: How would you define the collective psychology of SLORC?

ASSK: My impression of them as a whole is that they do not know what communication means. They don't communicate, either with the people or with the opposition. And I wonder whether they even communicate with each other. If everybody in SLORC shares this minister's attitude, that money is what decides everything, then I have this rather unhappy image of them simply shoving dollar bills at each other.

AC: Is it fair to say that the regime—SLORC—are Buddhists?

ASSK: I would not like to comment on other people's religious inclinations. It's not for me to say who is Buddhist or who is not. But I must say that some of their actions are not consonant with Buddhist teachings.

AC: For example?

ASSK: There's so little loving-kindness and compassion in what they say, in what they write and what they do. That's totally removed from the Buddhist way.

AC: Removed from people?

ASSK: Yes. This is the problem with a lot of authoritarian regimes, they get further and further away from the people. They create their own isolation because they frighten everybody, including their own subordinates, who feel unable to say anything that would be unacceptable.

AC: Yes, I've noticed that. Back in 1990, when I was in the jungle along the Thai-Burma border, I witnessed SLORC's "ethnic cleansing" campaign against the Karens, and to an extent against the Mons and Shans, as well as their attempt to exterminate the armed democracy forces based in the hills near Mannerplaw. At that time I interviewed a SLORC commander who had been captured after a fire-fight...

ASSK: How did they treat him?

AC: Humanely. This, I can testify to. Not only the SLORC officer but also the privates who had been captured. But I asked this commander, "Why are you killing your own people?" He brought out of his pocket a picture of himself as a monk and said, "I don't like killing, but if I don't kill, I will be killed." He then started to cry. His tears looked real...

ASSK: Why did he enter the army if he was so against killing? Was there nothing else he could do?

AC: I asked that same question to a group of young SLORC conscripts who were being held in the stockade; "Why do you kill?" And they replied, "If we don't kill we're killed." Then I asked what you asked me: "But why did you enter the army?" They all said the same thing: "If we don't join the army our families are abused. We have no money, there's no other source of income, there's no work, it's the only way we can give money to our parents, otherwise they can't eat."

ASSK: Yes, I have heard that in some parts of the country there is a lot of forced conscription—they do force villages to produce a certain number of conscripts for the army.

AC: Thousands of Burmese students have fled the country as well as hundreds of thousands of refugees from the time of SLORC's coup in 1988. Obviously, you're here in Rangoon struggling with your people for democracy but what about all those other disenfranchised people living in squalor, many of them weakened by starvation, or dying of disease? What are your feelings about those citizens of the nation?

ASSK: It is so they can come back that we're fighting for democracy in this country. Where will they come back to if we can't make this place safe for them? The people need a country where they can feel safe.

AC: What are your feelings specifically towards the young students?

ASSK: We have said from the very beginning that the NLD will never disown students who are fighting for democracy, even though they have chosen to take up arms and we have chosen the way of non-violence. Because we are not in a position to guarantee their security, we do not have the right to demand that they do what we want them to do. We look forward to the day when we can work together again.

AC: Many peace settlements are occurring around the world—in the Middle East, in the former Yugoslavia, possibly in Northern Ireland and of course, the miracle that's occurring in South Africa. SLORC has a precious opportunity to follow suit—a reconciliation could occur. Now, you have repeatedly called for dialogue, but what is it that's preventing SLORC from saying "Daw Aung San Suu Kyi, let's say hello, have lunch together, and see where it goes from there?"

ASSK: This is exactly what I meant when I said they do not know how to communicate. I think they're afraid of dialogue. I think to this day, they do not and cannot understand what dialogue means. They do not know that it's a process that is honorable, that it can lead to happiness for everybody—including themselves. I think they still see dialogue as either some kind of competition in which they might lose or as a great concession which would disgrace them.

AC: It sounds like fear. What do you think this fear is rooted in?

ASSK: When you really think about it, fear is rooted in insecurity and insecurity is rooted in lack of *metta* [loving-kindness]. If there's a lack of *metta*, it may be a lack in yourself, or in those around you, so you feel insecure. And insecurity leads to fear.

AC: In South Africa, Archbishop Desmond Tutu is leading the Council for Truth and Reconciliation. Already, the former Defense Minister under the apartheid regime has been indicted for his complicity in the murder of thirteen people while in power. Now, if we were to put ourselves in the minds of some of SLORC's main players—I would think that fear would be a legitimate concern. In other words, they have good reason to be insecure. Won't the people seek revenge after democracy is won?

ASSK: I think here they [SLORC] underestimate both the people and us as a movement for democracy. Obviously, there is some hatred among the people, especially among those who have suffered. However, we are confident that we can control this hatred. But there is no hate among the leaders of the NLD. The authorities find this difficult to understand. There are many in SLORC who feel strongly against Uncle U Kyi Maung,* Uncle U Tin U,** and even U Win Htein [Aung San Suu Kyi's personal assistant who spent six years in Insein Prison and was re-arrested on 21 May 1996],

---

* "Uncle" is used here as a term of respect.
** As above

23

because they are ex-military men who are actively involved in the democratic process.

I think SLORC's reading of the situation is this: if these men, who themselves were in the military, are opposing them, they must be doing so out of vindictiveness. I do not think it occurs to them that these ex-military officers are supporting the democracy movement because they believe in certain principles. It goes back to what I just told you about waving a dollar note above a grave: people who think that any-body can be bought, that human minds and hearts are mere com-modities subject to the laws of supply and demand, such people would not be able to understand other human beings who work for a cause and are prepared to sacrifice themselves for that cause.

Mind you, none of these people we are talking about have done well out of joining the movement. They've suffered and their families have suffered, but they're still going on. And it's not as though they are unaware that they could be subjected to even more suffering.

AC: When and if "genuine dialogue" begins between you and SLORC, what would be the first item of discussion?

ASSK: Well, if we got to the dialogue table, the first thing I would like to say is, "You tell us what you have to say." I would like to lis-ten to them first. Why are you so angry with us? What is it that you object to? Of course, they may say, we object to your criticisms. But we've always pointed out that we've been very careful not to attack anybody personally. But criticize we have to, that is part of our duty. Otherwise how can we hold our heads up as a political party that represents the interests of the people? We have to point out whatever is against the interests of the people. If we know that something is detrimental to the good of the people and we don't say anything about it, that would be sheer cowardice.

AC: Many peace settlements have been brokered by middle people, a mediator or intermediary. Have you ever thought about offering that as an option?

ASSK: We don't need an intermediary because we're always prepared to open dialogue at any time.

AC: Is Ne Win [Burma's "retired" dictator] really the person you want to open a dialogue with?

ASSK: I don't know...I really don't know. That is what some people say. But I have no hard evidence either for or against the theory that he is still the power behind the throne.

AC: When you call for dialogue, are you calling for a dialogue with Ne Win or with SLORC?

ASSK: We're calling for a dialogue with SLORC. But if we had absolute proof that he's behind everything that SLORC is doing, then perhaps we would decide to seek dialogue with him.

AC: Yesterday, before your public talk began, a Rangoon University student asked me bluntly: "Should Burma's democracy movement engage in an armed struggle rather than continuing in a non-violent way?"
I told him I would ask you the question.

ASSK: I do not believe in an armed struggle because it will perpetrate the tradition that he who is best at wielding arms, wields power. Even if the democracy movement were to succeed through force of arms, it would leave in the minds of the people the idea that whoever has greater armed might wins in the end. That will not help democracy.

AC: Daw Suu, how effective is non-violence in the modern world, and more specifically, with regimes that seem devoid of sensitivity or any sense of moral shame and conscience?

ASSK: Non-violence means positive action. You have to work for whatever you want. You don't just sit there doing nothing and hope to get what you want. It just means that the methods you use are not violent ones. Some people think that non-violence is passiveness. It's not so.

AC: Let me ask the question in another way. In your country there were numerous brave young men and women who literally faced the bullets and bayonets, in their willingness to be non-violently active, yourself included. And the results left at least 3,000 dead.

25

Do you ever have doubts about the effectiveness of non-violent political activism in the face of armed aggression?

ASSK: No, I don't have any doubts about it. I know that it is often the slower way and I understand why our young people feel that non-violence will not work, especially when the authorities in Burma are prepared to talk to insurgent groups but not to an organization like the NLD which carries no arms. That makes a lot of people feel that the only way you can get anywhere is by bearing arms. But I cannot encourage that kind of attitude. Because if we do, we will be perpetuating a cycle of violence that will never come to an end.

AC: It's a matter of debate, but politics and religion are usually segregated issues. In Burma today, the large portion of monks and nuns see spiritual freedom and socio-political freedom as separate areas. But in truth, *dhamma* and politics are rooted in the same issue—freedom.

ASSK: Indeed, but this is not unique to Burma. Everywhere you'll find this drive to separate the secular from the spiritual. In other Buddhist countries you'll find the same thing—in Thailand, Sri Lanka, in Mahayana Buddhist countries, in Christian countries, almost everywhere in the world. I think some people find it embarrassing and impractical to think of the spiritual and political life as one. I do not see them as separate. In democracies there is always a drive to separate the spiritual from the secular, but it is not actually required to separate them. Whereas in many dictatorships, you'll find that there is an official policy to keep politics and religion apart, in case I suppose, it is used to upset the *status quo*.

AC: The Burmese monk U Wisara, who died years ago while in prison, after 143 days of a hunger strike, was an outstanding example of politically motivated non-violent protest. Indeed, Burma has a long history of monks and nuns being actively engaged in political areas when it concerns the welfare of the people. However, I wonder about today. With the crisis at such a critical moment, do you think that the *Sangha*—the order of monks and nuns—can play a greater role in supporting the democracy movement? After all, it's their freedom too.

26

ASSK: Well, there are a lot of monks and nuns who have played a very courageous role in our movement for democracy. Of course, I would like to see everybody taking a much more significant role in the movement, not just monks and nuns. After all, there is nothing in democracy that any Buddhist could object to. I think that monks and nuns, like everybody else, have a duty to promote what is good and desirable. And I do think they could be more effective. In fact, they should help as far as they can. I do believe in "engaged Buddhism," to use a modern term.

AC: How might they be more effective?

ASSK: Simply by preaching democratic principles, by encouraging everybody to work for democracy and human rights, and by trying to persuade the authorities to begin dialogue. It would be a great help if every monk and nun in the country were to say, "What we want to see is dialogue." After all, that is the way of the Buddha. He encouraged the *Sangha* to talk to each other. He said, "You can't live like dumb animals. And if you have offended each other, you expiate your sins and offenses by confessing them and apologizing."

AC: What do you think is preventing the *Sangha* from saying to those SLORC generals who visit their monasteries, "What we want to see is dialogue?"

ASSK: I don't know. I do not think there is anything in the *Vinaya* [monastic discipline] that says that monks should not talk about such things, or is there? I do not know. You're more familiar with the *Vinaya* than I am because you were a monk. Is there anything that says that you cannot say such things?

AC: I don't know of any rule that says you can't tell the truth. But perhaps, there's some blind separation going on...

ASSK: I see...

AC: I know that you occasionally pay your respects to the Venerable Sayadaw U Pandita at his monastery, here in Rangoon. May I ask you to share some aspect of his teachings that you have found helpful?

ASSK: I remember everything he has taught me. The most important of which was that you can never be too mindful. He said you can have too much *panna*—wisdom—or too much *viriya*—effort; but you cannot overdo mindfulness. I have been very mindful of that (*laughing*) throughout these last seven years.

Also, he advised me to concentrate on saying things that will bring about reconciliation. And that what I should say should be truthful, beneficial, and sweet to the ears of the listener. He said that according to the Buddha's teachings, there were two kinds of speech: one which was truthful, beneficial and acceptable; and the other which was truthful, beneficial but unacceptable, that is to say that does not please the listener.

AC: Throughout my years of lecturing on both Buddhism and Burma's struggle for democracy, I've encountered many people who wish to label you in heroic terms. Even the recent *Vanity Fair* interview with you was entitled on the cover as "Burma's Saint Joan"...

ASSK: Good heavens, I hope not.

AC: Which raises my question. In strictly Buddhist terms, I have heard you referred to as a female *Bodhisattva*—a being striving for the attainment of Buddhahood—the perfection of wisdom, compassion and love, with the intention of assisting others to attain freedom.

ASSK: Oh, for goodness' sake, I'm nowhere near such a state. And I'm amazed that people think I could be anything like that. I would love to become a *Bodhisattva* one day, if I thought I was capable of such heights. I have to say that I am one of those people who strive for self-improvement, but I'm not one who has made, or thought of myself as fit to make a *Bodhisattva* vow. I do try to be good (*laughs*). This is the way my mother brought me up. She emphasized the goodness of good, so to speak. I'm not saying that I succeed all the time but I do try. I have a terrible temper. I will say that I don't get as angry now as I used to. Meditation helped a lot. But when I think somebody has been hypocritical or unjust, I have to confess that I still get very angry. I don't mind ignorance; I don't mind sincere mistakes; but what makes me really angry is hypocrisy. So, I have to develop awareness. When I get really angry, I have to be aware that I'm angry—I watch myself being angry. And I say to myself, well,

I'm angry, I'm angry, I've got to control this anger. And that brings it under control to a certain extent.

AC: Is it ironic that you're dealing with one of the world's most hypocritical regimes?

ASSK: But you know, I have never felt vindictive towards SLORC. Of course, I have been very angry at some of the things they've done. But at the same time I can sense their uneasiness—their lack of confidence in good, as it were. And I think it must be very sad not to believe in good. It must be awkward to be the sort of person who only believes in dollar bills.

AC: How do you perceive their uneasiness? Is it a sense of moral shame or moral conscience in them?

ASSK: I'm not talking about moral shame or moral conscience. I do not know if all of them have it. I have sadly learned that there are people who do not have a moral conscience. All I'm saying is that I think there must be a lot of insecurity in people who can only believe in dollar bills.

AC: When you speak to your people who gather in front of your house on weekends, do you in fact speak to SLORC, trying to appeal to that place in them that might make them pause and reflect on their actions? Or are you just speaking to your people?

ASSK: I'm talking to the people, really. Sometimes, of course, I'm also talking to SLORC, because a lot of the issues that I address are so closely linked to what the authorities are doing throughout the country. But basically I'm addressing people and I do think of SLORC as people. They do not always think of us, who oppose them, as people. They think of us as objects to be crushed, or obstacles to be removed. But I see them very much as people.

AC: During the last month I've spoken with a lot of Burmese people in markets, shops, vendors on the street, and construction workers. I've asked them how they feel about the conditions of their country under SLORC. Almost everyone says that they are afraid of SLORC's wrath; afraid of retribution; afraid that if they speak out they'll pay for it with imprisonment. So in time, I've come to appreciate the importance of your words, "Fear is a habit; I'm not afraid." But is that true, Daw Suu, are you not afraid?

ASSK: I am afraid. I'm afraid of doing the wrong thing that might bring harm to others. But of course, this is something I've had to learn to cope with. I do worry for them though.

AC: Several thousand people attend your weekend talks in front of your house. Three students were recently arrested and sentenced to two-year prison terms...

ASSK: Yes. But one must ask why the USDA [Union Solidarity Development Association], which is supposed to be a social welfare organization but is in fact used by SLORC as its political arm, besides disrupting the activities of the NLD, is having enormous rallies which people are forced to attend.

AC: U Kyi Maung was telling me about this. Are people fined if they don't attend these SLORC-instigated rallies to chant slogans in support of their National Convention?

ASSK: Yes. I had a letter from somebody from Monywa saying that they were made to attend this rally. And every household that could not send a member had to give fifty kyats. For poor people these days, fifty kyats is a lot of money.

AC: How poor is poor in the countryside?

ASSK: You don't have to go to the rural areas...just go out to a satellite township like Hlaingthayar [near Rangoon] and take a look. They can't afford to have two meals of rice a day. Some can't even afford to have one. So they are forced to drink rice water instead of eating rice.

On the other hand, some have gotten very rich in Burma—rich as they have never been before. This is an aspect of life today that disturbs me very much—the gap between the rich and the poor has gotten so wide. You must know that there are restaurants and hotels in which people throw away tens of thousands of kyats a night [the official bank rate is 6 kyats to $1]. And at the same time there are people who have to drink rice water to survive.

30

AC: I know that 80 percent of Burma's population live in the rural areas, and most are farmers. What are their conditions like?

ASSK: The peasants are really suffering. Farmers have told us that they have been forced to eat boiled bananas because they don't have rice to eat. If they can't grow enough rice to provide the quota they [are forced] to sell to the government, then they have to buy rice on the open market and sell it to the government at a loss because the government buys at a fixed price which is lower than the market price. And farmers who refuse to grow the second crop of rice have their land confiscated. The only reason why they refuse to sow a second crop is because they lose so much on it. Not only do they lose what little profits they've made on the first crop but they end up with huge debts. Yet the authorities insist that they must grow a second crop.

You see, when people start deceiving others, in the end they deceive themselves as well. And the authorities seem to imagine that if they make people grow two crops of rice they will get twice the amount of rice to export, without considering the fact that the second crop of rice may well affect the next crop.

AC: Does torture still go on in Burma's prisons? And do you have evidence for this?

ASSK: Yes, torture goes on in all the prisons of Burma. And yes, I do have evidence of this. But it is more important to try to understand the mentality of torturers than just to concentrate on what kind of torture goes on, if you want to improve the situation.

AC: How many political prisoners are still being detained by SLORC?

ASSK: I think it's in the four figures. We can't be certain because we are not even certain how many political prisoners there are in each of the prisons of Burma. The prisoners themselves do not know everybody who is there. They are kept apart.

AC: There is a lot of pent-up anger among some people in this country towards the SLORC. When and if your struggle for democracy succeeds, and perhaps you assume a major leadership role in a democratic Burma, can you guarantee that SLORC will not face criminal charges?

ASSK: I will never make any personal guarantees. I will never speak as an individual about such things. It is only for the NLD to speak as an organization—a group that represents the people. But I do believe that truth and reconciliation go together. Once the truth has been admitted, forgiveness is far more possible. Denying the truth will not bring about forgiveness, neither will it dissipate the anger in those who have suffered.

AC: Could you envision a Truth and Reconciliation Council in Burma after she gains her freedom?

ASSK: I think in every country which has undergone the kind of traumatic experience that we have had in Burma, there will be a need for truth and reconciliation. I don't think that people will really thirst for vengeance once they have been given access to the truth. But the fact that they are denied access to the truth simply stokes the anger and hatred in them. That their sufferings have not been acknowledged makes people angry. That is one of the great differences between SLORC and ourselves. We do not think that there is anything wrong with saying we made a mistake and that we are sorry.

AC: Are there listening devices in your house?

ASSK: Perhaps there are, I don't know.

AC: Does it concern you?

ASSK: No, not particularly. Because I'm not saying anything that is underhand. Whatever I say to you, I dare to say to them, if they would like to come to listen to me.

AC: Is your telephone tapped?

ASSK: Oh yes, probably. If it is not I would have to accuse them of inefficiency (*laughing*). It should be tapped. If not, I would have to complain to General Khin Nyunt [SLORC's Military Intelligence Chief] and say your people are really not doing their job properly.

AC: What does it feel like to be under such scrutiny all the time?

ASSK: I don't think of it. Most people I speak to on the telephone are just friends and we don't really have anything particularly important to say to each other. You say hello, how are you, I'm so happy to be able to speak to you. Then there are people ringing up for appointments. And my family rings me every week. But it's just, how's everybody, how are they getting on, what are your plans, can you get this for me, can you send me that (*laughing*)—that sort of thing. Nothing that I mind the Military Intelligence personnel hearing.

AC: So you feel no pressure whatsoever from all the unseen eyes, a tapped telephone, the Military Intelligence men everywhere, and of course, that ever present threat of re-arrest—nothing at all?

ASSK: I'm not aware of this pressure all the time. But sometimes, of course, I am. For example, somebody from America, whom I had not met for years, rang up. His brother had been in Rangoon recently, and he started talking about his brother's meetings with some people in the government. I said, "You do realize that my telephone is tapped. Do you intend that everything you say be heard by the MI?" And he said, "Oh, yes, yes." But he hung up pretty quickly after that, so it was quite obvious that it had not entered his head that my telephone would be tapped. On such occasions, I am aware of my unusual circumstances.

AC: Are measures taken by your colleagues for your security?

ASSK: You see the students who are outside at the gate, on duty as it were. They don't have weapons or anything like that. We screen people who come in to see me. I don't see everybody who says they want to see me. Apart from that, what else are we supposed to do?

AC: Well, you're dealing with a rather violent regime. Has SLORC either directly or indirectly ever verbally threatened your life?

ASSK: You do hear the authorities saying "We'll crush all these elements who oppose whatever we are trying to do," and so on and so forth. One hears that sort of thing all the time.

AC: Soon after Nelson Mandela was released after his imprisonment, the international media began labeling you "the world's most famous political prisoner." May I ask your comments about that?

ASSK: I'm not one of those people who think that labels are that important. Recently somebody asked if I felt that I had less moral authority now that I was free. I found it a very strange question. If your only influence depends on you being a prisoner, then you have not much to speak of.

AC: So despite your years of detention, you never felt like a prisoner?

ASSK: No, I have never felt like a prisoner because I was not in prison. I believe that some people who have been in prison also did not feel like prisoners. I remember Uncle U Kyi Maung saying that sometimes he used to think to himself when he was in prison: "If my wife knew how free I feel, she'd be furious." (*laughing*) And just yesterday, somebody interviewing me for a television program asked, "How does it feel to be free? How different do you feel?" I said, "But I don't feel any different." He asked, "How is your life different?" I said, "In practical terms my life is different, of course. I see so many people; I have so much more work to do. But I do not feel at all different." I don't think he believed me.

AC: U Tin U* told me that being imprisoned for his love of freedom was one of the most dignified fruits of his life. But he seems to be quite happy to be out and about again. Was it the same for you? Were you happy to reconnect to life and intimate relationships?

ASSK: I never felt cut off from life. I listened to the radio many times a day, I read a lot, I felt in touch with what was going on in the world. But, of course, I was very happy to meet my friends again.

AC: But Daw Suu, you were cut off from life in a fundamental way. You were cut off from your family, your husband, your children, your people. Cut off from your freedom of movement, of expression.

ASSK: I missed my family, particularly my sons. I missed not having the chance to look after them—to be with them. But, I did not feel cut off from life. Basically, I felt that being under house arrest was just part of my job—I was doing my work.

AC: You have been at the physical mercy of the authorities ever since

---

* See Appendix 2.

you entered your people's struggle for democracy. But has SLORC ever captured you inside—emotionally or mentally?

ASSK: No, and I think this is because I have never learned to hate them. If I had, I would have really been at their mercy. Have you read a book called *Middlemarch* by George Eliot? There was a character called Dr. Lydgate, whose marriage turned out to be a disappointment. I remember a remark about him, something to the effect that what he was afraid of was that he might no longer be able to love his wife who had been a disappointment to him. When I first read this remark I found it rather puzzling. It shows that I was very immature at that time. My attitude was—shouldn't he have been more afraid that she might have stopped loving him? But now I understand why he felt like that. If he had stopped loving his wife, he would have been entirely defeated. His whole life would have been a disappointment. But what she did and how she felt was something quite different. I've always felt that if I had really started hating my captors, hating the SLORC and the army, I would have defeated myself.

This brings to mind another interviewer who said that he did not believe that I was not frightened all those years under house arrest. He thought that at times I must have been petrified. I found that a very amazing attitude. Why should I have been frightened? If I had really been so frightened I would have packed up and left, because they would always have given me the opportunity to leave. I'm not sure a Buddhist would have asked this question. Buddhists in general would have understood that isolation is not something to be frightened of. People ask me why I was not frightened of them. Was it because I was not aware that they could do whatever they wanted to me? I was fully aware of that. I think it was because I did not hate them and you cannot really be frightened of people you do not hate. Hate and fear go hand-in-hand.

AC: Your country's prisons are filled with prisoners of conscience. Perhaps copies of this book will be smuggled into the prisons. What might you say to those men and women?

ASSK: They're an inspiration to me. I'm proud of them. They should never lose faith in the power of truth. And they should keep in mind what Shcharansky once said, "Nobody can humiliate you but your-self." Keep strong.

AC: One final question. Daw Suu, back in 1989, days before you were placed under house arrest, you made the statement: "Let the world know that we are prisoners in our own country." It has been a few months since the time of your release. Has anything really changed?

ASSK: The world knows better that we are still prisoners in our own country.

Chapter 2

"Running away is not going to solve any problems"

ALAN CLEMENTS: Daw Suu, I would like to ask you more about engaged Buddhism. I spent a few months in Vietnam this year and outside the city of Hue I visited the monastery of the first Vietnamese Buddhist monk who immolated himself back in 1963. A young monk gave me a photograph of his burning and explained that the "immolation was not an act of destruction or suicide but an act of compassion; his way of drawing world attention to the staggering suffering the Vietnamese people were forced to bear during the war." There is no doubt that such an act of engaged Buddhism is extreme. But that image prompts me to ask you how engaged Buddhism, in whatever expression it may take, could be more activated today, especially among the 1,000,000 monks and 500,000 nuns in your own country?

AUNG SAN SUU KYI: Engaged Buddhism is active compassion or active *metta*. It's not just sitting there passively saying, "I feel sorry for them." It means doing something about the situation by bringing whatever relief you can to those who need it the most, by caring for them, by doing what you can to help others.

Of course, the "sending of loving-kindness" is very much a part of our Burmese Buddhist training. But in addition to that we have got to do more to express our *metta* and to show our compassion. And there are so many ways of doing it. For example, when the Buddha tried to stop two sides from fighting each other, he went out and stood between them. They would have had to injure him first before they could hurt each other. So he was defending both sides. As well as protecting others at the sacrifice of his own safety.

In Burma today, many people are afraid to visit families of political prisoners in case they too are called in by the authorities and harassed. Now, you could show active compassion by coming to the families of political prisoners and offering them practical help and by surrounding them with love, compassion and moral support. This is what we are encouraging.

AC: But fear so often overwhelms the heart before compassion has a chance to become active. As you have said, "fear is a habit." Just the other day I was at a shop in the city xeroxing a letter to a friend and accidentally dropped the paper on the floor. The shopkeeper picked it up and while he was handing it back to me he noticed in capitals the letters "NLD." He panicked and began ripping the paper into small pieces. I asked him, "Why?" and he replied with a rather frightened face, "NLD means prison."

ASSK: You should have told him not to be ridiculous.

AC: I don't think he's the only one who is afraid. But how can this "active compassion" express itself out on the street, to the common folk, among those where "fear is a habit"?

ASSK: These things are happening because there is not enough active compassion. There is a very direct link between love and fear. It reminds me of the biblical quotation, that "perfect love casts out fear." I've often thought that this is a very Buddhist attitude. "Perfect love" should be *metta* which is not selfish or attached love. In the *Metta Sutra* [a discourse by the Buddha] we have the phrase "like a mother caring for her only child." That's true *metta*. A mother's courage to sacrifice herself comes out of her love for her child. And I think we need a lot more of this kind of love around the place.

AC: I don't mean to challenge you, but I was mugged earlier this year while waiting in a Paris subway station. And if my aggressor hadn't sprayed me in the eyes with mace I certainly would have put up a fight. Afterwards, it made me think of the magnitude of violence in the world. We do need a lot more love around the place, but love is often an ideal. You use the metaphor of a mother's courage to sacrifice for her child and a love that embraces even his faults, but this "child" is slitting the throats of his neighbors...

ASSK: I think you have not quite understood what I've been saying. You see, we've got to make *metta* grow. We've got to make people see that love is a strong, positive force for the happiness of oneself, not just for others. A journalist said to me, "When you speak to the people you talk a lot about religion, why is that?" I said, "Because politics is about people, and you can't separate people from their spiritual values." And he said that he had asked a young student who had come to the weekend talks about this: "Why are they talking about religion?" The student replied, "Well, that's politics."

Our people understand what we are talking about. Some people might think it is either idealistic or naïve to talk about *metta* in terms of politics, but to me it makes a lot of practical good sense. I've always said to the NLD that we've got to help each other. If people see how much we support each other and how much happiness we manage to generate among ourselves, in spite of being surrounded by weapons, threats and repression, they will want to be like us. They might say, well, there's something in their attitude— we want to be happy too.

AC: Presuming the day comes when the NLD and SLORC come to the table for dialogue, with a regard for truth and reconciliation, who will in fact determine the truth from fiction?

ASSK: What we need when we come to dialogue is confidence, in ourselves as well as in each other. Truth does not become such a problem if there is confidence in each other. Quite often people tell lies because they are afraid to tell the truth, which means that they don't have enough confidence in the other person's understanding or sense of compassion. When we talk about the connection between truth and reconciliation, we have also got to remember that another very necessary ingredient is trust in each other. With trust, truth and reconciliation will follow naturally.

AC: You've said that the core psychological quality which drives a repressive authoritarian regime is "insecurity." How could someone who fundamentally operates from fear, which is really a mistrust of oneself, ever expect to bring genuine trust to a truthful dialogue?

ASSK: That's a very thought-provoking question. Perhaps what they should try to do is to love themselves better. Not in the selfish sense, but to have *metta* for themselves as well as for others. As you put it, if fear is motivated by lack of trust in oneself, it may indicate that you think there are things about yourself which are not desirable. I accept that there are things about me, as for the great majority of us, which are undesirable. But we must try to overcome these things and improve ourselves.

AC: I wonder if, when you call for a dialogue with SLORC, you're perhaps indirectly inviting them to have a more honest dialogue with themselves, with that long-forgotten place inside of them that yearns, like inside all of us, to be trusted and loved?

ASSK: I hope so. You know...I understand that they do not like it when I criticize what is going on. As a politician—as somebody representing a political party working for democracy—it's my duty to say what needs to be said. Not criticizing implies either that you can't find anything to criticize, in which case there is no point in asking for change; or that you know that there are things which are not right, but you're too frightened to point them out. If you're working for democracy or a cause in which you believe, you ought to have the courage to speak up. Of course, nobody enjoys being criticized but I think you can learn to be more objective about it.

AC: Do you criticize with compassion or resentment?

ASSK: We have no time to feel resentment. And we help each other not to be vindictive. We have good relationships within the NLD, and I think it's our genuine care for each other that keeps out the nasty feelings, which as human beings we are all prone to.

AC: How do you help each other keep out feelings of vindictiveness?

ASSK: It's partly because we have a sense of humor. We've always had a great laugh over all the problems we've had to face, and all the (*laughing*) injustices and abuses that have been heaped on us.

AC: But it can't be just the humor. These generals have been vicious, abusive and slanderous. Then of course, your six years under house arrest and the separation from your family. When you lay on the mass of suffering your people have been forced to bear, imprisonment, torture...

ASSK: It's also because we, in the NLD, have been given a lot of *metta* by the people at large—our supporters. And when you receive so much, you have to give in return. If you're very much loved, in the right way, then you cannot help but respond. That does not mean that we're totally free of negative feelings. And as long as we are not free of them we will be subject to them. But the goodwill and the *metta* we've received have done a lot to push out these feelings from within us.

AC: Yes, the love you receive from the people at your weekend talks is quite evident.

ASSK: Yes, when I look at them I see how intelligently they follow everything that we are saying. They are interested and very sharp. We have an expression in Burmese: "You show them the shadow and they see the substance," as it were.

AC: Why do you think the people love and trust you so much?

ASSK: I think the very first reason why the Burmese people trusted me was because of their love for my father. They had never doubted his goodwill towards them. And he had proved with his life that he was ready to sacrifice himself for them. Because of that they loved him and I think a lot of that love was transferred to me. So I started off with an advantage—a ready-made fund of *metta* on which to build. So you cannot separate the fact that I'm my father's daughter from the fact that the people and I have managed to build up solid bonds of *metta* between us.

AC: I've read that you have an enormous affection for the army and would like it to be an institution the people could respect. With that statement, and assuming Burma becomes a democratic nation with you as her leader, I ask, how can you, "Burma's Gandhi," a woman politician firmly rooted in non-violent principles, become Chief of Staff of the army? It would be hard to imagine Gandhi walking past saluting columns of armed soldiers.

ASSK: Of course, in politics there are bound to be inconsistencies. But as I see it, the main responsibility of the army is to protect and defend the people. If we lived in a world where it was not necessary to defend ourselves, there would be no need for armies. But I do not envisage that in the near future the world would be such that we can afford to be without protection. I would like to think of the army as a force of protection rather than a force of destruction.

And there's always the question of *cetena* [right intention]. The *cetena* of the army should be right. I once had a talk with an army officer who was full of hatred for the Communists whom he had fought. And I said, "I find this very disturbing that you fought them out of a sense of hatred. I would like to think that you were fighting motivated by a love for the people you were defending rather than out of hate for those whom you were attacking." That's what I mean by *cetena*. Of course, one may argue this is splitting hairs. If you are killing the enemy, can you be motivated by love?

AC: The war that I've seen didn't look loving. What do you think?

ASSK: This is a very interesting question. I would have thought that in the heat of the battle few people would be motivated by love for those they wish to defend, by love of justice. This is the motivation with which you should enter the army and go into battle, but we are mere mortals and not *arahants* [enlightened ones]. I wonder though, whether it would be possible for anybody to keep this sense of love in the heat of the battlefield. But I'm not sure whether you're motivated by any sense of hate either. I'm inclined to think that you are taken through it by training. You must ask the ones who've actually been to battle, Uncle U Tin U and Uncle U Kyi Maung. They've fought in the war and must have killed people.

AC: I've seen professional soldiers in combat and even though I was there as an non-combatant, it was a twilight zone...soldiers strung out on adrenalin.

ASSK: Was it hate that motivated them, or love? Or something else altogether?

AC: Well, in one instance the armed democratic forces were simply defending what little ground they had left to survive on. It was, I suspect, out of love for their people, homeland and principles that they were defending from SLORC's genocidal campaign. They acted as anybody would, I think, when faced with such brutality. It seemed like common sense.

ASSK: One could say that to maintain a professional, honorable army would be an act of common sense.

AC: I've heard that your weekend public talks are videotaped by SLORC. Is that true?

ASSK: Oh yes, I'm sure.

AC: The reason I ask is that I was told by quite a reliable source that a SLORC general's wife is eager to see your tapes.

ASSK: Oh, how nice!

AC: This gave me an idea. You ask for a dialogue with SLORC, who are obviously all hardened military men. Perhaps you could seek a dialogue with the generals' wives. You could have a chat with them, talk things over casually.

ASSK: (*laughs*) That's an idea isn't it? I've never thought of that.

AC: Burma is a matriarchal society…despite appearances.

ASSK: Well, I would very much like to have tea with them. It's so much nicer to be friends, isn't it? It's exhausting being enemies. I often think to myself: I wish they would all stop behaving like enemies. Why can't we all be friends? It would be so much better for everybody concerned.

AC: Your telephone number is in the phone book. It's just a call away…

ASSK: I know. And I'm one of those people who can never resist smiling at somebody who smiles at me sincerely.

AC: Was Ne Win the one behind your incarceration in 1989?

ASSK: I don't know. But it is a fact that I was incarcerated after I started criticizing him for the ruin he had brought on the country.

AC: Have you ever met him?

ASSK: When I was a young girl.

AC: I bring Ne Win's name into the situation for one reason. In the bigger picture, what we see in Burma today is rather archetypal. On the one hand, there's Ne Win—the man—and perhaps the longest-standing dictator in the world today—thirty-five years and counting. And you, the woman, who stands firmly for the principles of freedom and non-violence. There are enormous polarities between you and Ne Win. The masculine against the feminine. Weapons versus warmth. Repression embraced by forgiveness. It's all about that old male-dominated model of repressive rule, where "might is right," being challenged by a new feminine vision of equality, human dignity and power from kindness. From within the crisis could arise a biblical-like redemption. Or like King Ashoka's change of heart during the third century, a change from a violent monster to the most famous Buddhist king in history. Do you think that Ne Win is Buddhist enough to concern himself with redemption—going down in the annals of Burmese history as potentially a modern day King Ashoka? An opportunity is there. He has the moment.

ASSK: I think most Burmese regard themselves as Buddhists but a lot of us are Buddhists by inheritance, because our parents were Buddhists. I think there are a lot of Burmese who have not really studied Buddhism very deeply, beyond the basic Five Precepts,* and take it very much for granted. I think it would be a great idea if we all took a far deeper interest in our religious heritage and were serious about practicing our Buddhism, not simply professing it.

AC: What aspect of Buddhism could be more intimately embraced rather than intellectually conceived?

ASSK: You know, if we simply abided by the Five Precepts we would be home and dry (*laughing*).

AC: Maybe just the first precept, not harming sentient beings?

ASSK: That's not quite enough.

AC: The second too—not stealing?

---

* To undertake the Five Precepts of Buddhism is to abstain from taking life, taking what is not given, wrong conduct in sexual desires, telling lies and drinking intoxicating liquors which occasion heedlessness.

ASSK: The first two would be along the road, quite a lot. The first three, almost home and dry. Almost, but not quite, actually we need all five.

AC: It probably goes without mentioning but it seems rather obvious that among many SLORC generals you are dealing with some primitive emotions—a Stone-Age level of consciousness. But, as I said, I do believe in redemption. But perhaps it's wishful thinking. What do you think? Are some people just too far gone, that no matter what, they remain unredeemable?

ASSK: According to Buddhism, there were people whom the Lord Buddha himself could not redeem. So who are we to claim that we would be able to redeem everybody? Since we don't know who's redeemable and who's not, we have a duty to try. We can't just write off somebody as beyond the pale. We should give people the benefit of the doubt.

AC: I've watched many hours of videotape that were smuggled out of Burma, showing you traveling the country, speaking to the people, walking through rural villages as you campaigned for the elections. Of course, this was all prior to your incarceration. I was struck by the level of SLORC's harassment of you and your NLD colleagues.

ASSK: I've forgotten the harassment. In what way? Oh yes, in the Irrawaddy Division, particularly, there was a lot of harassment.

AC: The military gunboats packed with armed SLORC soldiers...

ASSK: That's right, when we were going down to the Irrawaddy, they [SLORC soldiers] would come up to us and play army music.

AC: Also, there were many other instances of SLORC soldiers with automatic weapons, brandishing bayonets, scolding people to return to their homes and not to greet you. Then of course, there is that famous Danabyu incident of you walking head-on towards a row of soldiers with their rifles aimed to shoot, with the captain in his countdown to fire. Could you recount that experience?

ASSK: I have never really dwelt on it very much nor have I written about it. From what I remember...my NLD colleagues and I had just come back after having spent the day traveling downriver to various towns and villages. We were accompanied by an army major of the troops in the area and by officers in their boat. We came back in the evening and were walking towards the house where we were to stay for the night. They were behind and I was in front. And in front of me was a young man holding our NLD flag. We were walking behind him in the middle of the street heading home for the night, that's all. Then we saw the soldiers across the road, kneeling with their guns trained on us. The captain was shouting to us to get off the road. I told the young man with the flag to get away from the front, because I didn't want him to be the obvious target. So he stepped to the side. They said, well, they were going to fire if we kept on walking in the middle of the road. So I said, "Fine, all right," we'll walk on the side of the road and we would divide forces. He replied that he would shoot even if we walked at the side of the road.

Now that seemed highly unreasonable to me (*laughing*). I thought, if he's going to shoot us even if we walk at the side of the road, well, perhaps it is me they want to shoot. I thought, I might as well walk in the middle of the road. While I was walking back the major came running up and had an argument with the captain. We just walked through the soldiers who were kneeling there. And I noticed that some of them, one or two, were actually shaking and muttering to themselves but I don't know whether it was out of hatred or nervousness.

AC: What happened between the SLORC major and the captain?

ASSK: Apparently, the captain tore the insignia off his shoulder. He threw it down and said, what are all these for if I'm not allowed to shoot? Or words to that effect. I had already gone. Those who were there told me what had happened.

AC: What went through your mind when it was happening?

ASSK: I was quite cool-headed. I thought what does one do? Does one turn back or keep on going? My thought was, one doesn't turn back in a situation like this. I don't think I'm unique in that. I've often heard people who have taken part in demonstrations say that when you are charged by the police you can't make up your mind in advance about what you'll do; it's a decision which you have to make there and then. Do I stand or do I run? Whatever you may have thought before, when it comes to the crunch, when you're actually faced with that kind of danger, you have to make up your mind on the spot…and you never know what decision you will make.

AC: Was that the only occasion that you experienced such a direct violent threat?

ASSK: It once happened in Rangoon, but not quite like that. There was an incident in Myenigon when a person was shot. We had come back from a ceremony at an NLD office. It was the anniversary of the day some demonstrators had been killed and I wanted to lay a wreath in memory of those people. We had chosen to do that on our way back at a rather isolated place on the road so that there would be no problems. But some students who were not part of the NLD had come along with us. They decided to lay a wreath at a place where it was far more controversial and there were lots of troops around. When these students laid down their bouquet a lot of troops poured in and started grabbing them. I was already starting to leave and I said, "We've got to turn back. We can't just leave those students because they were not members of our NLD youth." I turned back and I also laid my bouquet there, which was not our original intention. But I felt we had to demonstrate solidarity with others who are in the movement for democracy. I do not like this attitude, that if they don't belong to a political party we have no responsibility for them. And as we were driving away, the soldiers started shooting. So I said, "Turn back. We do not run away when people are shooting." We turned back and there was a policeman who was waving his gun, and shouting rude remarks, saying, "Don't run away." And we said, "We're not running away. In fact we have just come back."

AC: Is that your policy, when you hear gunshots, to go back and face the fire?

ASSK: Yes, don't run away. Running away is not going to solve any problems. We just wanted to know why they were shooting. What was it that they were so angry about? So we went back and asked them. But they didn't answer. They went away.

AC: Actions speak louder than words...

ASSK: We need to ask a lot of questions in this country and to answer them as well. That's the only way we will resolve our problems.

AC: A direct question. How are you affected by the SLORC's hatred towards you?

ASSK: It's just boring. What's that phrase?—"the banality of evil."

AC: People the world over have come to associate your name and life with bravery and fearlessness. Nevertheless, you consistently defer such compliments by saying that your NLD colleagues have suffered and been much more courageous than you...

ASSK: You know, when I was a child I was afraid of the dark, whereas my brothers were not. I was really the cowardly one in the family. This is probably why I find it very strange when people think I'm so brave.

AC: You really do find it strange, don't you?

ASSK: Yes, I find it rather strange (*laughing*). Some of the things that I do that others consider brave just seem normal to me.

AC: Like walking into a line of armed soldiers ready to shoot you?

ASSK: No, not that sort of thing.

AC: You don't see that as courageous?

ASSK: I don't know if I think of that as very courageous. There must be thousands of soldiers who do that kind of thing every day. Because unfortunately, there are battles going on all the time in this world.

AC: So the issue of your courage never arises in your mind? Not even a whisper of self-congratulation? Nothing?

ASSK: Perhaps it is only in the sense of my attitude towards the unjust actions of the authorities that makes me realize that, maybe, I have less fear than a lot of people in Burma. This is probably because I have lived in free societies for most of my life, that fear of the authorities has not become a habit. It's normal for me not to answer questions which I do not think other people have the right to ask me.

But a lot of people in Burma are so frightened that if the authorities question them, they just submit to the interrogation. They're conditioned to this kind of behavior.

AC: Daw Suu, is there a place in yourself—your inner edge—where you need to bring greater courage?

ASSK: There's always courage involved in making decisions, especially in our circumstances. It's not only because you think that it may harm you, but it's that your decisions may have wide-ranging consequences that you have to face and take responsibility for. Accepting responsibility is an act of courage.

AC: Given the escalating intensity of the crisis in Burma, that must keep you rather finely balanced on the razor's edge, so to speak.

ASSK: Well, we're always in the process of having to make decisions which entail a lot of responsibility, and in so doing we're always open to harsh actions by the authorities. But as I've said before, I'm very fortunate in having supportive and caring colleagues. We make decisions by consensus. So our courage is collective courage—individual courage which we pool together and the whole becomes larger than the sum of the parts.

AC: In one of your speeches, back in 1988, you said, "I always tell people to have high aspirations. Have the highest aspirations." If I may ask you, Daw Suu, what is your own highest aspiration?

ASSK: My highest aspiration is very much a spiritual one: purity of mind.

Chapter 3

"Truth is a powerful weapon"

ALAN CLEMENTS: Daw Suu, here in your country, speaking the truth is regarded as a punishable crime against the state, if that truth is unacceptable to the authorities. But why is "truth" so threatening?

AUNG SAN SUU KYI: Because the power of truth is great indeed. And this is very frightening to some people. Truth is a powerful weapon. People may not think so but it is very powerful. And truth—like anything that is powerful—can be frightening or reassuring, depending on which side you are on. If you're on the side of truth, it's very reassuring—you have its protection. But if you're on the side of untruth—then it's very frightening.

AC: What are your views on having the uncompromising conviction that speaking the truth is imperative, no matter what the circumstances or the consequences may be? Is honesty always the best policy?

ASSK: Honesty is the best policy. One should just do it openly. This is how I've always operated. It doesn't mean that I tell everybody everything. But if I'm asked about something, either I say what it is, or I just bluntly say: "I will not tell you." For instance, when the military intelligence came to try to interrogate me I just said that I would not answer. If I had answered I would have implicated other people, because what they were doing was trying to find out who was helpful to me, so they could get them.

AC: So the criteria for you in truth-telling are the implications for others?

ASSK: Yes. It's better not to answer than to deceive. Deceiving is an exhausting activity. It's true what Scott said, "O what a tangled web we weave, When first we practice to deceive!"

AC: Even when the challenge of honesty means weighing the risk of imprisonment, harassment to family, loss of job or even torture?

ASSK: You lose more by deception—that, you can be sure of. But, it's true that nothing comes without a price. However, it's always easier to accept the consequences of honesty rather than the consequences of deceit. All the times you have ever deceived anybody will stay with you for your entire life, whereas the consequences of honesty, in the long run, are never burdensome.

AC: How would you advise others to challenge the habit of deception?

ASSK: What I would say would be so simple, most people would not be able to accept it. I think you're just happier for not indulging in deceit. That's it.

AC: What, in essence, does truth mean to you?

ASSK: In the end, truth cannot really be separated from sincerity and goodwill. I cannot claim that in every situation I am able to see the truth. But one does one's best to be sincere in evaluating a situation, making an honest distinction between what is right and what is not. If you do so you are on the side of truth. But truth is a large concept. Pure truth—absolute truth—is beyond ordinary beings like us because we cannot see things absolutely and as a whole. But we try our best. I think of all of us who are on the side of truth as struggling towards it, rather than in full possession of it. Truth is something towards which we struggle all the time.

AC: To what extent is truth subjective, *vis-à-vis* ultimate truth?

ASSK: The search for truth is in a sense the struggle to overcome subjectivity. By that I mean that you've got to remove as far as possible your own prejudices and distance yourself from them in assessing any given situation.

AC: Learning the art of objectively relating to our subjectivity?

ASSK: The search for truth has to be accompanied by awareness. And awareness and objectivity are very closely linked. If you are aware of what you're doing, you have an objective view of yourself. And if you are aware of what other people are doing you become more objective about them too. For example, awareness means that when you are aware of the fact that somebody is shouting, you don't think to yourself: "What a horrible man." That's purely subjective. But if you are aware you know that he's shouting because he's angry or frightened. That's objectivity. Otherwise, without awareness, all kinds of prejudices start multiplying.

AC: I think it was Carl Jung who said that he "would prefer to become whole rather than good." What does it mean to you to quest towards "wholeness"? Does it have any relevance to you?

ASSK: Well, in the first place, one's got to find out what "good" means. When Jung said, "I'd rather be whole than good," what does he mean by "good"? Also, when one says that he wishes to be pure, you have to first discover what he means by purity. Like truth, it's a very large concept. It's something towards which you aspire and struggle all the time. If anybody says, "I have achieved purity," he or she is probably not that pure. I doubt that anybody who is not an *arahant* [enlightened one] could actually say, "There's no impurity in me." But I think that if you are in search of purity, you've got to know what impurity means. For people brought up in Buddhism, I don't think it's so difficult, because we have our concepts of greed, hatred and ignorance which create impurity. So anything that you can trace to ill-will and greed, that is impure. And anything that you can trace to ignorance, now that's a problem. How do you know that you are ignorant, if you are ignorant?

AC: It's rather difficult to be objective about what you don't see. It's a type of mental blindness, isn't it?

ASSK: Yes. But how do we recognize the areas of our own ignorance?

AC: Through awareness of our mistakes, and, of course, having good friends always helps.

ASSK: Yes. Good friends point it out.

AC: Of course you know the story of Ananda [the Buddha's attendant] when he asked the Buddha, "Venerable sir, it seems to me that half of the spiritual life is good friendship." And the Buddha corrected him by saying, "No, Ananda, the whole of the spiritual life is good friendship." What constitutes "good friendship" to you? You seem blessed to have many warm and generous people near to you.

ASSK: I have to say that I have been very fortunate in having been blessed with good teachers and friends all my life. But it's difficult to generalize about what forms the basis of friendship. I think first of all, you have to be interested in people, to see them as individuals, with their own worth and value. If you're interested in people and respect their point of view, you want to know more about them, which means that you listen to them, observe them, and learn from them. I think that is how friendship begins. Otherwise, if you're not interested in them, you don't notice what they are doing. Whatever they say or do makes no impression on you, and you learn nothing from them. I find my friends interesting. I value them. That's how they became my friends. We wanted to know more about each other, not out of a sense of vulgar curiosity but simply because we appreciated each other as individuals and were prepared to listen to each other. So in that sense, one of the important ingredients of friendship is the desire to know more about the other person. And the more you know, the more there is to appreciate about them.

AC: Is that another way of saying *mudita?*

ASSK: Whatever your friend achieves is a matter of joy for you. Because *mudita* is translated as sympathetic joy, isn't it?

AC: Normally it is, but I've always translated it as the ability to resonate and elevate with another person's happiness.

ASSK: Yes, that's a nice way of putting it.

AC: It's a rather obvious point to some, but it seems to me that many people often unconsciously use their friendships as a place to hide or escape. They play it safe, rather than engage the edge of truth and discovery together. I'd call it a collusion to maintain mediocrity—the status quo—and not to rock the boat.

<u>ASSK:</u> People do long for security. But your best friends are the ones who bring out the best in you, who make you feel good, because they encourage you to develop what is good in you, rather than what is bad. True friends have a way of pointing out what you should not do. Not in a hurtful or abrasive way, but totally constructively, encouraging you towards what is good for you and for others around you. That does not mean that friends are never critical. Sometimes it might be necessary for a friend even to be abrasive, just to bring one to his senses. But the intention must be based on *metta*.

<u>AC:</u> Is this where the priority in friendship becomes truth itself, rather than a blind alliance to protect each other from a painful truth?

<u>ASSK:</u> I don't think that people who are incapable of facing the truth are capable of making real friends. How can you make genuine friends if you are hemmed in by pretense and deceit?

<u>AC:</u> Daw Suu, it seems obvious that you're dedicated to facing the truth, but from where did it start? Or let me ask it this way: as a child did you have a vision of your future? Did you have a dream?

<u>ASSK:</u> I don't think I had such visions as a child. I was much more interested in playing. But later I went through phases. I think the first serious ambition I had was wanting to be a writer. That was when I became a bookworm and started discovering the world of books. Before then, I only read children's books and had not yet discovered what I would call real books. It was only when I was about twelve or thirteen that I started reading the classics. So by the time I was fourteen I was a real bookworm. For example, when I went shopping with my mother I would bring a book along. I could not read in a moving car because it always made me feel rather sick, but the moment the car stopped anywhere, I would open my book and start reading, even if it was at a traffic light. Then I would have to shut it and I couldn't wait for the next stop.

<u>AC:</u> Was becoming a writer the only real ambition that you had?

<u>ASSK:</u> Actually, when I was ten or eleven I wanted to enter the army. In those days the army was an institution which we thought of as very honorable because it was the institution founded by my father.

And everyone referred to my father as *Bogyoke*, which means General, so I wanted to be a general too because I thought this was the best way to serve one's country, just like my father had done. But things changed. So this is why I can say with absolute truth that I have great affection for the army—I'm not making it up. I really thought at one time that this was the way to serve my country. Up to then, of course, we had democracy in Burma, and the army was an institution that served the people and not one that took from them.

AC: Was it even possible to serve in your father's army as a woman?

ASSK: No.

AC: Being in Burma these last few months has made me think a lot about this issue. Do you feel that one's weaknesses or foibles can become strengths?

ASSK: You can turn anything into a strength, if you know how to go about it. Most people know that when somebody loses his sight his sense of hearing can become acute. But I think he's got to work at it. If somebody just sits there feeling glum because he's blind, he's not going to help himself in any way. But if he takes an interest in sounds and develops sensitivity of touch, then his weakness will not turn into a strength as such, but will help him to develop other strengths to compensate for the weakness. However, there has to be endeavor. You can't just sit there and hope that things will happen. You've got to work at it. I am a great believer in action, endeavor and effort.

AC: You have written: "Fearlessness may be a gift but perhaps more precious is the courage acquired through endeavor, courage that comes from cultivating the habit of refusing to let fear dictate one's actions." If truth is the basis of genuine dialogue, what is more precious than truthfulness itself?

ASSK: Sincerity and goodwill. I think they can carry us very far along the path of dialogue. People who are full of sincerity and goodwill tend not to be afraid of facing others. And I can say with full confidence that I've always been sincere in my dealings with SLORC.

There have been times when I have been very angry at things they've done, but I have never lost my goodwill towards them. I don't say that I am always in the right and I am prepared to be convinced by them that I have been wrong in certain ways. But I'm not afraid of facing them, at any time.

Also, I don't think any of them can say that I have ever deceived them in any way. There are those who have said to me: "You can't afford to be so honest with SLORC—they are not honest people. You've got to play by their rules." But I have always refused that line of reasoning. If they're deceiving me and I retaliate by deceiving them, how can we ever get to a position of trust? If they are deceiving me, it's all the more important that I don't deceive them.

AC: When you really delve into the recesses of your being, how do you determine that which is sincere from that which is deceptive?

ASSK: But don't you know?

AC: Well, generally yes, but in all honesty, I've been fooled more than once by my own false certainty. There are some fairly subtle, insidious voices inside. Delusion is a rather distorting and manipulative quality of consciousness, isn't it?

ASSK: That is something that I do not myself quite understand. When I was young, I was a normal, naughty child, doing things that I was told not to do, or not doing things that I was supposed to do. Like running away and hiding instead of doing my lessons. I didn't like to work or study. I preferred to play all the time. But I always knew when I was not doing what I should be doing. I might not have admitted it, but I knew when I was in the wrong. And I thought that older people too always knew when they were doing something that they felt they ought not to, even if they did not admit it. But since I have grown up I wonder whether there are people who actually do not know that what they are doing is not right. What do you think?

AC: Quite frankly, I think some people enjoy doing wrong convinced it is right. I've interviewed torture victims who speak about the perverse joy they witnessed in their torturer's face, the delight in inflicting pain. I think of genocidal psychopaths, rapists and murderers who in fact think of their atrocities as joys. Take for example this young Israeli who assassinated Prime Minister Rabin. I've watched news clips of him on the BBC and listened to his comments. He seems pathologically proud that he murdered Mr. Rabin. You see his face and it's bright, almost rapturous, and he speaks of his special liaison with God...

ASSK: Well, there are people who think that it's right to do anything in the name of their religion, their race, their family, or any organization to which they may belong. Does it come back to a matter of training?

AC: Training helps, but of course not every psychopath has parents who were also deranged. There are some people who seem devoid of moral shame. For example, let's take the case of SLORC who as a matter of policy oppress and torture at will. How could a sense of moral shame be fostered in them?

ASSK: In many ways, I find it quite difficult to accept that they're that different from us. After all, they are Burmese brought up in a Buddhist society. They could not be unaware of the Five Precepts—every Burmese person is aware of them. Even those who are Buddhist only because their families are, who don't even delve into the philosophy of Buddhism, are aware of the Five Precepts. That's basic.

AC: They might be able to recite them but to put them into action? Isn't *ahimsa* or harmlessness the root of the Five Basic Precepts?

ASSK: The Five Precepts do not really include *ahimsa*, but of course it is at the root of things—not just not killing but also not robbing. Robbing is violating somebody else's right to his own property. So you could also consider theft as violence, of a kind. But not everybody thinks in that way. They see the Five Precepts very simply: do not kill, do not steal, do not tell lies, do not commit sexual aberrations, and do not take intoxicating drinks and drugs. They see them in a superficial way. Of course, most people would be able to easily associate killing or rape with violence. But not everybody will immediately see theft as an act of violence. Then again, the telling of lies, I think many people would have doubts whether that's violence. Telling a lie is not really an act of violence. But you could take it further and say you are violating another's right to hear the truth and in that sense it is a form of violence. And with the business of intoxicating drinks and drugs, some people could argue that as long as you don't get wild and start abusing anybody else, what harm do you do to others? It's not an act of violence. Then there are others who could say this is an act of violence towards your own self—you are harming yourself by taking these drinks and drugs that intoxicate you, destroy you physically and affect your mental judgment. When you say that *ahisma* is at the root of the Five Precepts— this is probably how you are interpreting each one. But not everybody thinks that way.

AC: Do you believe in intrinsic evil?

ASSK: I have spoken about this to a number of people and I always quote something that Karl Popper said when he was asked, "Do you believe in evil?" He said, "No...but I believe in stupidity." And I think this is very near to the Buddhist position. I don't think there is a word for "evil" as such, in Buddhism, is there?

AC: No, I've not come across it. I think it's a Christian concept.

ASSK: I have not come across it either. But of course, we talk of greed, anger and ignorance. That's stupidity, isn't it? Ignorance is stupidity. There's also something very stupid about greed. Greed is very short-sighted. Anger also. And short-sightedness is stupidity. I've always said that one of my greatest weaknesses is having a short temper. I tend to get angry quite quickly. This is a lack of ability to raise yourself above the immediate situation. This is where I have found that meditation helps—it gives you a sense of awareness that helps you to observe and control your feelings. This feeling which is so destructive is all tied up with ignorance.

AC: It's fair to say that it's significantly easier to feel compassion for "victims" who are "legitimately" suffering, while it is far more challenging for the majority of people to feel genuine compassion for the perpetrator of such violence. And without having compassion for the perpetrator, one so easily demonizes that person into an unredeemable evil force that imprisons them, so to speak, outside of oneself. Whereby, we unconsciously perpetuate this vicious cycle of the oppressed and oppressor. How do you advise your people not to "demonize" the SLORC?

ASSK: I encourage people to focus on deeds, rather than on people. I was once speaking about Angulimala [a mass murderer at the time of the Buddha]. I said, even he changed, his deeds were horrendous but the Buddha himself was able to separate the person from the deed. Once Angulimala had been made to understand that what he did was wrong and was genuinely repentant, he set out to follow the right path. And the Buddha was the first one to take him under his wing, as it were.

AC: But Angulimala was the most famous case of redemption during the lifetime of the Buddha. As you know, he attained enlightenment. However, after having become a monk, everywhere he went he was stoned and beaten by the people. Do you think that once democracy is won, SLORC fears the same situation? Will people seek revenge?

ASSK: I would think it's quite natural that some of them should fear that a democratic government would in some way persecute them, or allow others to persecute them.

AC: Do you have safeguards to minimize this possibility, that you've discussed among your colleagues?

ASSK: My colleagues and I are simply not interested in vengeance.

AC: I know SLORC has made, and continues to make, repeated attempts to smear your character. What are their most frequent criticisms?

ASSK: They focus on the fact that I'm married to a foreigner and have spent many years abroad. They also say other things, such as, I have not kept my promise of not founding a political party. I never made such a promise. I've only said, "I do not wish to have to found a political party." Before SLORC took over in 1988, I said this was not the time to found political parties...we should all be united. Nor did I say anything about not contesting the elections. I would always say "This is something that I do not want to do at the moment." I have always been very careful never to commit myself because I know that in politics you cannot always predict what is going to happen. That is why I've promised the people only that I'll be honest with them. I have not promised that I will bring democracy. I have said, "I will always work and do my best to bring democracy and will go on working for it as long as I'm alive or until we get it."

<u>AC:</u> From what I've read of your speeches, you not only take SLORC's criticisms without retaliation but explain that such criticisms are in fact advantages. For example, they criticize you for having lived abroad for twenty-eight years...

<u>ASSK:</u> Yes, it's because I have lived in free countries for a large part of my life that I'm not easily frightened. Fear is very much a habit. People are conditioned to be frightened.

In free countries it is quite normal to ask "why?" if anybody, even a security officer, asks you to do something which seems unreasonable. In an authoritarian state asking questions can be dangerous so people simply do what they are told to do. So those in power get more oppressive, and the people get more frightened. It's a vicious circle.

<u>AC:</u> Honestly, have any of their criticisms really annoyed you?

<u>ASSK:</u> No, they haven't. Their attacks are so crude that they win my sympathy rather than anything else. At one time I thought they were actually rather funny (*laughing*). Before I was placed under house arrest, we found that every time one of them attacked me viciously, we gained more support than ever. We used to jokingly say to each other, "We have to present them with special certificates of honor, for helping us with our campaign for democracy." Later, I realized this was not a good idea. It was rather serious, not because it was an attack on me, but because it was creating a greater gap between us and them—between those who wanted democracy and those who wanted to stand by the authorities. So I was against this form of propaganda warfare.

<u>AC:</u> Are these SLORC attacks—their slander and lies—strictly the result of their misogynistic expression of hatred for you, or is it conceived as propaganda in support of their holding on to power?

61

<u>ASSK:</u> Basically, they [SLORC] do not like the fact that I have so much public support. So they attempt to diminish support for me and our movement for democracy.

<u>AC:</u> As you said, SLORC has repeatedly used against you the fact that you are married to a British citizen, Dr. Michael Aris. What's wrong with that?

<u>ASSK:</u> That's exactly how I feel. What's wrong? Sometimes I think it's just as well I'm not married to a Burmese, because if my family and his were here, they might have come under a lot of pressure. That might have been an extra burden for me. I'm aware of this from what has happened to my colleagues—how much pressure their families are under and how much more they must bear.

<u>AC:</u> I was told that prior to your arrest, during your campaign in rural Burma, someone asked you why you had married a foreigner and you replied, "It's quite simple. I was living in a foreign country at the time I was ready to marry…so I married the most suitable foreigner." Is there any truth to that?

<u>ASSK:</u> I don't think I said that. I was speaking in a village, and they asked me why I had married a foreigner. I said, "Well, I happened to be there and I met him. If I had lived in this village I would probably have married somebody from this village."

<u>AC:</u> But it is true that the new constitution SLORC is attempting to draft, stipulates that anybody who contests the Presidency of Burma cannot be married to a "foreigner."

<u>ASSK:</u> That's right. There are other things to it as well. Even if his or her children are citizens of a foreign country, etcetera.

<u>AC:</u> Obviously, SLORC's way to eliminate you from the Presidency.

<u>ASSK:</u> That's what people say. But I have always said that if it is intended for me then it's a great pity—no constitution should be written with one person in mind.

<u>AC:</u> Daw Suu, you're an extremely charismatic figure to your people, which easily allows those with aspirations of a free country to project their hopes and dreams upon you. How do you encourage

your people to take greater responsibility for the success of achieving democracy and not to depend on you?

ASSK: I keep telling the people that I cannot do it alone. Nor can the National League for Democracy. Everybody who really wants democracy has to do his or her own bit—you can always find a way.

AC: Do you feel burdened by the immense projection placed upon you?

ASSK: No. I have never pretended that I could do it alone and I do not believe in assuming unnecessary burdens. I have always told them that I'm not free from fault and I've made mistakes. But I've been very lucky in having very good teachers in my life. Otherwise, I do not consider myself to be an exceptional person.

AC: From the time after SLORC's takeover in 1988, you advocated and used civil disobedience against what you called "unjust laws." In so doing, you explained that, "What I mean by defying authority is non-acceptance of unlawful orders meant to suppress the people." Eight years have past since that time and "unjust laws" still exist in Burma. Are you still encouraging your people to defy authority?

ASSK: I've always said that they really must learn to question people who order them to do things which are against justice and existing laws. Ask, according to which law are you forcing me to do this? What right do you have to make me do this? They've also got to ask themselves, should we do this? People must ask questions and not just accept everything.

AC: So am I right in saying that you and your colleagues within the NLD are trying to educate the people of Burma to think and inquire, to stand for the truth, and defy these "arbitrary" and inconsistent laws or injustices?

ASSK: Let me put it this way. We are trying to help them to educate themselves, to understand the situation better and to see clearer. Not to be blinded by fear.

AC: Take for example, the boy in the village, who is being forced into the army, or into some kind of slavery to build this or that

SLORC project. Now, this boy is faced with a difficult dilemma. If he doesn't acquiesce to the soldier's command, he will most likely face imprisonment or even torture. Even his family may face violent consequences. How do you think this boy should handle the crisis?

ASSK: We can't expect that boy to stand up for himself alone. We've all got to help him. When we say that everybody should develop a true sense of responsibility—part of that is to accept one's responsibility to others, and never leave anybody to suffer by himself.

AC: If, as you said, "we've all got to help him," what should the villagers do to help the boy? Should they intervene and say no to the authorities? Should they all come out in unison and throw down their shovels? Should they develop a solidarity, so that one becomes two, then three, until everyone comes out, and perhaps sit on the earth in a meditative posture in defiance to the injustice?

ASSK: It depends on what happens to them when they sit down and put away their shovels. If they're dealing with armed troops, it might not be reasonable to say no. It could result in quite a disastrous situation. This is why I say that there are certain situations where you can't expect people to stand alone. We've all got to help. The whole country has to stand up against such cruel practices. We can't expect one boy, or one village, to stand up. But if one boy, one village, two villages, a hundred villages, a hundred towns, the whole country, decide this is it—we're not going to condone this practice of forced labor—then we'll get somewhere. Every one of us has a responsibility in helping others to escape from such an unjust, cruel situation.

AC: Let's look at the issue from another angle. SLORC has a 400,000-strong army that has been trained to oppress its own people, so it seems by their repeated behavior. Obviously, within a democratic Burma you will need an army. Assuming democracy is achieved, what will happen to SLORC's army, of course with the generals removed?

ASSK: It will be a better and more honorable army and one that will be loved by the people. That is what you want an army to be. When my father founded the army he meant it to be an honorable one that was loved and trusted by the people. The kind of army we want is an army in which the soldiers themselves will be much happier.

AC: But Daw Suu, up to now that army is very much in the habit of oppressing its own people—they seem trained to do so...

ASSK: I don't think soldiers are generally trained to oppress. They are simply trained to obey and if they are trained to obey something that is good, then they can change very quickly.

AC: I wonder. A personal question. In Buddhism it's understood that it's more difficult to conquer oneself than to conquer one's enemy. What are the inner struggles that you face in conquering yourself?

ASSK: Oh...I'm soldiering on. And it's constant. It's always a matter of developing more and more awareness, not only from day to day, but from moment to moment. It's a battle which will go on the whole of my life.

Chapter 4

"Working for democracy"

ALAN CLEMENTS: When you reflect back over the years of your life, what have been the most important experiences and personal lessons that have had a significant effect on your growth as an individual?

AUNG SAN SUU KYI: It's very simple. What I have learned in life is that it's always your own wrongdoing that causes you the greatest suffering. It is never what other people do to you. Perhaps this is due to the way in which I was brought up. My mother instilled in me the principle that wrongdoing never pays, and my own experience has proved that to be true. Also, if you have positive feelings towards other people they can't do anything to you—they can't frighten you. I think that if you stop loving other people then you really suffer.

AC: How would you characterize yourself as a person?

ASSK: Well, I see myself sometimes quite differently from how other people see me. For example, all this business about my being so brave...I had never thought of myself as a particularly brave person at all. And when people say: "How marvelous it is that you stuck out those six years of detention," my reaction is, "Well, what's so difficult about it? What's all the fuss about?" Anybody can stick out six years of house arrest. It's those people who have had to stick out years and years in prison, in terrible conditions, that make you wonder how they did it. So I don't see myself as all that extraordinary. I do see myself as a trier. I don't give up. When I say, "I don't give up," I'm not talking about not giving up working for democracy. That too, but basically I don't give up trying to be a better person.

AC: So it's this inner drive, this determination towards perfection or wholeness that most characterizes you?

ASSK: Yes. People talk quite a lot about my determination but I don't think of myself as a very determined person. I just think of myself as a trier.

AC: What is it in your life that provides you with the greatest sense of meaning and purpose?

ASSK: At the moment, of course, it's our cause for democracy. In that sense...I am very fortunate. A lot of people here in Burma are. I have spoken about this to members of the NLD: "Don't feel sorry for yourselves. Don't think of yourselves as being unfortunate because of having to live through these times. Think of it as fortunate, because you have an opportunity to work for justice and the welfare of other people. This sort of opportunity does not come to everybody all the time." You may desire it but you may not get it. So I think of myself as fortunate, because I have been able to work for something which is worth working for—democracy. I think this is what is behind the sacrifices made by so many of my colleagues. They believe that their sacrifices are worth what they are fighting for.

AC: Let's broaden the issue. What might be the common bond that allows others in the world to feel and understand that your people's struggle for freedom is not different or separate from their own pursuit of happiness? Might there be an intimate link that binds all humankind together?

ASSK: Yes, of course. Everybody understands the fundamental human desire for freedom and security. What we want in Burma is both security and freedom; freedom from want and freedom from fear; freedom to be allowed to pursue our own interests—obviously, without harming other people's interests. At the same time we want the security that allows us to pursue these interests without fear of other people's interference. Real freedom cannot exist without security. An insecure person is never really free.

AC: What are the most prevalent fears among the Burmese people today?

ASSK: I think most people are afraid of loss. They're afraid of losing their friends, their liberty, their means of livelihood. Basically they are afraid of losing what they have or losing the opportunity to be able to get something they need in order to live decent lives. What people want is freedom from that sort of fear. For instance, they should not be afraid that anybody at any time can take away their right to practice their own profession. This has been done in Burma. Many lawyers of the NLD, when they came out of prison, had their licenses taken from them. They must find other ways of earning their livelihood.

AC: Could you explain the variety of ways SLORC oppresses the NLD?

ASSK: The very fact that you are an NLD member makes you vulnerable. If you are active as an organizer you are constantly harassed. In many townships NLD [members] are not allowed to hold their own meetings in their own offices. In some places NLD organizers are not allowed to go out of town without the consent of the authorities. And of course they are constantly watched and questioned by the MI [Military Intelligence].

AC: On a more personal note: Daw Suu, when you consider your life, would you say that there are distinct periods that are definable by some dramatic emotional or psychological changes?

ASSK: No, I don't think it happens like that. It's more gradual. Except, I suppose, for people who've had very traumatic experiences. Perhaps such people suddenly change quite noticeably.

AC: I don't know how you use the word trauma, but the death of your father at such a young age would be considered by most standards to be rather traumatic. Or the witnessing of your brother's death by drowning when you were seven. He was your best friend too...

ASSK: I don't remember my father's death as such. I don't think I was aware that he died; I was too young. I felt my brother's death much more. I was very close to him...probably closer to him than to anybody else. We shared the same room and played together all the time. His death was a tremendous loss for me. At that time I felt enormous grief. I suppose you could call it a "trauma," but it was not something that I couldn't cope with. Of course, I was very upset by the fact that I would never see him again. That, I think, is how a child sees death; I won't play with him again; I'll never be able to be with him again. But at the same time, looking back, there must have been a tremendous sense of security surrounding me. I was able to cope—I didn't suffer from depression or great emotional upheaval.

AC: If I may make a personal observation...you seem so confident.

ASSK: I have never thought of myself as particularly confident. What I do know is that I want to do what is right. I don't claim that what I'm doing is always right. But I know for a fact that my intentions are good and that I don't want to hurt anyone.

AC: What has been the experience in your life that has caused you the most grief?

ASSK: I would say it was my brother's death. But looking back, it seems to me that I did cope with it very well. I've thought of it from time to time. I was not utterly devastated by it. I was grieved, but I did not go to pieces. So that seems to indicate that the family situation was such that there was enough support around for me to be able to cope with my grief.

AC: Have you ever been betrayed in such a way that it pierced your heart?

ASSK: I think all of us who have joined the movement for democracy have known betrayal. We have known people who have left our cause because it was too difficult and they just could not cope with it any more. But none of the really important people have done that—U Tin U, U Kyi Maung, U Aung Shwe, U Lwin—they have all remained staunch.

AC: From the time of SLORC's coup in 1988 up to the present, they have obsessively reiterated that their true intentions are to bring peace, tranquillity and a genuine multi-party democracy to Burma. Now I am curious, why haven't these generals just come out and said: "Listen, we're a totalitarian dictatorship. It's our show. We own the banks; we have the power, the armed forces and the weapons;

we have the seat at the United Nations; all foreign business contracts are with us—the SLORC. So, no more democratic jargon. No more lies." Why don't they just come out with the truth?

ASSK: They must know better than I why they have not come out with it. But basically, it's a recognition of the fact that dictatorship is wrong and democracy is desirable.

AC: So, you do feel that SLORC recognizes their shortcomings?

ASSK: Yes, of course, after all they promised multi-party democracy. That's a recognition of the fact that they see it as something good and desirable, even if they're not keen on it.

AC: Perhaps I'm naïve, but why would a totalitarian regime say they want a multi-party democracy, without believing in it themselves?

ASSK: Because they know that's what most of the people want.

AC: So they're just pandering in words to the people's desire?

ASSK: I wouldn't say that the term is "pandering to." I suppose the thing is that they can't entirely resist the will of the people.

AC: But the people utterly despise SLORC. And SLORC has proven time and again that repression of democracy is their true intention. So who is SLORC appealing to with all this democracy rhetoric? Are they trying to convince themselves?

ASSK: It's possible that they are appealing to those from whom they hope to attract investment. It could be as cynical as that. But it is a question that only they can answer. Nevertheless, sometimes there are questions that some people can't answer, even about themselves. Because their motives are so mixed.

AC: On to more evident truths. It's a well-established fact that SLORC uses corruption as both a political tactic to control people and out of sheer greed on their part. Could you shed some light on how their corruption functions and how widespread it is?

ASSK: Corruption exists everywhere throughout the country. You have to pay to get the most ordinary things done such as renewing a car license. You even have to bribe hospital workers to perform necessary little services for patients. Corruption is endemic. Whoever has the authority can do whatever they want. At the village level the authorities refuse to do what they should do, unless they are bribed. But that does not apply to everybody. I know that there are some Village or Ward Law and Order Restoration Councils, that are honest and try to help the people. This is why we need democracy. We need a system that does not depend on whether an individual wants to do what is right or not. The system should have checks and balances that prevent him from going along the wrong path.

AC: Just how pervasive is bribery in Burma?

ASSK: Very pervasive. And you can't really blame the civil servants who demand bribes, when you consider that their starting salary is about 670 kyats a month. You told me that a cup of tea at the Strand Hotel costs three dollars which is more than half that. In a system like that, can one be surprised that there's such widespread bribery and corruption?

AC: Not an easy question, but when democracy is achieved, how will you and the NLD tackle the problem of such widespread corruption?

ASSK: It will not vanish overnight. Measures will have to be taken to ensure that civil servants are adequately paid. Accountability is one of the best ways of checking corruption and a democratic system means accountable government. But corruption is also a state of mind which has been brought about by the political situation. If the people at the top are corrupt, then people below think it is all right to be corrupt. If the people at the top are not corrupt and if it becomes obvious that they are accountable, we will be able to check corruption. It's also a matter of education. We will try our best to make people understand that corruption is not a way of life and if it is a way of life then it is certainly not the best.

AC: Talking of education, what is the state of education in Burma?

ASSK: Abysmal. Education is in a very bad state indeed. The dropout rate in primary schools has been rising steadily since SLORC seized power. In schools, pupils are forced to make donations for all sorts of silly things and are not even provided with adequate textbooks. But there is something very interesting. I have mentioned this during my weekend meetings quite often. Last week, at the end of May, the schools reopened and at least two schools, perhaps more, had big signs saying: no donations of any kind and you can buy all your books in school—you don't have to buy them outside. So I think that our weekend meetings have a good effect because they always emphasize the necessity of good education.

AC: The SLORC is responding positively to your talks?

ASSK: They always respond. Always. This is why when some people ask me "If SLORC's policy was to try to marginalize you, what would you do?" I reply that they are not marginalizing us. They are not even trying. They keep me on the spot all the time. In a way, they are my unpaid PR.

AC: Back to business. All over Rangoon there are new imported cars. There are computer dealers selling the latest models from Apple, and Toshiba and Sony outlets selling state-of-the-art televisions and sound-systems. In an impoverished nation, who is buying these things?

ASSK: I don't know…but I was told that some have gotten very rich through the drug trade and they are laundering their black money…

AC: Are you saying that a large portion of the rich in Burma today are involved in the drug [heroin] trade?

ASSK: Not a large portion…but certainly a significant portion. Of course, if you investigate those who have become very rich over the last seven or so years [since SLORC's takeover], you will find that their wealth comes not as much from straightforward business, as it does from bribes.

AC: Burma's dictator, Ne Win, has ruled Burma for well over three decades. In so doing, he has systematically suppressed almost every form of freedom. The large majority of people in Burma were born under his rule. How has this psychologically affected the people?

ASSK: One dominant feature is the lack of confidence. And lack of confidence often means lack of honesty, because you don't know whom you can trust enough to be honest with. That is connected to fear. If you don't have confidence, you're filled with fear. This lack of confidence, of trust in each other, is a real sickness.

AC: People from all over the country, and from all walks of life, come to speak with you here at your home. Do you find that some of them are reluctant, or at times too scared to speak the truth?

ASSK: They are not afraid of telling me the truth because a lot of them trust me and know that I won't betray their trust. But what they say does demonstrate to a large extent how little they trust each other. I get a lot of information on who is not reliable and who is in contact with whom and therefore not to be trusted. But a lot of it is just genuine anxiety, not mischief-making. They really are afraid that somebody might be informing on somebody else.

AC: How pervasive is SLORC's Military Intelligence network?

ASSK: It's pervasive. We know for a fact that there are informers and that news sometimes does leak out, or get to the intelligence services. That is how it works in all police states. It's not unique to Burma.

AC: Is mistrust so widespread that it has reached a paranoia level?

ASSK: I think it's going along those lines.

AC: Daw Suu, at your weekend public gatherings you answer questions that have been submitted to you during the week. Almost every one of these questions reflects SLORC's numerous styles of repression and corruption—questions that speak of pain and struggle. Do you prepare your answers the night before or are they spontaneous?

ASSK: Sometimes I look over the questions the night before, that is if I have time. If I have no time, at least half an hour before. And it's only in case there's anything technical.

AC: From all the questions that are submitted to you weekly, who decides which questions are to be answered on weekends, and why?

ASSK: We get so many letters that I can't read them all myself. So our office staff read them first, weeding out the ones which we've answered before or ones that viciously attack someone personally or the government. We don't mind people criticizing the injustices of the government from which we are all suffering, but I never read to the public letters which viciously attack anyone in particular, even if the attack is justified in the sense that the injustice they are pointing out is true. For example, if a person writes a letter accusing a particular individual by name of corruption, I don't read it out. I'm against bringing personalities into politics. We do not like focusing on individuals, this is a very low kind of politics. Such letters are removed or we adapt them to leave out the names of individuals and say the authorities said or did such and such a thing on such and such a date. Also, we verify the facts before we read out anything. We don't just accept everything as it comes. This is not a place where you air your grievances without proper evidence.

AC: What would you say are the most positive qualities that have emerged among your people through their struggle for freedom under such harsh conditions of repression?

ASSK: Well...I think the Burmese people are much more hard-working than they used to be. They have been "forced" to work hard. I think those of us involved in the movement for democracy have learned to recognize our strengths and to build on them. I think it has also created very strong friendships.

AC: Could it be said that in your movement for democracy, you are ushering in a renaissance period in Burma, which is combining timeless Buddhist values with modern political principles?

ASSK: I don't think any individual can usher in a renaissance but I hope that we're heading for one. When people face troubles, they are forced to reassess their lives and their values, and that is what leads to renaissance.

AC: You've described your struggle for democracy as a "revolution of the spirit." In essence, what does this mean?

ASSK: When I speak about a spiritual revolution, I'm talking a lot about our struggle for democracy. I have always said that a true revolution has to be that of the spirit. You have to be convinced that you need to change and want to change certain things—not just material things. You want a political system which is guided by certain spiritual values—values that are different from those that you've lived by before.

AC: What shift in consciousness has been required in order to make the struggle a "spiritual revolution" from a socio-political one?

ASSK: Because of the tremendous repression to which we have been subjected it's almost impossible for it to be either a political or a social revolution. We're so hemmed in by all kinds of unjust regulations that we can hardly move as a political or a social movement. So it has had to be a movement very much of the spirit.

AC: Have you had a parallel passion to that of a political life?

ASSK: My other passion is literature, but it seems to dovetail with politics. In Burma, politics has always been linked to literature and literary men have often been involved in politics, especially the politics of independence.

AC: Before your arrival on to the political scene in Burma in 1988, did you feel that anything was missing from your life in Oxford?

ASSK: No. I think one should lead a full life wherever one is.

AC: Do you feel pretty complete wherever you are?

ASSK: Well, here and now I'm not part of my family and a family is part of one's life. So I cannot say that my life is complete. But I don't think anybody's life is. There is no perfection in this world. Once you accept that fact, you can lead a full life wherever you are.

AC: Do you live with demanding models of perfection in your speech and behavior?

ASSK: Oh yes, I do have perfectionist tendencies. I would very much like to be perfect. I know I'm not but that does not stop me from trying.

AC: Is striving for perfection a hardship?

ASSK: No. It's just part of everyday living. One tries.

AC: In essence what does "perfection" mean to you?

ASSK: My father once talked about purity in thought, word and deed. That's what I mean by perfection. Purity.

AC: Always the perfectly pure motivation?

ASSK: Yes. I think the greatest protection in life is absolute purity. I believe that nobody can hurt you except yourself, ultimately.

AC: Your father was assassinated when you were two years old. Then when you were seven years old you witnessed your brother's death by drowning. With the loss of your most intimate male figures at such a young age was there a dominant male—a father figure—who took over that important role during the years of your childhood?

ASSK: Not really. I never felt the need for a dominant male figure, because my mother's father who lived with us was the ideal grandfather. He was very indulgent and loving. During my childhood he was the most important male figure in my life.

AC: Do you have any actual memory of your father?

ASSK: Well, I have a memory of him picking me up every time he came home from work, but I think this may be a memory that was reinforced by people repeating it to me all the time. In other words, I was not allowed to forget. So it may be a genuine memory or it may be something I imagined from what people kept telling me. But I do seem to remember that whenever he would come back from work, my two brothers and I would come running around the stairs to meet him and he would pick me up.

AC: Do you think of your father every day?

ASSK: Not every day, no. I'm not obsessed by him, as some people think I am. I hope that my attitude towards him is one of healthy respect and admiration, not obsession.

AC: All the people compare you to him, from your physical appearance, your obvious leadership roles in Burma's independence, your articulation of similar and at times identical principles…the list goes on. What are your differences? What sets you apart? Not in the obvious ways but perhaps in policy choices—ways of thinking.

ASSK: I do not think we have any major differences. He was a better person than I am, and I'm not saying this just because I want to appear modest. My father was one of those people who was born with a sense of responsibility, far greater and more developed than mine. From the very moment he started going to school, he was a hard worker, very conscientious. I wasn't like that. I would study hard only when I liked the teacher or the subject. I had to develop my sense of responsibility and work at it. I think that's one of our differences. But in attitude, I don't think there are any fundamental differences between us. In fact, when I started doing research into my father's life I was struck by our similarities. I was surprised that we thought so much alike. At one time there were some thoughts and feelings that I thought were my own, and then I discovered that he had had them already.

AC: I read the following passage from a book you wrote about your father: "He was a difficult personality. There was much criticism about his moods, his untidiness, his devastating fits of silence, his equally devastating fits of loquacity and his altogether angular behavior. He himself admitted that he sometimes found polite, refined people irksome and would long to separate himself from them to live the life of a savage." It sounds like he was a straightforward wild man.

ASSK: My father was not really a savage. He was very angular, as I said, and got irritated by the outward trappings of certain fine society people. But at the same time, he was very refined in spirit, flexible and able to adapt. This is why, I think, he was the great man that he was. But all the people, because he was the leader, made a big deal of the fact that he was abrupt, stern and not always sociable. However, he was objective enough to see that this was not the way in which a head of state should behave. And towards the end of his life he maintained the dignity and honor of the nation, taking his responsibilities very seriously.

AC: What first comes to mind when you think about him?

ASSK: First of all the fact that he was a person capable of learning and who learned all the time. He also had an innate confidence in himself. Which did not mean that he was not aware of his own faults: he was conscious of them and of the need to improve. He was a person who went in for self-improvement all the time. There was at the core of his being a wholesomeness and a refinement that kept him together and made him an integrated person throughout all the phases he went through.

AC: You symbolize and embody for millions of people around the world a spiritually infused, non-violent approach to politics. On the other hand, your father as an army general advocated an armed struggle and used violence successfully in a revolution to free his country from foreign oppression. If your father were alive in 1988, at the time of SLORC's slaughter of unarmed pro-democracy demonstrators, and if he were a student leader—a young Aung San—how do you think he would have responded to the crisis?

ASSK: Don't forget that I was over forty-four when I entered the movement for democracy, and my father was thirty-two when he died. He entered politics when he was eighteen, and founded the Burmese army when he was twenty-six. Now, when I was twenty-six, I was not the person I was at forty-four. And it is possible that if I had entered politics much earlier I might have had a far more passionate approach and might not have followed the way of non-violence. I might have taken the same attitude he did, that any means used for gaining Burmese independence was acceptable. That was why he founded the army. At that time he thought that the most important thing was to achieve independence. But by the time he died, he understood that the problems of the country should be resolved through democratic politics and not through armed combat.

AC: How would you characterize your relationship with your mother?

ASSK: I treated my mother with a lot of love, respect and awe, as most Burmese children are taught to do. To me, my mother represented integrity, courage and discipline. She was also very warm-

hearted. But she did not have a very easy life. I think it was difficult for her to bring up the family and cope with a career after my
father's death.

AC: When you look back over your relationship with your mother,
are there aspects of her which were limiting to you? Perhaps values or attitudes that confined you? Or mistakes in the way she
raised you?

ASSK: I think she tried her best. She tried very hard to give us the
best education and the best life she could. I do not think anybody
is ever free from making mistakes. She was very strict at times. When
I was younger I felt that was a disadvantage. But now, I think it was
a good thing because it set me up well in life.

AC: How was she strict?

ASSK: Highly disciplined…everything at the right time…in the right
way. She was a perfectionist.

AC: Are you that way with your children?

ASSK: I'm not that much of a disciplinarian, but I am strict. My
mother was a very strong person and I suppose I too am strong, in
my own way. But I have a much more informal relationship with
my children. My mother's relationship with me was quite formal.
She never ran around and played with me when I was young. With
my sons, I was always running around with them, playing together.
Also, I would have long discussions with them. Sometimes I would
argue with them—tremendously passionate arguments, because my
sons can be quite argumentative, and I am argumentative too. I never
did this sort of thing with my mother.

AC: What do you argue about? Your values? Your Buddhist beliefs?

ASSK: It depends. I think my elder son, being more mature, tends
to discuss philosophical issues more, whereas with my younger son
we don't talk about that sort of thing much—at least not yet.

AC: Before we started our interview the other day, you mentioned
that your youngest son, Kim, is a bit of a rock 'n' roller.

ASSK: Yes, he's very fond of...do you call it "hard rock"?

AC: If it's electric and loud...

ASSK: He is very musical and I've learned a lot about the kind of music that he likes. I have no problems with him...it's his father who has arguments with him about the kind of music he likes. Michael objects to Kim playing his music so loudly. Whereas that never troubles me...I can tolerate it.

AC: So he's allowed to play hard rock music as loud as he wants in the house?

ASSK: Yes, I never stop him because I don't like him listening to this music on the earphones. I think that damages his ears. I'd rather put up with all that noise than have him damage his ears.

AC: Western music has invaded Burma...Music Channel V—Star TV's attempt at MTV—is beamed in by satellite. Rock concerts are now available on video for rental and purchase. There are even several discos and nightclubs in Rangoon with live music, including hard rock. Some of the cutting edge of western music with radical video images of sex, drugs and often violence, is mixing with an ancient mystical culture. What do you think of this in light of hoping to preserve traditional Burmese Buddhist culture?

ASSK: If it comes in too quickly in this way, we may end up with a very superficial kind of non-culture. I am very much for openness— people studying other cultures. But this kind of quick invasion can be unhealthy. There are many aspects of Burmese culture which are worth preserving. Foreign influences have come in so overwhelmingly and so quickly we might lose more than we should.

AC: What are the most important qualities of Burmese culture you wish to preserve?

ASSK: The Buddhist values of loving-kindness and compassion. A respect for education.

AC: Burma will soon have a major influx of tourists and along with them the "backpackers," who will inevitably bring in drugs—acid, marijuana, hashish, Ecstasy, and a loose, cool attitude towards travel.

What about the incoming travelers?

ASSK: It's worrying to me that they're coming in before the Burmese people have had a chance to develop self-confidence. The economy is in a terrible state and the Burmese people do not feel proud of their country at the moment. At such a time it is too easy for young people to grab at foreign ideas and values, simply because they think foreigners are better than they are and more successful. A people who have confidence in themselves have a better appreciation of both their own culture and that of others. They are more discriminating about what they should preserve, what they should discard; what they should accept, what they should reject.

Chapter 5

"It still surprises me that people think of me as an important person"

ALAN CLEMENTS: Buddhist philosophy explains the transformation of an apparently negative experience into its positive opposite. For example, seeing cruelty as an opportunity to love, or deception as an invitation to honesty. In other words, everything is workable. There are no obstacles, only challenges, if spiritual attitude is well-focused. To explain this point the Buddha once chastised his monks for criticizing his arch-nemesis Devadatta, upon his death. As you know, Devadatta attempted to kill the Buddha on several occasions. But if I'm not mistaken, the Buddha said that without Devadatta's aggression he would never have been able to become fully accomplished in patience. One could see this as praise for the adversary or the opposition.

In Burma today we have a nearly identical metaphor with SLORC's politics of repression being confronted by a spiritual revolution. May I ask you for your views on the transformation of negativity into freedom as it applies to your struggle for democracy?

AUNG SAN SUU KYI: In order to have a really strong, healthy democracy, we need a strong, healthy opposition. I always explain that you need a good opposition because they'll always point out your mistakes and keep you on your toes. In many ways, the opposition is your greatest benefactor. In worldly terms the opposition in a democracy plays the role of Devadatta for any legal government. It stops the ruling party from going astray by constantly pointing out its every mistake. The opposition as the potential next government keeps the current one from misusing its power.

<u>AC:</u> As you know, the Buddha used the concept *"samsara"* to point

out existence in its totality—the whole swirl of life, with birth, aging and death, as the backdrop of all else that we think of as important. Do you ever step back from the immediacy of the struggle and contemplate your anonymity or your unimportance to yourself within the bigger picture of existence?

ASSK: Yes. In fact, it still surprises me that I'm supposed to be an important person. I don't see things that way at all. I don't feel any different now that I'm in politics compared to what I felt before. Of course, I've got more responsibilities to discharge. But I had many responsibilities as a wife and a mother too. Things may appear big and important at times but I realize they are small when I consider the fact that we're all subject to the law of *anicca* [impermanence]. To put it in more blunt terms, I do contemplate my death. Which means to me an acceptance of the principle of chance. And by reflecting upon your own death some of the problems which seem significant to you just shrivel into nothingness. Do you ever think of your death?

AC: Yes, I do, sometimes. But by contemplating death, it hasn't brought me fear of death as such, the impression that something is ending, but a greater passion for living in the present. And you, may I ask how the contemplation of death has been of value to you?

ASSK: Few people really face the fact that they are going to die one day. If you contemplate your own death, in a sense it means that you accept how unimportant you are. It's a way of stepping back from the present, from the immediate concerns of the world in which you're engaged, realizing just how insignificant you are within the whole scheme of things—within this swirl of *samsara*. And yet, you are essential in your place, even if you may not be of great importance. Everybody is essential. But it is a matter of having a balanced view of your place in the world. Having enough respect for yourself to understand that you too have a role to play and at the same time, having enough humility to accept that your role isn't as important as you or some people may think it is.

AC: As you know the First Noble Truth of the Buddha's enlightenment was the truth of *dukkha*—the truth of suffering. A truth that was rooted in the realization that all things were *anicca* or changing; everything was in a constant flux and therefore unsatisfactory. In the ultimate sense, that there could be no "permanent" happiness in an "impermanent" world. Do you ever teeter on the edge of your own existential plight—your individual struggle for spiritual freedom and your socio-political struggle for your people's freedom?

ASSK: No. Since we live in this world we have a duty to do our best for the world. Buddhism accepts this fact. And I don't consider myself so spiritually advanced as to be above all worldly concerns. Because of this, it's my duty to do the best that I can.

AC: So you see no split or tension between your Buddhist pursuits and your political ones?

ASSK: No...no.

AC: Many years ago I interviewed Burma's former Prime Minister U Nu who stated as a matter of fact that he was a committed *Bodhisattva* [a being striving for Buddhahood]. I asked him what was it like being the Prime Minister with full control of the army and to have made the vow to become a Buddha. He said rather explicitly, if I remember correctly, that it was a major burden, a nearly constant moral dilemma. What he was saying was that being a devout Buddhist was incompatible with being a political leader who had a responsibility to use the armed forces. Don't you feel any such dilemma?

ASSK: No, I do not see a dilemma. I would not think that I'm in any position to even contemplate taking the *Bodhisattva* vow. My first concern is to abide by Buddhist principles in my worldly dealings. Of course, I do meditate. That's because I believe that all of us, as human beings, have a spiritual dimension which cannot be neglected. Overall, I think of myself as a very ordinary Burmese Buddhist who will devote more time to religion in my older years.

AC: Do you consider yourself a Theravada Buddhist [which means the school of the elders, and is practiced in Burma, Thailand, Cambodia, Laos and Sri Lanka]?

ASSK: I am a Theravada Buddhist but I respect Mahayana Buddhism as well [a school of Buddhism practiced primarily in Tibet and other Himalayan countries as well as in Vietnam, Japan and to an extent in China]. Also, I have a great respect for other religions. I do not think anyone has the right to look down on anybody's religion.

AC: What are the elements of Mahayana Buddhism that you respect?

ASSK: In Mahayana Buddhism there's much more emphasis on compassion than in Theravada Buddhism. I'm very sensitive to this, because we need a lot of compassion in this world. Of course, compassion is also a part of Theravada Buddhism. But I would like to see more of our people putting compassion into action.

AC: What motivates you to meditate as a daily practice?

ASSK: The main reason why I meditate is the satisfaction that I derive from the knowledge that I am doing what I think I should do, that is, to try to develop awareness as a step towards understanding *anicca* as an experience. I have very ordinary attitudes towards life. If I think there is something I should do in the name of justice or in the name of love, then I'll do it. The motivation is its own reward.

AC: When we consider those who perpetrate the injustices in the world, they often seem to have the assumption that they are immune to their own actions, that they are above the law, so to speak, and that their repressive actions have no real effect on themselves...

ASSK: But it does have an effect on them. I'm sure everything that everybody does has a psychological effect on them. For example, take the extreme case of a dictator who is in a position to do anything he pleases. He can just say: "Have that man executed." He may not have anything to do with the execution itself and he may not even think about it the next day. But the very fact that he's had another man executed means that his sensitivities have become much more hardened. He has been affected. Every time he does something to somebody, he is also doing something to himself. And if he's a man with any sense of a conscience, somewhere inside of him, something will make him feel uncomfortable. Another thing is that he will affect people's perception of him. To put it in the simplest way, those who are connected to the man who was executed will like him less. So every time he commits an injustice he is adversely affected, whether he realizes it or not. In fact, this dictator may die without ever realizing how much the people had hated him. But the effect remains the same.

AC: So no one is above the law, no matter how lawless they may be?

ASSK: They may be above human laws, but not above the law of *karma* because the law of *karma* is actually very scientific. There is always a connection between cause and effect. It's like the light of a star, isn't it? The light that we see now was initiated so many light years ago, but there it is. In science too, there can be a seemingly long gap between cause and effect. But there's always the connection between them.

AC: Or perhaps in the more immediate sense, like the Vietnamese Buddhist monk Thich Nhat Hanh said, "In the grain of rice see the sun." Do you see yourself as just a seed-sower of democracy?

ASSK: I'm thinking of a book I once read, by Rebecca West. She was talking about musicians and artists as a "procession of saints always progressing towards an impossible goal." I see myself like that—as part of a procession, a dynamic process, doing all that we can to move towards more good and justice; a process that is not isolated from what has happened before or what will come after. And I do whatever I have to do along the path, whether it's sowing seeds or reaping the harvest or (*laughing*) tending the plants half-grown.

AC: Do you ever feel inadequate for the role that you are in?

ASSK: I very seldom think of myself as playing a role. I always think of myself as part of a movement, so my adequacies or inadequacies don't come so much into the question. I know that a lot of people will find this hard to believe because so much media attention is focused on me it seems as though I am playing the central role.

The main role in which I have to cope alone is meeting the foreign media. The other EC [Executive Committee] members of the National League for Democracy don't do much of that. But in everything else we work together. I'm not alone. Perhaps because of that I don't feel inadequate. I do not think my role is as large as some people think it is.

At the meeting table, which is where it matters, we are very much on an equal footing. I don't have any more clout than anybody else. If my suggestions are better they will take them, but not for any other reason. Mind you, they give me a lot more work to do because I am the youngest so I think I'm rather at a disadvantage!

But it's a family feeling between us and I do feel almost a blood bond with them. There's a lot of affection between all the members of the EC, and the more we meet, the stronger this bond of affection between us becomes. We are happy to work together and are courteous to each other. I'm surrounded by gentlemen. And when we are together, even when we have enormous problems to cope with, we draw strength from each other.

<u>AC:</u> If I may make another personal comment about you, I would say that you're an extremely articulate woman, with a profound sense of what is right and wrong, and at the same time a very simple person. Am I right?

<u>ASSK:</u> Yes, (*laughing*) I have very simple attitudes and this is one of the problems. Some people want to make something extraordinary out of me, but I'm not particularly extraordinary. I suppose people think I'm extraordinary because I'm so simple they can't believe it.

<u>AC:</u> Do you even see yourself as a leader?

<u>ASSK:</u> No! I find it very embarrassing when people refer to me as *"gaungzamggyi"*—big leader.

<u>AC:</u> In a previous conversation I asked you whether you believed in intrinsic evil. What about its opposite? Do you believe in the inherent goodness of people?

<u>ASSK:</u> I believe in the inherent goodness of some people and I think there is both good and bad in everyone. It's a matter of which bits you cultivate. Also, I think some people are born intrinsically more serene, sensible and compassionate than others. And there are those who, because of their upbringing, are able to develop these qualities more than others. Then of course, there are those who have certain traits that are so strong that perhaps all training can do is curb them to some extent, but not remove them entirely.

<u>AC:</u> Does that mean that everyone is awakening despite appearances?

ASSK: That, one cannot say, because the seed of awakening may not come to fruition. Some people are naturally more inclined towards the good and some are more inclined towards the stupid or the bad.

AC: From where do you think does this inclination towards the "good" or the "bad" originate?

ASSK: Well, it's a combination of things. I think we're all born different. For example, the moment my eldest son was born, he had a distinctive personality. Something about him marked him out as an individual. It's not just the loving-mother syndrome, thinking my child is different from everybody else. He was different. Even his cry was different. In fact, every mother in the hospital ward learned to recognize their baby's cry easily and quickly. In the same way when my second son, Kim, was born, I knew immediately that he was not at all like Alexander. I just had to hold this baby in my arms and look at him and I knew that he was different from his brother.

But of course, our surroundings make a difference too. I read somewhere that psychologists claim that 80 percent is nature and 20 percent is nurture. But that 20 percent goes a long way. On the other hand, I have heard of children who have grown up in the most awful circumstances and yet...

AC: Who really shine?

ASSK: Yes. They've come out of it strong and compassionate.

AC: What do you think it is in the human spirit that allows one person to rise to new heights through traumatic experiences, while someone else descends into the abyss?

ASSK: There are those who rise to a challenge and achieve great heights in the face of adversity. It can even bring out the best in them. While in others, adversity seems to bring out the worst. But it is very difficult to know what makes them different. You can hardly say that it has anything to do with upbringing. Now some psychologists and psychiatrists blame all problems on childhood experiences. But I think there are people who have something innate in them that enables them to rise above the limitations of their environment. For instance, I've been reading about an Iranian woman who became blind when she was three or four years old. The mother found her a burden and treated her badly. In fact, she told her repeatedly; "I wish you were dead. What use are you being alive?" Furthermore, even her mother's friends would say that it would have been much better if she had died. But apparently the girl had a strong sense of her own existence. I suppose you could say that she never lost the sense of her own self-worth as a human being despite the fact that it was drummed into her all the time that she was a worthless burden to her family. This girl was totally deprived of parental love, but she became the first blind graduate in Iran.

AC: So you do believe that no matter how tragic one's circumstances may be, with courage and determination one can make it? And with intelligence they can transform the difficulties into strengths?

ASSK: Yes. But some really thrive on adversity while others go under. You can see this with people who have been in prison. I have to say that the majority of our people who have been put in prison have come out unshaken. But others have broken and turned away because they just couldn't take it any more.

AC: I understand that U Win Tin, the Secretary for the NLD who was arrested along with yourself and others in '89, is still in prison.

ASSK: Yes, he's still in Insein Prison, and I understand that his health is not very good. He was sentenced to four years' imprisonment. Then after he had been put in prison they added another seven years on to it. This is one of their [SLORC's] standard practices. In February 1996 he was tried again in prison, without benefit of counsel, and had yet another prison term—five years—slapped on him.

AC: But why wasn't he released too? SLORC had a personal vendetta against him?

ASSK: He's a very able man and as you said, he is the Secretary of the NLD. He works hard and is well respected. He's also extremely intelligent and he's incorruptible. I think the combination is too much for SLORC.

AC: Speaking of incorruptibility—what is it about someone that allows him to maintain his integrity and dignity, even in such extreme conditions as solitary confinement or even torture?

ASSK: I think most of the people I know who have not become corrupt have a real sense of self-responsibility. While those who become corrupt either cannot see, or do not accept, that they are responsible for the consequences of their actions. They don't understand the connection between cause and effect.

AC: Could it be that they're too frightened?

ASSK: It's self-deception. Basically it's an issue of honesty. If you accept responsibility for your actions, whether they are right or wrong, that's honesty. You're prepared to accept that your actions may have certain consequences. You may not be aware of all of them and your assessment of the consequences may not be correct. Nevertheless, you do try to see things honestly for what they are.

AC: Would you say more about the relationship between corruption and self-deception?

ASSK: Corruption is a form of dishonesty because it's rooted in self-deception. I don't think that people who are corrupt really admit it. They have other words for it. They may say, "Oh, it's what everybody is doing." Or, "There's nothing wrong with it." There're so many ways of explaining away their corruption. That in itself is a lack of honesty. A lack of honesty with oneself.

AC: So it's this quality of radical self-honesty that is the key. Which comes back to self-awareness. Have you found that meditation has been an essential force in protecting and strengthening you against any form of corruptibility?

ASSK: It has been a help. But I have to go back to my parents and the way I was brought up and taught. My mother always emphasized honesty and integrity. It wasn't just that she herself was honest and incorruptible but she was also upholding my father's values. So it does go back a lot to nurture. It's not that I didn't know these things before I started meditating. Meditation has helped me to uphold the values that I've always been taught since I was a child.

AC: What does Buddhist meditation mean to you?

ASSK: It's a form of spiritual cultivation—a spiritual education and a purifying process. Basically, it's learning awareness. By being aware of whatever you're doing, you learn to avoid impurities.

AC: How instrumental has meditation been in discovering new aspects of your interior life? Has it been a process of self-discovery?

ASSK: I don't know if it has been a process of self-discovery as much as one of spiritual strengthening. I was always taught to be honest with myself. Since I was quite young I had been in the habit of analyzing my own actions and feelings. So I haven't really discovered anything new about myself. But meditation has helped to strengthen me spiritually in order to follow the right path. Also, for me, meditation is part of a way of life because what you do when you meditate is to learn to control your mind through developing awareness. This awareness carries on into everyday life. For me, that's one of the most practical benefits of meditation—my sense of awareness has become heightened. I'm now much less inclined to do things carelessly and unconsciously.

AC: How did you learn meditation?

ASSK: I did go to the Mahasi Thathana Yeiktha meditation center but that was long ago, when I was in Burma on one of my visits. I was in my twenties. But I never really meditated very much. My real meditation took off only during my years of house arrest. And for that I had to depend a lot on books. Sayadaw U Pandita's book, *In This Very Life*, was a great help.

AC: As a Theravada Buddhist, are you still open in your spiritual attitudes to learn from other traditions, or are they fairly set?

ASSK: I'm very interested in hearing about other people's spiritual experiences and views. I've got a lot more to learn, from as many people as are prepared to teach me.

AC: You often refer to your democracy movement here in Burma as a "revolution of the spirit" that is rooted in Buddhist principles. How much, if at all, do you draw upon the wisdom of other religions in your approach to politics?

ASSK: I have read books on other religions but I haven't gone into any of them particularly deeply. But I find that the idea of *metta* is in every religion. The Christians say God is love. And when they say, "perfect love casts out fear," I think by perfect love they mean exactly what we mean by *metta*. I think at the core of all religions there is this idea of love for one's fellow human beings.

AC: You and your colleagues have set up a Welfare Committee for political prisoners. What is its main function?

ASSK: We help the families with funds, medicines and food for the prisoners. Some people can't even afford to go see their husbands or fathers in prison, because they are kept in jails far away from where the families live. As you know, fares are very high now. We help all political prisoners, not just those who belong to the NLD. We don't make any discrimination. We give help to those who have been pulled in on strange cases, like celebrating my winning of the Nobel Peace Prize and so on. I think those are practically all out now, because they were sentenced to three to four years' imprisonment and it's four years since I got the Nobel Prize.

I mentioned earlier that U Win Tin was subjected to another trial in prison. Twenty-two other political prisoners were tried with him and sentenced to additional terms of five to twelve years. Our Legal Aid Committee is preparing their appeals. We want to help political prisoners in any way we can—social, financial, legal.

AC: Speaking about the Nobel Peace Prize, how did winning the prize affect you?

ASSK: My immediate thought was that people would take a greater interest in our cause for democracy. And of course, when I wrote to the Nobel Committee, I did say that I was very grateful that they had recognized our cause. But at the same time, whenever I'm given any prize like that I feel a sense of humility. I think of all my colleagues who have suffered much more, but who have not been recognized. My recognition really stems from the courage and the sufferings of many, many others.

AC: You were the first person ever to receive the prize while under detention. How did you receive word of the award, and was it a surprise?

ASSK: I heard it on the radio. And it was not really a surprise to me because they had started saying a week or so before that I was on the shortlist. With President Václav Havel having nominated me, with such strong backing, it was not altogether a surprise for me that I did get the prize.

AC: Were you in any way looking forward to the results?

ASSK: No, not looking forward but of course, I was curious to know. When you are under detention alone, you are always curious to hear the next day's news. And yet, at the same time, you become much more objective. You become a little more distant from what's going on; you're not that passionately involved, in a sense.

AC: Coming back to the present circumstances in Burma under SLORC, is your party allowed to print anything?

ASSK: No, we are not allowed to print anything. You have to get a license in order to print anything as a political party and the license has to be renewed every six months. Our license has not been renewed since July 1990.

AC: What about other forms of censorship?

ASSK: Everything is censored. Look at some of the magazines. You'll find that some have silver ink blocking out passages, articles and even short stories—whether it's fiction or non-fiction. Anything can be censored. In 1993, when Nelson Mandela was given the Nobel Peace Prize, a magazine printed his photograph, and they made them ink out his picture. All because he was a Nobel Peace Prize winner.

AC: Well, that makes the picture clear...

ASSK: I think that they heard that some people compared me to him.

AC: And it's true that a Burmese writer can't even use your name as a fictional character in a novel?

ASSK: It's forbidden to even use the name "Suu" I hear. But I suppose that if that name were given to a really nasty character the censors might allow it to pass...

Chapter 6

"Each country is linked to the others
through the bonds of humanity"

ALAN CLEMENTS: The SLORC Chairman, General Than Shwe, has been in Bangkok attending the ASEAN [Association of South-East Asian Nations] conference at the invitation of Thailand. It seems that host members are seriously considering granting Burma membership status by the year 2000. If you had been there, how would you have addressed the leaders of your neighboring countries?

AUNG SAN SUU KYI: It really depends on the context. That time, I believe, they were going to sign a nuclear non-proliferation treaty, and I'm very much in favor of one. So it depends on what they are discussing.

<u>AC:</u> Let me ask the question in context. Often, such conferences as this one, ASEAN, neglect the role of "human rights" for the sake of economic interests, which generally means self-interest. Take for example the American administration's present policy towards China. Most educated people know of China's sorrowful human rights record, both internal and external to the country, as in the case of its genocide of the Tibetan culture. In relationship to this, President Clinton has made it clear that despite China's disregard for human rights, it will not affect their "most favored trade status." And it seems that ASEAN countries have also separated human rights and democracy in Burma from economic involvement and co-operation. What do you think of this need of some world leaders to separate money and profits from people and human values?

<u>ASSK:</u> It's a totally artificial separation.

<u>AC:</u> But why do you think so many political leaders insist on this

95

"artificial" separation as a matter of firm national policy?

<u>ASSK:</u> It's because certain systems which are not what one would call wholly democratic have achieved economic success. There has come about a school of thought that economic success is totally divorced from political freedoms. But, I think, there are other reasons for economic success. Take Singapore [a member of ASEAN] for example. I think there are two basic reasons for their economic success. One is that they have had a government which is not corrupt. Nobody can accuse them of corruption. They may not be wholly democratic in the way in which some of us see democracy but they are not corrupt. Secondly, they have put a great value on education and have done everything they can to raise its standard. So I think it's wrong to equate Singapore's economic success with the fact that it's not wholly a democracy. It makes much more sense to link its success to the fact that it has an intelligent, upright government, along with an excellent educational system. I think we're getting our values and equations wrong.

<u>AC:</u> But Daw Suu, isn't the situation a bit more insidious? It might be true that the Singaporean government is not corrupt, in an overt sense. But when you consider the fact that Singapore is one of the largest investors in SLORC's economy, totaling nearly 770 million dollars, doesn't that point to complicity?

<u>ASSK:</u> Yes, of course. That's what I'm saying. Because Singapore has succeeded economically, they think their success is because they're not wholly a democracy. But my argument is that this is not so. The reason for Singapore's success is not a lack of certain democratic rights but the fact that they have an upright government that is very intelligent. That you cannot deny. In addition, they have an excellent educational system which has made their people fit to cope with many modern-day economic issues. I think people are just barking up the wrong tree when they equate economic success with lack of democracy. There have been a couple of very interesting speeches by the Hong Kong Governor Chris Patten. He sees a belief in progress, economic freedom and free trade as the most important features of societies that have achieved economic success. He said it has not much to do with particularly Western or Eastern values.

AC: But one's complicity with the denigration of life is not "upright." I don't see the wisdom here. And by complimenting the Singaporean government as intelligent, well, it strikes me as a compliment for materialism at the least—setting aside the complicity factor.

ASSK: No. I'm not complimenting materialism at all. I'm just saying that they have what we would call in Buddhism *moha* [ignorance]. It's not the right understanding.

AC: What isn't the right understanding?

ASSK: The fact that they think their economic success is due to their lack of democracy.

AC: Let's be specific. How do you feel about Singapore's massive infusion of economic dollars into SLORC-controlled Burma? We all know that a vast percentage of these millions of dollars goes right into the bank accounts of the generals and their most favored friends.

ASSK: I don't think it helps the democratic cause and in the long run it will not help their economic cause either. Because I do not think that without a change in the political system Burma will be able to maintain its economic development. The reason why it seems as though Burma has developed economically over the last six years is that we started from less than zero, and it's very easy to show progress from that point.

AC: Can you explain how investing in Burma doesn't help the country from where the investment originates? Singapore thinks it is secure.

ASSK: The Singaporeans think that the lack of democracy is not an obstacle in the way of economic success. It may not have been so in their own country, but Singapore is very different from Burma. Here in Burma, the present system of government is such that there can be no economic progress. The system of education is such that there cannot be any sustained development. They have not looked at the factors that really matter. What they're looking at is the fact that Burma is virgin territory. Let's take the tourist industry as an example. People just want to go to a new place that others have not yet been. So they calculate that if they invest in the tourist industry of Burma they will be able to reap good returns. But as I understand it, the tourist figures are not good.

AC: Archbishop Desmond Tutu of South Africa has stressed his belief in the need for international economic sanctions against SLORC's Burma. He substantiated this "need" by pointing to the fact that it was only when sanctions occurred in his country that the apartheid government buckled. He also stressed that "engaged diplomacy" was gibberish and in no way reliable in bringing down an authoritarian regime. May I ask your views about the issue of "engaged diplomacy" *vis-à-vis* an international economic embargo as it applies to Burma?

ASSK: It depends on what they mean by "engaged." If they were truly engaged with both sides—the democratic forces as well as SLORC—I think it could help a great deal. But some of the countries which are said to be pursuing a constructive engagement policy seem to be only engaged with one side.

AC: I have spoken with a number of political attachés in several of the embassies here in Rangoon about the issue of imposing economic sanctions against SLORC. Most of them made the argument against sanctions stating that such measures would only hurt the people and not SLORC. I asked the obvious question: "How could the vast majority of the people become any more hurt than they already are?"

ASSK: Somebody said to me, "We're already crawling." There are some who think that it might have a positive effect if there were the type of economic sanctions that prohibited people from buying rice from Burma. In that case, the farmers would be in a much easier situation.

AC: So the argument that sanctions hurt the people just doesn't hold water?

ASSK: I wouldn't say that so glibly. One would have to study the situation quite carefully.

AC: Of course, you've studied the situation. Would you say more?

ASSK: For example, Burma depends a lot on imported medicines. The BPI [Burma Pharmaceutical Industry]—which produces high-quality medicines, just cannot produce enough. So there are certain sorts of imports that would really hurt the people if they were stopped.

AC: Please correct me if I'm wrong, but it seems that 99.9 percent of the cash in your country is owned by SLORC and their friends.

ASSK: Yes...

AC: Then wouldn't international economic sanctions awaken SLORC, so to speak, from their totalitarian nightmare and in fact ease the suffering for the vast majority of your people who want democracy?

ASSK: Yes. It is possible.

AC: With regard to medicines, sanctions could easily be tailored.

ASSK: Yes...

AC: So if economic sanctions were imposed it wouldn't hurt anyone except SLORC?

ASSK: Yes, I don't think it would really hurt the people very much. But I've always been very careful not to support economic sanctions without thought. Because certainly one does not want to do anything that hurts the people.

AC: The United Nations General Assembly has just issued yet another strong resolution against SLORC, citing the usual violations — forced labor, political prisoners, and so on. However, the United States Ambassador to the United Nations, Madeleine Albright, said she would have liked an even stronger statement...

ASSK: The resolution is quite good. It's a strong resolution...and it could have been stronger. But it's always good to leave room for stronger measures in the future.

AC: The SLORC seat at the United Nations has been repeatedly yet unsuccessfully contested by Burma's government-in-exile, the NCGUB, [the National Coalition Government of the Union of Burma] based in Washington, D.C. How is it that this respected body of men and women that comprises the United Nations allows an "illegal government" to hold a seat? After all, it was your party—the NLD—that won the free and fair elections, and not SLORC.

ASSK: SLORC is not the only government in this sort of situation. They've always allowed governments which came into power by force to sit in the United Nations, with the exception of the Khmer Rouge.

AC: As the rather well-known story goes, when Gandhi was asked what he thought of Western civilization he replied: "I think it would be a good idea." As an American, my country—as you must know—was founded upon a human, spiritual and cultural genocide of the native American population. I think it's also rather common knowledge that wherever European civilization spread around that time, it did so by decimating the indigenous peoples of the countries they invaded. Of course the British also oppressed Burma for over 150 years until she gained her independence in 1947. Don't you think there's some value in questioning the West's understanding of human rights, despite the fact that they have signed the Universal Declaration of Human Rights?

ASSK: Well, isn't it precisely because they have done these things that they are aware of the need for human rights?

AC: Of course, one would like to believe so—but the examples are numerous, that point to major and consistent contradictions to the West's awareness of human rights, post signing of the Declaration. America's invasion of Vietnam is but one example. However, setting aside my beliefs—do you have a real faith and trust in the value systems of the West?

ASSK: These are not just the value systems of the West. Human rights were quite recently enforced in the West because the Western world had suffered such utter devastation from World War II and the denial of human rights. Of course, we suffered in the East too from World War II. But don't forget that our sufferings were not imposed on us by any Western power, but by an Eastern power. Because of the power of pre-war Japan there was equal devastation in Asia. Just as there was tremendous devastation in Europe because of the power of pre-war Germany. The point is that it's encouraging that peoples and countries decided it was time to try to stop the same kind of disaster from ever befalling the planet again.

AC: Recently President Bill Clinton expressed his support for you and Burma's struggle for freedom and democracy. But I couldn't help thinking how much more he could do beyond a few words of support. I spent six months last year in the former Yugoslavia, and the feeling among the vast majority of people that I came to know, was that Bosnia was of "no strategic interest" to the West, and therefore expendable. Do you ever feel that Burma has been placed in the same category by some world leaders and therefore seems to them unimportant to defend?

ASSK: We are not depending on either the West or the East to help us through. But we know that in this day and age the opinion of the international community cannot be ignored. No country can survive by itself. No country can be an island unto itself. We know that. And we want to live in a world where each country is linked to the others through bonds of humanity. We will always try to promote such an atmosphere.

And yes, it is true, that in the old state of the Republic of Yugoslavia, the international community could have done more. And yet one asks, what more? Come in with arms? Of course, that's violence again and would not resolve the hatred between the Serbs, Croats and Bosnians. That is something they will have to address.

AC: But certainly armed intervention by the West would have stopped the atrocities perpetrated against the civilian population by the soldiers of each side. Are you saying that under no circumstance would you advocate armed intervention, or the use of arms at all?

ASSK: I would not say that. I never said that we do not need an army in Burma. I do accept that the situation of the world is such that there is still a need for military forces. But in their own place. And with regard to the former Yugoslavia what I'm saying is that of course the international community might have taken more positive action. But are you not saying rather that America should have taken more positive action? But then one asks why America? Why not Europe?

I'm just being the devil's advocate. Because what some Americans say is, "Why didn't the Europeans look after their own backyards? Why America, when there were many European countries quite capable of taking more positive action in former Yugoslavia?" And that becomes a difficult question to answer.

<u>AC</u>: Are you disappointed in America's response or role in Burma's struggle for democracy?

<u>ASSK</u>: No. I think in recent months the United States has been very firm in its support for democracy in Burma. We might want firmer action—depending on what happens. Not just on the part of the United States, but from the international community as a whole.

<u>AC</u>: Which might be?

<u>ASSK</u>: As you know, I never discuss our future plans.

<u>AC</u>: Some time ago, Mr. Burton Levin, the US Ambassador to Burma during 1988, sent me a video that showed some of the pro-democracy demonstrations that occurred in front of the embassy. Banners and placards held by the demonstrators clearly showed their enthusiasm for American support. Were the demonstrators at that early stage in the movement looking for American-style democracy as a role model?

<u>ASSK</u>: Some of them seemed to be. I think really one should depend on oneself, first of all. That's very Buddhist, isn't it? Whom do you have to worship but yourself, as it were?

<u>AC</u>: A fleet of American warships was just off the coast at that time. Was there any place in you that was hoping for intervention?

<u>ASSK</u>: No, no, I knew perfectly well that the American warships off the coast had nothing to do with our situation. I'm not that naïve.

<u>AC</u>: So the fleet was there only to potentially evacuate Americans?

<u>ASSK</u>: Of course!

<u>AC</u>: I was watching an interview on BBC with a Rwandan refugee who said, "Because it was a genocide in Rwanda it meant nothing to the international community. But if we were gorillas it would have

moved heaven and earth to intervene."

ASSK: I'm not sure that remark is absolutely accurate. If gorillas were massacred, there are animal rights associations which would have worked very hard to stop the massacre. It's just that the issue of genocide is so much more complex that the international community hesitates to get involved.

AC: I know that it's a complex issue, but the reality remains that genocide occurred and the world community only watched. The "hesitation" was at the price of 700,000 deaths. Don't you think that some leaders of powerful countries rather consistently wobble when it comes to assisting the powerless in their time of need?

ASSK: It depends on the country. There are some countries that are always ready to speak up for human rights and others that hesitate much more.

AC: Are you disappointed by the international response to Burma?

ASSK: No. Of course, we always hope that it will get better and there will be more sympathy and support for the principles and values that we're struggling for. However, we should consider the fact that very few people in the world even knew where Burma was before 1988.

AC: Do you feel that it is ever appropriate or justified for one country to intervene in the internal affairs of another country whose powers are creating hell for the population? Is it the duty of a powerful country to help the weaker one in such instances?

ASSK: I think it is better that the international community carries out this responsibility as a whole. There are far too many complications that arise when one country is given either the responsibility or the right to interfere in the affairs of another country. But I do think that the international community as a whole should recognize that it has got responsibilities. It can't ignore grave injustices that are going on within the borders of any particular country.

AC: Back to the issue of foreign investment in Burma. Hundreds of millions of dollars are pouring into your country, with more waiting in bank accounts. I assume that many of these business people want the truth. What would be the most appropriate way for these potential investors to cut through SLORC propaganda, and get to the facts about what's really going on in your country?

ASSK: They could always start by talking to us. We could give them a good idea of what is going on...if they're interested in finding out the truth. But I think a lot of people just don't want to know.

AC: So potential investors should seek appointments with you?

ASSK: Not necessarily with me. They can also seek appointments with other people in our organization and other people in the democratic forces who would be in a position to explain to them what is really going on in this country.

AC: Certain business people and politicians argue that investment in Burma is good because it creates a middle class and therefore the most expedient way to usher in democracy. How would you respond to this argument?

ASSK: Investments in Burma during the last seven years [from the time of SLORC taking power] have done nothing to create a stronger middle class. There are a few people who have gotten very rich, and a rapidly increasing pool of the very poor. The great majority of civil servants, who should normally be part of the middle class, are struggling to get on with their lives. Their salaries are so low compared to the cost of living they have to choose between corruption and starvation.

AC: SLORC presents a grotesquely inaccurate picture of reality in your country to its own people. No one believes SLORC's newspaper or television reports. The vast majority of the population today rely on your weekend talks for the truth and an analysis of the facts. Are tapes and videos of your talks getting out into the rural areas?

ASSK: I believe so. But people can learn the truth in a variety of ways. For example, everybody was very grateful because the official Burmese media broadcast the whole speech of their Ambassador to the United Nations. It gave them a chance to find out what was actually in the resolution (*laughing*). Otherwise, they would not have known. So truth "won out" in some way or another.

AC: What happens if someone is caught by the authorities listening to one of your tapes or watching one of your videos?

ASSK: In some instances people have had their television sets and video decks confiscated. While in other places the authorities have actually issued orders that no one is to watch my videotapes.

AC: What are your feelings about the use of non-violent demonstrations in Burma today? Are you advocating them? Considering them? Discouraging them?

ASSK: At the moment I'm not advocating anything. I've always said that one works according to a changing situation. You cannot have one fixed policy for all time.

AC: Are you aware of any radical, left-wing militant groups within the country that advocate urban guerrilla tactics as we have seen in Northern Ireland or in the Middle East?

ASSK: I'm not aware of them. But there are probably individuals who would like to work along those lines.

AC: Do you have students who plead with you to engage in an armed struggle with SLORC?

ASSK: Not just students, there have also been elderly men who have advocated armed struggle. They think this government is so lacking in good intentions that the only way to get democracy is by crushing them through force of arms. I think it's sheer frustration that drives them to this conclusion and the fact that the attitude of the authorities is so extreme. Extremism begets extremism.

AC: I can easily understand their attitude. In Nigeria, Ken Saro-Wiwa [a writer, human rights and environmental activist] summed it up bluntly in a letter that was smuggled from his prison cell several months prior to his execution: "Do I think I'll be executed? Yes. I expect it. We're dealing here with a group of Stone-Age military dictators addicted to blood."

What turned your father away from the use of weapons to overthrow fascism and imperialism towards a non-violent political solution? Did he study Gandhian principles?

<u>ASSK:</u> He didn't advocate a non-violent, non-cooperation movement the way Gandhi did in India. My father was very intelligent and he used it in an extremely practical way. He was also quite ready to admit his mistakes. For example, he acknowledged that it was because of his—not just his—but a general political immaturity of the younger people involved in the independence movement that made them look to a fascist military power [Japan] for help. But he was quick to learn and decided later that the best way to go about achieving independence was through a political solution that hurts no one.

<u>AC:</u> Do you consider yourself more of a Gandhian-styled political leader? Or does your approach to non-violence come more from your understanding within Buddhism?

<u>ASSK:</u> I don't think of myself as either a Gandhian or Buddhist politician. I am Buddhist of course, and I would be guided by all the Buddhist principles that I have absorbed throughout my life. The fact that I admire the men who led Burma's "first independence movement" also means that I'm influenced to some degree by their principles and actions. But primarily the reason why I object to violent means is because I think it would perpetuate a tradition of changing the political situation through force of arms.

<u>AC:</u> All of your most intimate colleagues—the EC members within the NLD—are ex-military men, mostly retired or sacked generals with a long history of appreciating the combatant's role in life. Do you find in your discussions together that they struggle perhaps to understand or appreciate your conviction in the use of non-violence in achieving a political solution?

<u>ASSK:</u> For me it's very practical. If you want to establish a strong tradition of democracy in this country one of the basic principles of achieving it is that you bring about political change peacefully through consulting the will of the people via the ballot box and not through force of arms. If you want democracy you must demonstrate its principles; you need to be consistent in politics.

AC: Would you say more about consistency in political policy?

ASSK: If you say that you want to change a system where might is right, then you have to prove that right is might. You can't use might in order to bring about what you think is right and then still insist that right is might. People are not fooled by that. I was told a story by a monk in the Inlay Lake area when I went up there in 1989. Have you ever heard of U Po Sein? He was a very well-known dancer in a Burmese theater troupe. There was a comedian in U Po Sein's troupe who would say before the beginning of a performance: "Look here, U Po Sein, nobody in the audience can dance as well as you. But there is nobody in this audience who will not know if you make a wrong move." It's like that in politics too. People may seem apathetic and indifferent but they know if you make a wrong move, or that you've been inconsistent.

AC: Do you ever feel, perhaps in one of your more private moments, overwhelmed in your position of non-violence, say in relationship to the global addiction to violence? Do you feel like a lone star, so to speak, in the midst of the darkness? Leaders the world over generally believe that "might is right" and the greater the might usually determines who wins in the end.

ASSK: I don't think I'm the only one who does not believe that weapons are the way to change. But yes, if you really conjure up an image of all the weapons in the world it would be much higher than Mount Everest, don't you think?

AC: I have heard an image used to describe the amount of nuclear weapons on the planet. If you were to translate nuclear warheads into TNT, you could fill successive train cars that would extend to the moon and back eight times.

ASSK: I really wonder why people waste so much time, energy and money on producing that kind of stuff.

AC: Do you know specifically where all the weapons are coming from that SLORC consumes?

ASSK: I know that the government buys a lot of arms from China. But I think it buys arms from other places as well. There was a rumor some time ago that some high-ranking officials in SLORC were going around to various countries—including some in Europe—trying to buy arms.

AC: What would you say are the main qualities of consciousness that you try to foster in yourself and encourage others to embrace, as the foundation of your struggle for democracy?

ASSK: First of all, what we would like is vision. We would like the people to see and understand why a political system is tied up with our daily lives. Why we cannot ignore politics and just concentrate on economics, as the authorities would like us to do. We want them to understand that our struggle for democracy is a struggle for our everyday life, that it's not removed. It's not something that you do when you have a bit of free time, or when you feel like it. You have to work at it all the time, because it affects your life all the time. You can never separate the political system of a country from the way in which you conduct your daily life. This is basically the spirit that we want—an awareness that what we are struggling for is not some distant goal or ideal. What we are struggling for is a change in our everyday lives. We want freedom from fear and want. There are people today who enjoy materially secure lives, but they can never be sure when this will be taken from them. There must be a sense of security that as long as we're not doing harm to others, as long as we are not infringing the laws which were brought about so that we should not harm each other, we should be able to rest secure in the knowledge that we ourselves will not be harmed. That the authorities cannot remove you from your job, kick you out of your house, throw you in prison, or have you executed, if you have done nothing to warrant such actions.

AC: SLORC seems to have a fetish for forcibly evicting people from their homes and relocating them to more "desirable" areas. I know that in 1990, the *New York Times* reported that the authorities "forcibly relocated over 500,000 people from Rangoon alone" and trucked these people to their "new towns," that turned out to be nothing more than malaria-infested swamp land. Apparently this happened all over the country and I'm told that it continues today. Could you explain what's behind these current SLORC evictions and confiscations of property?

ASSK: Whenever they [SLORC] think they need a particular piece of land for a building project, then off these people go...

AC: These people have no rights whatsoever?

ASSK: No. People have no rights.

AC: So they are simply told by the authorities to get out of their homes on such and such a date and that's it?

ASSK: That's right.

AC: Where do they go?

ASSK: Most of them are just dumped in fields and told to put up their huts.

AC: How widespread is this today?

ASSK: It happens all over Burma.

AC: And the reason?

ASSK: Forced relocations are mostly carried out with a view to making a place more attractive for tourists.

AC: I know that the American government has a two-million-dollar ransom on the Burmese citizen Khun Sa, known by most people as the world's most notorious heroin drug lord—supplying approximately 60 percent of the global heroin supply. And just recently SLORC cut a deal with him; however, the nature of the deal remains somewhat of a mystery. Which leads to my question. Khun Sa's 13,000 soldiers are seen every day on SLORC-controlled television handing over their weapons, but where is the beef, in other words—the tens of thousands of tons of heroin?

ASSK: I've absolutely no idea where the heroin is. Let's wait and see, perhaps the heroin will emerge...

AC: Is it as simple as the SLORC having cut an amnesty deal with him? I mean this guy makes Noriega look like a drug-store cowboy.

ASSK: Well, you've seen photographs of Khun Sa. Does he look like a man who is in fear of his future?

AC: He looks like a pretty happy camper to me.

ASSK: Exactly. He does not look at all nervous. He's on equal terms with the [SLORC] ministers and commanders. He seems very much like a man who has got nothing to worry about.

AC: I guess I've once again been outsmarted by SLORC's stupidity. I could never have imagined that they would go public with it.

ASSK: It comes back to that same old question we were talking about, are they really that stupid? Or is there some deep thought behind it? Tell me what you think. Everyone is absolutely mystified as to why they've done something so silly.

AC: How would the NLD go about resolving the opium and heroin problem in Burma? And would you in fact grant America's request to extradite Khun Sa to stand trial in the US?

ASSK: Let us talk about the drug issue—how we are going to try to eradicate this problem. Those people who actually grow opium pop-pies are not that rich. The reason they grow poppies is because they have no other means of income or because they are afraid of the drug runners who force them to grow them. If we provide them with alternative sources of income, then they won't be so keen to go on. It is all a matter of education. They have to understand why it is better for them not to continue growing opium. We don't believe in just telling people to stop doing something. We want them to understand why they should stop. We, at the NLD, are great believ-ers in education. We want to make the people understand that they do not need to grow opium poppies. So we will give them practi-cal help and also educate them so that they will not want to go on with opium production.

AC: As we know, habits run deep, it'll take quite some time...

ASSK: It will take time but perhaps it will not take as long as people think it will, because do not forget that in these days of international communications revolution, you can get across to people very quickly if you really want to try—if you are really intent on doing so.

AC: And regarding Khun Sa?

ASSK: We shall have to go into that very carefully. We are not the government of this country. We are not in a position to do anything about him and we do not believe in making premature comments.

AC: What do you think would be Burma's unique expression of democracy?

ASSK: I don't know because we have not started our democracy yet. But I would like to think that it would be a democracy with a more compassionate face. A gentler sort of democracy...gentler because it's stronger.

AC: Would it be a capitalistic form of democracy?

ASSK: We've never thought of it as a capitalist democracy as such. We do not see why democracy should be made a part of capitalism or vice versa. We think that democracy means the will of the people. It means certain basic freedoms, which will have to include basic economic freedoms that would allow for capitalism. But that does not mean that the state would not have the responsibility for other aspects of the nation, such as education and health.

AC: Last year His Holiness the Dalai Lama said that what the Chinese are doing to his people "is a kind of cultural genocide and that time is running out." He went on to say that if the Chinese continue this, "there will be no Tibet to save." Could the same be said of Burma? Is time running out? Is there a time limit to how...

ASSK: No, of course not. Why should there be a time limit?

AC: I don't know, perhaps the desperation level of the people will peak and exceed their fears and they'll rise up again like in 1988...

ASSK: There's always a limit to what people are prepared to take. That doesn't necessarily mean that they'll express their discontent through demonstrations. But I don't think people will go on forever accepting injustice.

Chapter 7

"Saints are sinners who go on trying"

ALAN CLEMENTS: I think it was His Holiness the Dalai Lama who said that we should "foster an appreciation—a real love for our shared human status." There is something beautiful and appealing about the notion. And yet it seems foreign.... When I conjure up ghastly images of Auschwitz and death camps, the sea of cracked skulls from Pol Pot's killing fields, hacked-up bodies of Rwandan Hutus, or women screaming in Serbian rape camps, my heart closes. I wonder if the perpetrators of such atrocities can even be considered as human beings. Quite frankly, they seem sub-human. And Daw Suu, you seem to live and breathe your country's suffering. How do you manage to keep your heart open to the pain?

AUNG SAN SUU KYI: It depends on the circles in which you move. I think I'm very fortunate that the people around me have such open hearts. Because we can afford to be loving with each other, the habit of opening our hearts is always there. Also, if you know that there are people in the world who are worthy of love, and whom you could open up to without danger, I think you are more ready to accept that there are others too who could be lovable.

<u>AC:</u> I'll be specific. How do you look into the eyes of SLORC without feeling a sense of outrage, really?

<u>ASSK:</u> People often come to me and ask the same question: "Why don't you feel any sense of vindictiveness?" I think some of the people who ask this question don't believe that we are actually free from such feelings. It's very difficult to explain. The other day Uncle U Kyi Maung, Uncle U Tin U and I were talking with a group of our NLD delegates and we were laughing over this. Apparently, you had

113

asked Uncle U Kyi Maung how he felt the day he heard I was going to be placed under arrest. And he replied that he didn't feel anything at all. And you were surprised by that...

AC: Not only surprised, but I was shocked. Because what he said was that despite the fact that armed soldiers had surrounded your house, and it was likely that you would be taken to Insein Prison, you all just laughed about the crisis and started cracking jokes.

ASSK: Yes, and we didn't feel anything at all. So many journalists have asked me; "How did you feel when you were released?" I have said, "I felt nothing at all." (*laughing*) I had a vague idea that I should feel something, but my real concern was what should I do now? Then a journalist asked if I were elated or felt happy. I said, "No...none of these things. I always knew that I was going to be free one day. The point was, well, what do I do now?" But a lot of people don't believe me.

AC: They assume that it's some form of denial or repression in you?

ASSK: Exactly. (*laughing*) It's very strange.

AC: When you speak of "feeling nothing at all" after your release from detention, are you saying that the past is simply irrelevant?

ASSK: I don't think you can just forget the past but one should use experiences of the past to build up a better present and future.

AC: What about the victims who don't have the resiliency or the depth of spirit that you and your colleagues have, and do feel violated and made resentful by the atrocities committed towards them?

ASSK: Of course. Of course. This is why we are talking about the connection of truth and reconciliation. I think that first of all, their sufferings have to be acknowledged. You can't just wipe away the past. If you try, there will always be this ocean of festering resentment within those who have truly suffered. They will feel that their sufferings have been pushed aside, as though they've suffered for nothing; as though they've undergone torture for nothing; as though their sons and fathers had died for nothing. Those people must have the satisfaction of knowing that their sufferings have not been in vain, and this very fact, that there's an admission of the injustice done, will take away a lot of the resentment. Mind you, people are different. Some will always want vengeance and will keep on thirsting for it even if everyone says: "Yes, we know how you've suffered; we acknowledge the wrong that has been done to you or your father, or your son or daughter." There will always be people who can never forgive. But we must always try to. In Chile they had a Council for Truth and Reconciliation and there's one now in South Africa, under Archbishop Desmond Tutu. I very much believe in it. The admission of injustice, to a certain extent, will prevent it from happening again. People will realize that if you do such things, they get known. You can't hide them.

AC: Do you think it's essentially a human right that some form of justice is still required, beyond just an acknowledgment of the anguish and suffering a family or an individual has been forced to bear?

ASSK: Let's consider it as satisfaction rather than as a need for justice. If you talk about justice as a "human right" it could be misinterpreted as something done under the law. In many countries where dictatorships have fallen and democracies have arisen, you will find that it's not always possible to take full legal action against those who have perpetrated injustices. For various reasons there have had to be compromises. So if one talks about "justice," it might give the wrong impression that everything that has happened must be tried in a court, and that justice must be done in the legal sense. I would rather say that something must be done to satisfy the victims and the families of those victims.

AC: I was speaking to a Burmese friend of mine the other day and he gave an impassioned appeal on behalf of what he called the "88 generation," those university students who spearheaded the mass demonstrations. He said, "We feel hopeless, despairing and aimless. SLORC crushed our hopes of freedom." I would like to take the issue beyond Burma. What advice might you offer to such people living in such psychological pain?

ASSK: The only cure is work. I think that those who are really doing everything they can, whatever it is, do not feel either despair or hopelessness, because they're involved in the doing. To those who say that they are in such states of mind, one must ask: "Are you doing everything you can?" And I think, if the answer is truly "Yes," then you feel neither hopeless nor despairing.

AC: Experience shows that there is often a lag period between the trauma and the action to overcome it. It's a temporary paralysis of the spirit, so to speak. How can one breathe positive significance into despair and hopelessness? How might one give it spiritual meaning and value and turn it around to make it work in his favor?

ASSK: Let me try to explain this with a very down-to-earth example. I have often noticed this: when there is a simple household crisis, such as for example, the pressure-cooker bursting and throwing soup all over the kitchen ceiling, my first reaction is: "All right, calm down." Just tackle it. Because if you just stand there saying, "The pressure-cooker has burst and it's spurting all over the place," you can get into an absolute tizz. But my reaction is to say, "Well, there's no point getting into a tizz. I can't wish the soup back into the pressure-cooker simmering away in safety. I've just got to get on with cleaning it up." So I turn off the gas, and then I get a rag to clean up the mess. That in itself calms you down. You've got to work. If you're apathetic or filled with hopelessness and despair you've got to do what you can. I can't do anything about the fact that I have lost half the soup. But I can certainly clean up all traces of the disaster. Then I can start thinking, "Now, should I cook a bit more soup? Or should I supplement it with something else?" You get down to work and don't just stand there despairing. That's what I would say to people who feel hopeless and despairing: "Don't just sit there. Do something."

AC: So, in other words, the positive action itself is the healing?

ASSK: Yes. There's always something you can do if you really put your mind to it. I do believe that.

AC: Do you feel that there is ever a need for intimate discussion about the often traumatizing emotions of despair and grief without being indulgent?

ASSK: Of course there is. After all, the bursting of a pressure-cooker is a very minor crisis. But with big crises, for example the loss of a loved one, I believe that people must be allowed to talk about it and work through their feelings. But at the same time, you must encourage these people to get on with life; not to just sit and grieve over the person they have lost. So you have got to give them all the emotional support you can, but also try to find something practical for them to do. Such as, to think of those who are still alive and to do something for them.

AC: On the opposite side of things, with your enormous regard and compassion for the victims of suffering, are you also considering how to create safe conditions for the authorities when the struggle for democracy is successfully achieved? Because in a sense, they too are victims, so to speak, of their own fear and self-deception.

ASSK: It is too premature to talk about these things. Such matters should only be discussed when one enters into dialogue. But we do not want to penalize anyone, as such. We want a society where the healing process can take place quickly and that process must involve the satisfaction, to some extent, of the victims.

AC: Healing implies the perception of wound—a psychological trauma or series of them that occurred in the past. But the Buddha insisted that he could not see a first beginning to suffering nor a first cause for the arising of afflictive emotions. Therefore, he encouraged his followers to seek liberation only in the present and not by delving into the past. To explain this point, he used the simile of a man shot with a poisoned arrow. You might know it...

ASSK: That's right...

AC: So. This man is lying on the ground wounded and dying. As the Buddha attempts to save the man's life by pulling out the arrow, the man stops him and says: "Before you remove the arrow I want to know who shot me? Why did he shoot me? From what tree was the shaft of the arrow carved?" And so on and so forth, until the man dies. So my question is, how do the Buddha's teachings of "non-postponement" to the release of suffering fit into your idea of the healing process?

117

ASSK: There are some things that have to be done immediately and there are other things that have to be done later. Take something similar to the story of the arrow; if somebody is brought in as an emergency case—you immediately give him emergency treatment. But later, it may be necessary to go into the origin of whatever it is he's suffering from, in order for the healing process to be more effective. Now using the simile of the poisoned arrow, the first things to be done would be to pull it out, clean the wound, and dress it. Of course, that's not the moment to be inquiring into what kind of poison it was. But afterwards, it will be necessary to find out what sort of poison was on the arrow in order to give it the right antidote. So everything at the right time.

AC: In your "Freedom from Fear" essay* you quoted somebody, I'm not sure who it was, who said, "Saints are sinners who go on trying..."

ASSK: Yes. I can't remember who said or wrote it but I came across it a long time ago and I've always liked it very much.

AC: I like it too. Which brings me to the question. Prior to becoming a disciple, Saint Paul, known then as Saul of Tarsus, killed many people, including children, who espoused Christianity. Within the Buddhist tradition we also have examples of archetypal redemption, such as Angulimala—the mass murderer who changed and became a monk, and later achieved enlightenment...

ASSK: I wonder how old they were when they were converted? Do you know how old Angulimala was when he was changed by the Buddha?

AC: Well, from some of the temple paintings I've seen of him he's depicted as rather young...

ASSK: I think he was supposed to be quite young. Because he had started on his finger-collecting business quite early, hadn't he?

AC: To have cut a finger off every victim and to have reached 999

---

* "Freedom From Fear" first published July 1991 in various newspapers and journals worldwide, including *The Times Literary Supplement*, the *New York Times*, the *Far Eastern Economic Review*, the *Bangkok Post*, the *Times of India* and the German, Icelandic and Norwegian press. Reprinted in *Freedom from Fear*, published by Penguin Books, revised edition 1995.

murders he must have started early. But such dramatic spiritual conversions...

ASSK: You mean the blinding flash of light kind of conversion?

AC: No...how should I say it? It's so easy to segregate life into neat little ethical compartments of right and wrong, good and bad, moral and immoral, as if someone really had a hold on omnipotence. And if we don't open to a bigger picture, say as in these examples of redemption, the power of this quote is drastically reduced, if not lost altogether. I would like to understand how to feel more compassion for those who are considered as a menace to society? At times I have considered that capital punishment would be a good thing...

ASSK: Do you really think so?

AC: Would I want, on a personal level, someone to die for his crime? The closest I can get to that issue in truth, is no, I don't think so. However, I do know that if a killer hacked up my loved ones I'd be pressed to the edge and might seek revenge...

ASSK: But if you're a good Buddhist, shouldn't you be trying to change yourself rather than wishing that capital punishment would get rid of them?

AC: Well, all I'm saying is that some people do seem irredeemable. They're "natural born killers" who seem to have a perverse pleasure in making others suffer.

ASSK: How do you know they are irredeemable?

AC: I don't. It just seems rather likely from their behavior.... What do you think?

ASSK: I'm not in a position to decide who is redeemable and who's not. Just because I'm not able to redeem people doesn't mean that they are irredeemable. There are others who may be able to.

AC: Violence is just about everywhere we turn today. Many of our inner cities are war zones. Crime is the number one fear among most Americans. And in Burma today, the repression is escalating all the time. What is the driving force that allows one to keep on going when faced with cruel repression?

ASSK: My colleagues and I have been discussing this issue quite a lot lately. I think it's difficult to find an answer, but there is something innate in every human being. Although this is something that can be adapted, or changed, or made to take a more positive direction, some by nature are more inclined than others to taking a strong position. Of course, the social and political climate has a lot to do with it too. It is amazing to me how so many people simply do what they're told by the authorities. They've been conditioned to obey without questioning the situation. Which is why I always tell them to keep a questing mind. A questing mind is a great help towards withstanding violence or oppression, or any trend that is contrary to what you believe is right and just.

AC: What about the issue of turning away in the face of suffering, especially for those who're responding to their instinct to serve? Is it self-deception, yet another face of fear that masquerades as legitimate avoidance whereby one is paralyzed in spirit and soul from actually doing something to help? I know good people who want to serve, to give back to life, to support the oppressed, but the discussion often ends with who gets what, where, when and how?

ASSK: Well, if you have a mind that is always "questing" you'll find the answers; if you're always thinking of the ways and means of doing something to serve, you will. The "seeker" has the kind of mind that is not just questioning, but actually seeking answers. That is why I say a "questing mind" rather than a questioning mind.

AC: I've seen that many people pressure themselves when the "questing mind" turns rancid, into guilt or fear. Then one hurts to serve, so to speak, and loses the love of service. So is it fair to say that people should not pressure themselves into service but just keep an active inquiry?

ASSK: It's a beginning. Action comes out of thought. It should not be the kind of impulsive action that has no principle behind it. So I think, a first step is the questing process of looking for answers and searching for a way out of any problem. The second step is to put the answers into action.

AC: Going back to 1988. From what I understand, when the National League for Democracy was founded there were three factions that joined into one, and the group that you headed represented Burma's intellectuals—the artists, musicians, lawyers...

ASSK: Yes.

AC: I brought with me a quote from Václav Havel in which he explains the role of the intellectual within society. When I first read it, I instantly thought of you. He writes: "The intellectual should constantly disturb, should bear witness to the misery of the world, should be provocative by being independent, should rebel against all hidden and open pressures and manipulations, should be the chief doubter of systems...and for this reason, an intellectual cannot fit into any role that might be assigned to him...and essentially doesn't belong anywhere: he stands out as an irritant wherever he is."

ASSK: I would agree with everything that Václav Havel says. I would say that basically, in order to become an intellectual you've got to have a questioning mind. I think everybody is capable of having a questioning mind, but not everybody who has one can be described as an intellectual. To be an intellectual also requires some kind of scholastic discipline—that's essential. Intellectuals are very important in any society. Because they are the ones who, like in the quotation, are provoking people, opening them to new ideas, pushing them along to new heights. This is one of the tragedies of Burma—the intellectual is not allowed any place within society. And the real intellectual, of the kind described by Václav Havel, would not be allowed to survive in Burma.

AC: Why?

ASSK: He would either have to repress his instincts as an intellectual, or he would have to leave Burma, or he would have to go and sit in prison. He's got to choose between those three.

AC: So by function, a totalitarian regime attempts to create a mind-

121

less, featureless society by crushing the intellectual?

ASSK: The intellectual with his questioning mind threatens the totalitarian mind which expects orders to be carried out and decrees to be accepted without question. There will always be clashes between the authoritarian mind and the questioning mind. They just cannot go together.

AC: But of course, that's the very task you're confronted with in seeking genuine dialogue and potential reconciliation with SLORC.

ASSK: It doesn't mean that because you are part of an authoritarian regime, you don't have a spark of questioning in your mind.

AC: What is the chief factor that promotes the questioning mind?

ASSK: To begin with, you must have an interest in the world around you. If you're deaf and blind to it you won't question what is going on.

AC: Is the non-questioning mind an issue of unrecognized fright?

ASSK: No, I don't think it's just fright. Obviously, we're all born different and upbringing comes into it as well. One may be born with a questioning mind, but it may not have been encouraged, so it could get blunted. If you're bludgeoned every time you raise a question then you learn not to raise questions. And in time, you probably forget how to question. Even if you're not born with a questioning mind, you could be encouraged to acquire the habit. My mother did not encourage me to question, but she certainly never discouraged me either. She didn't say, "Ask questions." But when I asked questions she was always there even if she could not provide the answers.

And then of course, we were brought up on the legend of Pauk Kyine. One of the maxims that we learned from the legend was that if you go on questioning, you receive answers. If you go on traveling, you will reach your goal. If you keep alert and don't sleep much, you will have a long life. This is what we were taught as children. And most Burmese children know this story so well they've learned the maxims by heart. See in that story, the hero saves his life by staying alert throughout the night and by keeping close watch on the world around him.

AC: Perhaps it's impossible to know, but how have you come to have such a love of truth?

ASSK: I was not born with it. It was a matter of training. My mother was insistent on my being honest. In fact, she would get very angry if I didn't tell the truth...

AC: Did she actually explain to you an underlying principle or logic as to why honesty was preferable to deception?

ASSK: She did not always explain why it was necessary to be honest. She just made it very clear that honesty was good and dishonesty was wrong. This was something that I accepted at a very early age. My mother was naturally brave and honest—all those things I had to work to be. That was really good for me because it gives me the confidence that other people too can work towards such qualities.

AC: You seem to keep a relentless pace, meeting hundreds of people weekly. Also, there's a nearly endless line of foreign journalists seeking interviews with you. There are your weekend public talks and then your NLD EC meetings, with decisions that might affect millions of lives. How do you keep up the intensity? Do you ever have to stop and reconnect to that place of inner calm, in order to keep on going?

ASSK: I stop every evening, because in the evening I'm all alone and it's an automatic way of standing back from the action. Of course, there are times when I have to work very late into the night. Then I don't have much time to sit and take stock. The moment I finish work I just go straight to bed. But normally I get a few days a week when everything is quiet by seven o'clock at night and I'm alone in the house. It makes me realize there is always change. Life, in a sense, is lived on two levels, the hurly-burly of the world outside and the quietness of your inner life. And that's brought home to me practically every evening.

AC: When you do have these precious few moments alone at night, what do you normally do?

123

<u>ASSK:</u> It depends. Sometimes I have to do the most mundane things, like tidying my clothes or my desk. Sometimes I sit and read. I have to say that quite a lot of the time when I finish early, on those two or three days a week, would be taken up with tidying up the mess that has accumulated. But it's quite peaceful. It's manual work. I just put the right things in the right place, that's all. It's almost mechanical.

<u>AC:</u> Are you super-organized?

<u>ASSK:</u> I used to be super-organized. I knew exactly where each book or each magazine was. But I'm afraid I'm not so super-organized since my release. I've just had no time to put everything away in its own place.

<u>AC:</u> Do you ever get to a point and say, the heck with it, I'm exhausted, enough for today?

<u>ASSK:</u> Sometimes I am exhausted. I would like to sleep for about twelve hours at a stretch or just stay in bed for a whole weekend, two days of nothing—except reading for pleasure. That would be my idea of a really good holiday. But, I just don't have the time to do that.

<u>AC:</u> Since the time of your release—do you ever do anything just for the fun of it?

<u>ASSK:</u> There's a lot of fun in my daily life. The people I work with are so nice and they all have such a good sense of humor. Yesterday we had a joint birthday party for two of my cousins, Dr. Sein Win [the Prime Minister of Burma's government-in-exile] and Ko Cho. We had our *lugyi's* come over—our elders as we call them—U Aung Shwe, U Kyi Maung, U Tin U, U Lwin [EC members of the NLD] and our aunties—their wives. It was a simple party; not much apart from cake, tea and potato chips. But it was fun. We all had a really nice time. And every day too, there is a lot of joy and happiness—speaking with my colleagues, having lunch together with the office staff—just being with such good people struggling together, is in itself nourishing and replenishing. So I'm lucky to be surrounded by such great people.

<u>AC:</u> Besides being NLD colleagues, who are U Tin U* and U Kyi Maung** to you? Since they are both quite a bit older than you, are they your mentors or father figures as well?

<u>ASSK:</u> I look upon them as my uncles. Uncles are people who stand in for your father. So I do look upon them, in a sense, as father figures. But at the same time, when we work together they are very much my colleagues. On a daily basis they're friends too. Except I don't like to talk to them as friends, because that puts them on the same level as me. I like to think of them as higher, because they're older, and in that sense, I do look up to them. And yet, friends are the most precious things in the world. Friends mean more than anything else to me. So without intending any disrespect perhaps I could say they are two of my best friends—or to use that old phrase, "guide, mentor and friend." They are very different in character but both are equally endearing and equally trustworthy.

---

* See Appendix B for conversation with U Tin U.
** See Appendix A for conversation with U Kyi Maung.

Chapter 8

"I never learned to hate my captors"

ALAN CLEMENTS: Prior to your return to Burma in March 1988, you had been living a classic householder's life in Oxford. That is, until you received word that your mother had suffered a stroke, at which point you flew to Rangoon to be with her. Five months later you were at the center of a nationwide revolution with you as the principal leader. Was it a dramatic transformation for you, or was it a more gradual transition?

AUNG SAN SUU KYI: I was gradually drawn into the movement. To begin with, I was sitting in the hospital looking after my mother and I heard what was going on. Then people would come and talk with me about it, how bad the political and economic situation was. I did not say much, I just listened.

AC: There was no moment of epiphany when you realized that this was the moment for you to enter your people's democracy struggle?

ASSK: No. I don't remember such a moment. It was much more gradual.

AC: So when you came back to Burma to be with your ailing mother, you had no idea whatsoever that you would enter politics?

ASSK: I hadn't even an idea that the democracy struggle was going to take place like that. I don't think anybody did. I did know that things were going to change in Burma because people were extremely unhappy and restless by 1987. They were also more out-spoken and openly dissatisfied with the situation. And before I came in at the end of March, the problems with the students had already begun. On 13 March, Maung Phong Maw [a student from the Rangoon Institute of Technology] was killed. So by the time I arrived I knew that things were happening. In that sense, I knew as others did, that Burma was not going to remain quiescent. But I don't think I knew any more than anybody else that there would be such widespread demonstrations for democracy.

AC: During your years abroad, knowing well the conditions your people were living under, did you feel a constant angst, wanting to do something for your people but not knowing how to go about it?

ASSK: No. Of course, I did not like the situation. During my visits to Rangoon I would sometimes spend three or four months with my mother, and always when friends came over, at some time or the other, the conversation would inevitably turn towards the situation of the country.

AC: When you look back to that period, reflecting on the crisis in your country, could you envision the light of political change? It had such a rock-solid dictatorship for over three decades.

ASSK: Always throughout those years I had been very well aware of the fact that the majority of Burmese were growing more and more dissatisfied with the situation. So a lot of us believed that there would have to be a change.

AC: Did you have any idea of how or when that change would occur?

ASSK: No.

AC: Once the demonstrations began, were people prepared for such a violent military response? Did anyone anticipate it? Then again, as I think about it, Ne Win has had a long history of quelling dissent with violence.

ASSK: There had already been a couple of students who had been shot dead. So I don't think it was entirely unexpected.

AC: Did you participate in the demonstrations?

ASSK: No.

AC: Was it a matter of policy?

ASSK: No. It was partly because I was constantly looking after my mother in the hospital when the demonstrations took place. But I don't think I would have taken part in the demonstrations anyway. If you ask why, I'm just the sort of person who generally does not like to take part in demonstrations. Although if I felt that there was a need to do so, I probably would have.

AC: But you obviously expressed your regard for the vision, the courage and the determination of those students who organized and led them.

ASSK: Oh yes. I admired those who did what they did. I was totally behind what they were doing.

AC: Even though you didn't participate in the demonstrations were you in any way involved in their organization?

ASSK: No. I was just one of the large silent majority who were supporting them.

AC: When did your home become the central coordinating headquarters of the struggle?

ASSK: That was much later—only after about mid-August.

AC: You gave your first public speech at the Shwedagon Pagoda in August 1988, in which you announced your entry into politics. It is said that 500,000 people attended. With so many supporters who came out to see you, did you think that a shift from a dictatorship to democracy was near at hand? Or did you predict it would be a long protracted struggle?

ASSK: At the time I don't think anybody knew how long it was going to take. In fact, a lot of people expected it to come sooner than it has and thought that it would just be a matter of months before democracy was established.

AC: Did you have any prior knowledge of SLORC's takeover on 18 September 1988?

ASSK: There were lots of rumors about a projected military coup.

AC: Did that alter your way of thinking about what would be the best way to approach your non-violent struggle? And were there preparations you made in anticipation of the coup?

ASSK: What preparations could we make? We were just organizing a more cohesive force for democracy, and that is what we continued doing.

AC: On 19 July 1989, you called off a march for the following day, Martyrs' Day, stating: "We do not want to lead our people straight into a killing field." When you think back to that day—the day before your arrest—and the day commemorating the death of your father—what comes to mind? How do you feel, almost seven years later and after several months of freedom?

ASSK: Well, it was not an easy decision to make. I realized that I would not get hurt...others would have. To carry on would have been irresponsible. If others would have got hurt and I had remained unhurt, it would have been a responsibility I could not have lived with.

AC: Did you know at that time that you would be arrested any day?

ASSK: We had heard for some time that I would be arrested after the 19th of July.

AC: How did you hear?

ASSK: Just rumors, lots of rumors.

AC: May I ask you to describe what actually took place on the day of your arrest?

ASSK: Well, I think in the morning...I'm just trying to remember the exact sequence. One of my cousins came in at one point and said that there were soldiers all over the place and something was happening that was not quite right. Then Uncle U Tin U's son drove over and said his father had tried to go out for a walk in the morning and had been forbidden to leave his compound. He thought we were all going to be arrested. So we all took it for granted.

AC: How did you feel emotionally in such a difficult moment?

ASSK: I'm not sure that anything was going on emotionally. I just packed a bag with things to take to prison with me. Because we all thought that we would be taken to Insein Jail.

AC: Was your husband with you at the time?

ASSK: No. But Kim and Alexander were.

AC: Was there some degree of shock or panic within your children?

ASSK: No, not at all. I just explained to them—you know, Michael was due to arrive in a few days' time—that if their father did not arrive in a few days because he was not given a visa or something like that, then arrangements would be made for them to be sent back. I told some relatives that if Michael was not allowed to come in, they should just arrange for the children to be sent back. That's all. They understood.

AC: Once it was clear that you would not be taken to Insein Prison and that you were being placed under house arrest, you undertook a hunger strike. Were you prepared to go the distance, if necessary?

ASSK: I never say I'm going to do this or that. That is something I've never done, because I know that in politics one has to be flexible. I'm not one of those people who would ever say, hunger strike until death. I think of that as trying to create a zero-sum solution.

AC: Obviously you did it with a very clear purpose in mind.

ASSK: Well, you do it with a particular end in view.

AC: Was there anyone assisting you? Caring for you?

ASSK: My sons were with me. Then Michael arrived a few days later.

AC: That must be a rather dramatic event to watch your wife or your mother go on a hunger strike...

ASSK: Well, you know, we don't go in for melodrama in our family. We just think of the practical aspect of it. I do not encourage melodrama. I don't like it.

AC: You're extremely rational in that regard...

ASSK: No, I just think that melodrama is very silly. One has to live life on an even keel.

AC: What about the simplicity of pure emotions without melodrama?

ASSK: Well, there is nothing to get emotional about. And how is getting emotional going to help? It just uses up more energy.

AC: How long did your hunger strike continue?

ASSK: Eleven days.

AC: What prompted you to end it?

ASSK: Because I came to an arrangement with the authorities, with regard to the young people [NLD youth workers] who had been taken away from the house.

AC: Did the authorities honor that arrangement?

ASSK: Yes, I must say that they did honor it. They said they would treat these young people well, and they did so. They were not tortured. At least the ones who were taken from here.

AC: Did your house arrest essentially mean the cutting of all outside communication? The cutting of the telephone?

ASSK: We found the cutting of the telephone line funny. Because I always thought that it simply meant they switched it off somewhere at the main exchange. Actually no, they just came and cut off the wires of the telephone with a pair of scissors and carried it away. We found that very funny (*laughing*).

AC: Your house arrest was an archetypal sacrifice, if you will. On the one hand were your family and on the other your principles. The SLORC offered you freedom to leave the country if you wanted on the condition that you remain in exile, but obviously you had a deeper conviction in staying in Burma to further the struggle for freedom.

ASSK: As a mother, the greater sacrifice was giving up my sons, but I was always aware of the fact that others had sacrificed more than me. I never forget that my colleagues who are in prison suffer not only physically, but mentally for their families who have no security outside—in the larger prison of Burma under authoritarian rule. Prisoners know that their families have no security at all. The authorities could take action against their families at any time. Because their sacrifices are so much bigger than mine I cannot think of mine as a sacrifice. I think of it as a choice. Obviously, it is not a choice that I made happily, but one that I made without any reservations or hesitation. But I would much rather not have missed all those years of my children's lives. I would much rather have lived together with them.

<u>AC:</u> Has your family been supportive?

<u>ASSK:</u> Well, my family has been very supportive, which helps a great deal. And also, of course, I have not really been cut off entirely from my family. We don't live together, but it did not happen in one fell swoop. When I first entered politics, my family happened to be here with me tending to my mother. So it was not a case of my suddenly leaving them, or they leaving me. It was a more gradual transition which gave us an opportunity to adjust. Apart from the two years and four months during my house arrest when I had no contact with them, there has not been a sharp break.

<u>AC:</u> Do they have any interest in moving here and living with you?

<u>ASSK:</u> No, not at the moment. Nor do I encourage them, because I don't think the authorities would be particularly keen on making life happy for them.

<u>AC:</u> Are you able to stay in communication with them?

<u>ASSK:</u> Yes, they telephone me once a week and write whenever they can.

<u>AC:</u> Daw Suu, if I may I'd like to ask you a personal question. How has all that you have been through affected your marriage?

<u>ASSK:</u> I won't ever talk about my personal relationship with my family members. I believe in privacy.

<u>AC:</u> I fully respect that, but if I may ask you to clarify what are your basic thoughts behind the need for privacy?

<u>ASSK:</u> I believe in people's right to make their own choices, and people's right to their own privacy. It's for them to decide how much

they wish to reveal about their private life. It's freedom of choice. There are some people who like to talk about their private lives— they really love it. I have nothing to say to such people. It's not the way I do things, but of course, that is their choice.

AC: But what distinguishes the separation between that which is for the public and that which is private?

ASSK: That which has no bearing on my political work is private, and I only talk about things that concern the public. As I said, personal privacy has to be respected whether it's mine or that of others. I think my colleagues also believe in this. This is why we've never made personal attacks on anybody or referred to their personal lives, or even their foibles.

AC: As a matter of integrity you avoid speaking negatively about people in general?

ASSK: On a personal basis, yes. Of course, we have had to speak about people when it involves political actions.

AC: You posted excerpts of your father's speeches on the walls of the downstairs foyer. What was the purpose of this?

ASSK: I thought it would be educational for the [SLORC] security men who were here.

AC: Did you ever speak with them? Were they friendly?

ASSK: Of course, I talked to them. They were always very polite and some were very friendly.

AC: In a previous conversation of ours, you said: "I never learned to hate my captors, so I never felt frightened." Was your realization of not learning to hate your captors gained through mental reasoning or was it a sudden insight that developed one day when you looked them in the face?

ASSK: I think it has partly to do with my upbringing again. I may have mentioned to you that my mother never taught me to hate even those who killed my father. I never once heard my mother talk with hatred about the men who assassinated my father.

AC: Never?

ASSK: No…and she certainly never said anything to me that would have even made me feel resentful, let alone filled me with hate. Of course I thought before I entered politics in Burma that I was as capable of hate as anyone. However, later I realized that I did not know the feeling of real hatred, but it was something that I could see in my captors.

AC: You could actually see the hatred in the eyes of your captors?

ASSK: Yes, real hate and malice.

AC: May I ask then, what were your feelings towards your captors?

ASSK: I liked most of them as human beings—I could never help seeing the human side of them, what is likable. This is not to say I liked what they did. There are lots of things that they did and they are doing which I do not like at all. You must not think that I was very angelic and never got angry. Of course I got angry. But I never lost sight of the fact that they were human beings. And like all human beings, there's a side to them which must be likable.

AC: Did you turn your house arrest into a monastic-like life?

ASSK: I started off on the basis that I would have to be very disciplined and keep to a strict timetable. I thought that I must not waste my time and let myself go to seed (*laughing*). In fact, I did not find it at all difficult. I found it very easy to adjust to a regular timetable and I had enough to fill my days.

AC: What was your daily schedule?

ASSK: I would get up at 4:30 and meditate for an hour. Then I would listen to the radio for about an hour and a half. Then came my exercises, followed by a bit of reading before I bathed. After that came the day's program of reading, cleaning, mending or whatever it was I decided would be my chores for the day.

AC: How did you sustain yourself while you were under house arrest?

ASSK: I had a lot of things to do. It's not like sitting in a prison cell. I had a house to look after that had to be kept tidy and clean. I could listen to the radio and read. I could sew. I could do all the normal things that I would have imagined that many people do every day, with the exception of going out and having friends come in.

AC: So your life under incarceration was a huge silence filled with personal interests—household tasks, reading, radio, and sewing?

ASSK: No, I didn't think of it as a huge silence at all. They were just ordinary days. You know, people do like to dramatize things. It's not as dramatic as all that. I'm sure it's much more dramatic for people who are suddenly taken away from their homes and put in a prison cell. But I just continued to live in the house where I was before they put me under house arrest.

AC: Did you have any idea how long the authorities had planned to keep you under detention?

ASSK: The first detention order said one year, but we knew it was renewable.

AC: Did you think that your detention could go on indefinitely, maybe even for life?

ASSK: Yes. After the first extension I had a pretty good idea that this was something they could go on doing indefinitely. Especially after they changed the law.

AC: Did the authorities ever make it perfectly clear that you could be free if you left the country and did any SLORC members ever come to you directly to negotiate a settlement?

ASSK: No, but at one time they did make a suggestion that it might be a good idea. But they never put it to me in quite the way in which they put it to other people: "If she leaves the country...she can be free." But they knew that I knew because it was publicized on the BBC.

AC: You were never tempted by their offer of freedom?

ASSK: No.

AC: What was your reaction to their offer?

ASSK: My main reaction was surprise that they ever thought that I

Aung San and Daw Khin Kyi, Aung San Suu Kyi's parents, on their wedding day. PRIVATE COLLECTION

Aung San Suu Kyi, at about seven years of age, with her mother and eldest brother, Aung San U. COLLECTION OF THE BURMA PROJECT USA

Aung San.
COLLECTION OF THE BURMA
PROJECT USA

Aung San Suu Kyi
at age 6.
PRIVATE COLLECTION

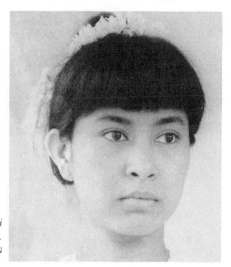

Aung San Suu Kyi
at about age 18.
PRIVATE COLLECTION

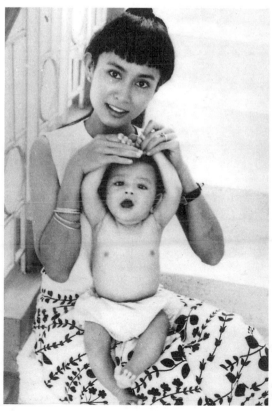

With her first-born son, Alexander,
in Nepal, 1973.
PRIVATE COLLECTION

Students on hunger strike demanding democracy and an end to one-party rule,
Rangoon, 1988. ZUNETTA LIDDELL

A student kissing the boot of
a soldier during demonstra-
tions in Rangoon, August
1988. RYO TAKEDA

With her two sons, Alexander (left) and Kim, May 1993—a rare photo of Aung San Suu Kyi while under house arrest. PRIVATE COLLECTION

From behind Aung San Suu Kyi's residence overlooking Lake Inya and one of the many luxury hotels under construction. ALAN CLEMENTS/THE BURMA PROJECT USA

Aung San Suu Kyi's family residence at 54 University Avenue in Rangoon.
ALAN CLEMENTS/THE BURMA PROJECT USA

*Chained forced
laborers in Burma.*
PETER CONRAD

would take up such an offer. And to a certain extent it indicated that they did not know me at all. I don't think this applies only to me. They do not really get to know people in general. I think it's very difficult for those who work by intimidating and using their power to repress others, to ever have the opportunity to get to know people really well. They have not learned the technique, so to speak, of getting to know people. Perhaps they have gotten into the habit of thinking that all people can be either intimidated or bought.

AC: We all have our dark moments where we have to wrestle with our demons. Did you ever get so frustrated that you just wanted to bang the wall with your fist?

ASSK: I did bang the keys of my piano the day I heard that Uncle U Tin U had been condemned to four years' hard labor. That put me in a bad temper. I thought that was highly unjust. It was sheer anger.

AC: Was there any period during your detention that you went into a more intensive period of meditation practice? Say for a few weeks or months, perhaps longer?

ASSK: No. But there were times when I did more meditation because I was getting better at it. I think this is the same with all those who meditate. Once you have discovered the joys of meditation as it were, you do tend to spend longer periods at it.

AC: May I ask what were the joys that you discovered?

ASSK: The stages I went through are the ones that Sayadaw U Pandita described in his book, *In This Very Life*. I'm just like any other meditator—nothing out of the ordinary.

AC: Your radio was your link to the world. What did you listen to?

ASSK: The news. I listened primarily to the BBC World Service, BBC and VOA [Voice of America] Burmese programs and The Democratic Voice of Burma. I also listened to the French radio but this was more to keep up my French than for any other reason. Sometimes I listened to the Japanese radio but I couldn't always fit it in; there were other things I wanted to listen to on the BBC World Service. So after some time I stopped listening to the Japanese radio. It just came on at the wrong time.

AC: Your period of incarceration obviously coincided with numerous and dramatic world changes, events that changed the political face of the world. Of course, these are too numerous to mention them all, but what were the ones that sparked the most interest in you?

ASSK: Anything that had to do with a democratic movement interested me tremendously. Everything that happened in Eastern Europe, in the Soviet Union, in South Africa, the Philippines, in Bangladesh, in Pakistan, in Latin America—anywhere and anything that had to do with the development of a democratic system of government or a more democratic way of life interested me very much.

AC: Did you have a television?

ASSK: I had a television which I had actually borrowed with a video deck to show some of the students an English Language program. That stayed with me throughout the six years (*laughing*).

AC: Were you allowed correspondence in and out?

ASSK: I carried on correspondence with my family for about the first year. But not after May of 1990. But that was more my choice.

AC: Based on?

ASSK: Two things. One was that they [SLORC] seemed to think they were doing me a tremendous favor by letting me communicate with my family. It was in fact my right. I've never accepted anything as a favor. So I would not accept any favors from them. Also, I did not think that they had a right to keep me under house arrest for longer than a year. In fact, they had no right to arrest all those NLD who had been successful in the elections. So it was a form of protest against injustices they were perpetrating as well as an indication that I would accept no favors from them.

AC: So you accepted nothing from the authorities, not even a penny?

ASSK: No.

AC: How did you survive?

ASSK: I sold some of my furniture.

AC: How did you manage to sell it?

ASSK: The security people sold it for me. Well, not that they sold it, they kept it in the warehouse. They paid me for it and the day of my release they brought back the whole lot. They were going to return it to me, but I said I couldn't accept it until I had paid for it. So I asked them to take it away until I gathered enough money.

AC: And how did you eat? Who did your shopping?

ASSK: I had a girl who'd come in during the week, every morning, and she did my shopping. She arranged all my food and everything.

AC: I've learned that your funds were so scarce that you had barely enough to eat and that your hair began falling out, and there were times you were too weak even to get out of bed.

ASSK: Yes, there were periods.

AC: How desperate did it get? Were you concerned with starvation?

ASSK: My theory was that if I died of anything it would probably be of heart failure from weakness, rather than from starvation.

AC: You had heart problems?

ASSK: No, but it's always a probability if you're undernourished.

AC: How would you say your incarceration has changed you? Do you feel it has matured you in some ways?

ASSK: One could say it matured me, but on the other hand I might have matured in any case. One gets more mature as one gets older, whether or not one is under house arrest.

AC: Where there any favorite books that you read?

ASSK: There were a number of books I liked quite a lot. I enjoyed Nehru's autobiography. I had an old copy of *Pride and Prejudice*, which I enjoyed reading again, but that was just for the enjoyment of the language more than for anything else. But a lot of the books were purely in the line of work, as it were—politics, philosophy, etcetera.

145

AC: Did you write during your incarceration?

ASSK: No. I didn't see the point in writing unless I could get my writing out to be published.

AC: Obviously some things did get out—your *Towards a True Refuge** essay.

ASSK: Yes. I wrote when Michael came and when I wanted to send out speeches or when arrangements were made for me to send out speeches through the authorities, which happened twice. The other speeches I just sent out through Michael.

AC: How were you informed of your release?

ASSK: The Head of Police and two other security personnel came at about four o'clock in the afternoon and told me about it.

AC: Were you given any prior notice?

ASSK: Well, I was told about one o'clock that they would be coming at about four o'clock.

AC: What was your first reaction when you were told?

ASSK: Well, my first reaction, I suppose, was that they're coming about my release. Then I thought, what should be my first move...

AC: What did you decide?

ASSK: I decided that I would ask Uncle U Kyi Maung and Auntie Kyi Kyi to come and see me because I have very good friendly relations with both of them. And of course, Uncle U Kyi Maung was the leader of the NLD who led our party through the elections.

AC: Did you immediately recommit yourself to a unified NLD and the continuation of the struggle?

ASSK: Of course. I asked Uncle U Kyi Maung to come over because I had every intention of continuing with it.

---

* Composed by Aung San Suu Kyi in the fourth year of her house arrest, as the Eighth Joyce Pearce Memorial Lecture, delivered on her behalf by Dr. Michael Aris on 19 May 1993 at Oxford University. Published in pamphlet form, Oxford 1993; reprinted in *Freedom from Fear* (Penguin Books, revised edition 1995).

<u>AC:</u> How soon after your release did you begin your public talks?

<u>ASSK:</u> The very next day. But I just went out to say hello, as it were, a few words of greeting.

<u>AC:</u> Are there any positive effects that have come from your period of incarceration?

<u>ASSK:</u> Well, I think if the SLORC had not put me under house arrest, our movement would not have attracted so much interest. It's always wrong to repress somebody whom you see as an enemy and who is without weapons. And SLORC, by being so harsh and oppressive in the way they have handled the opposition, has brought us a lot of sympathy in the country as well as throughout the rest of the world.

Chapter 9

"Violence is not the right way"

ALAN CLEMENTS: I'm struck by a major distinction among leaders of non-violent political movements. There appear to be two basic
paradigms of non-violence. One version is rooted in the belief in
God; meaning that its power and inspiration come from a theistic
or monotheistic understanding of the universe, life and humankind,
as seen in the movements led by Martin Luther King, Mahatma
Gandhi, Václav Havel and Nelson Mandela prior to his formation
of Umkhonto [the military wing of the ANC's struggle in South
Africa]. Each of these leaders, to a greater or lesser extent, had conviction in either a Christian or a Hindu conception of existence.
Whereas the second version is rooted in the belief in *anatta*—the Buddhist concept of emptiness, or interrelatedness, without any permanent god, entity, or "thing-figure" behind the veil. His Holiness
the Dalai Lama of Tibet is one example. Another one is the Vietnamese Buddhist monk, Thich Nhat Hahn who, as you may know,
led a non-violent peace movement during the Vietnam war and was
nominated for the Nobel Peace Prize by Martin Luther King in 1968.
And of course there's you, Aung San Suu Kyi, a dedicated Buddhist.

When you look at these examples, all the theistic expressions
of non-violence have been successful in their struggles, whereas the
Buddhists have not been successful in bringing about political
change—Thich Nhat Hahn admits this in his writings and the Dalai
Lama states that "time is quickly running out in Tibet." While in your
own struggle here in Burma, the results remain uncertain as SLORC
repression tightens daily. May I ask you for your impressions on this
distinction that I've raised?

AUNG SAN SUU KYI: But in Vietnam, especially in South Viet-

nam, there are so many Christians, and so many of them were in
key positions during the war. Ngo Dinh Diem was a Catholic. I
think that's one of the reasons for the failure of the Buddhist movement, because there were so many non-Buddhists holding power.
The Buddhist movement could not activate those who were crucial to the situation.

AC: Well, coming back to the question, is there anything to be said
about the conviction of those who have God in their souls *vis à vis*
those who see *anatta* as their abiding truth?

ASSK: I wonder whether it isn't something more practical than that.
Organized movements are essential to the way in which Christianity
works. Their churches are organized that way, whereas Buddhists
are not really organized around their monasteries. Although one
might go to the local monastery, or have one's favorite monastery
in which to worship, one does not necessarily stay confined to that
one monastery only. It's not like Christians who go to the same
church for years and years, and in so doing develop congregational
relationships. Perhaps your parents too went to the same church and
you know a lot of people through your ongoing association with
them. You also know what their parents were like and what affili-
ations they had. I think this is the way the base for organized movement is formed.

I have often thought that this is probably one of the reasons why
Christian-based political movements tend to take off quickly and
efficiently. The organization is already there. Look at Latin America, you'll find that a lot of their political movements against the
dictatorships, although they were not non-violent, were church-
based, which made them take off rather quickly. Even in Islamic
countries they have the mosque, which is formally organized, with
regular mosque meetings taking place weekly. This sort of formal
organization does not exist in Buddhist countries.

AC: So obviously you don't think that the success of these movements had anything to do with their convictions in God.

ASSK: I think that it's just the fact that they can meet regularly. Even
in India the government cannot say that Muslims must not go to

the Mosque. It would create such a reaction. They must allow them to go to the Mosque, so they can always meet regularly a minimum of once a week. Whereas, where can Buddhists meet? If the Buddhists started meeting once a week at a particular monastery, the MI [Military Intelligence] would be on to them immediately to find out what the meeting was about. But you can't stop people from going to church. In the Eastern European countries they tried this but once the focus of Western countries was on them and they needed Western loans, they could not tell people any more: "Don't go to church." It was so in Poland. There was a great deal of church-based political activity.

Now take an example in Burma. Last June Uncle U Kyi Maung started meeting a few elderly friends every Thursday for tea and a good discussion. What happened? They were hauled off by the MI and detained and interrogated for a few days. And if anybody thought of meeting regularly at a monastery in numbers of a hundred or two, there would be serious consequences. Whereas in Christian countries, the government may infiltrate the church with informers, but they would still have to allow these congregations to meet regularly. That's a great plus in favor of any popular movement.

AC: President Nelson Mandela writes in his autobiography, *Long Walk to Freedom* that in 1961 "the days of non-violent struggle were over.... We had no choice but to turn to violence." To substantiate his turn away from non-violence to violence he cited an old African expression: "The attacks of the wild beast cannot be averted only with bare hands." Nevertheless, there were some within the ANC who argued that non-violence was an inviolate principle, not a tactic that should be abandoned when it no longer worked. To this Mr. Mandela countered: "[I] believed exactly the opposite...non-violence was a tactic that should be abandoned when it no longer worked.... And it was wrong and immoral to subject our people to armed attacks by the state without offering them some kind of alternative." But if I am correct, you see non-violent political activism as a moral and spiritual principle and not merely as a political tactic?

ASSK: No, not exactly. It's also a political tactic. Military coups, which have happened enough in Burma, are violent ways of changing situations and I do not want to encourage and to perpetuate this tradition of bringing about change through violence. Because I'm afraid that if we achieve democracy in this way we will never be able to get rid of the idea that you bring about necessary changes through violence. The very method would be threatening us all the time. Because there are always people who do not agree with democracy. And if we achieve it through violent means, there will be the hard core of those who have always been against the democracy movement who will think, "It was through violence that they changed the system and if we can develop our own methods of violence which are superior to theirs, we can get back the power." And we'll go on in this vicious cycle. For me it is as much a political tactic as a spiritual belief, that violence is not the right way. It would simply not assist us in building up a strong democracy.

AC: But when you perceive that non-violent methods are no longer effective, do you as a leader have a duty to shift your non-violent tactic to sharpen the point so to speak, of your struggle, or do you adopt the attitude, come what may, to maintain non-violence, because of a moral affinity?

ASSK: You know we always take collective decisions...

AC: Yes, I know that...

ASSK: And as long as I'm part of a democratic organization I will have to abide by collective decisions.

AC: Then let me ask the question in another way. Daw Suu, I would like to understand you. Is non-violence an immutable ethical and spiritual principle that will never alter in your approach to the struggle?

ASSK: We have always said that we will never disown those students and others who have taken up violence. We know that their aim is the same as ours. They want democracy and they think the best way to go about it is through armed struggle. And we do not say that we have the monopoly on the right methods of achieving what we want. Also, we cannot guarantee their security. We can't say, "Follow us in the way of non-violence and you'll be protected," or that we'll get there without any casualties. That's a promise we can't make. We have chosen the way of non-violence simply because we think it's politically better for the country in the long run to establish that you can bring about change without the use of arms. This has been a clear NLD policy from the beginning. Here, we're not thinking about spiritual matters at all. Perhaps in that sense, we're not the same as Mahatma Gandhi, who would have probably condemned all movements that were not non-violent. I'm not sure. But he did say at one time that if he had to choose between violence and cowardice, he would choose violence. So, even Gandhi, who was supposed to be the great exponent of non-violence, was not somebody who did not make any exceptions...

AC: But what about choosing violence out of compassion, if it's the right word, rather than using it as an option instead of cowardice? Nelson Mandela writes: "Leadership commits a crime against its own people if it hesitates to sharpen its political weapons where they have become less effective." Isn't he saying that one's attachment to non-violence becomes in fact an act of violence towards one's own people, when the non-violent approach is no longer effective?

ASSK: It depends on the situation and I think that in the context of Burma today, non-violent means are the best way to achieve our goal. But I certainly do not condemn those who fight the "just fight," as it were. My father did, and I admire him greatly for it.

AC: So it's accurate to say that you're keeping your options open and that you're not confining yourself to one particular approach?

ASSK: We keep all our options open. It is very important that one should be flexible. We've chosen non-violence because it is the best way to protect the people, and in the long term assure the future stability of democracy. This is why my father changed from violence to non-violence. He knew that it was far better for the future of the country to achieve a democratic state through political means and negotiation, rather than through military means. It's the same with Nelson Mandela. He changed back to non-violence when this was possible. Of course, before then he used violence because the non-violent way was not paying off and it was seen as a weakness rather than a strength. But in those days things were different. When

153

Nelson Mandela and the other South Africans were first trying out the non-violent approach, the world was so busily engaged in the ideological battle between the East and West, they were not that interested in human rights. In a brutal world, Nelson Mandela and other South Africans felt that they had to choose means that would make an impact and that would move their position forward. In this day and age we can use non-violent political means to achieve our ends. But if you have a choice and feel that you have an equal chance of succeeding, I think you certainly ought to choose the non-violent way, because it means that fewer people will be hurt.

AC: I don't think that violence and non-violence are such clearly separate domains, really. Of course, people often compartmentalize them into black and white categories, but is it possible to have an armed force motivated by the philosophy of non-violence, or is it completely a contradiction in terms? Can you philosophically foster the mind state of a non-violent activist even though you may be a combatant and use violence when called upon to do so?

ASSK: You have to define what you mean by violence. If we define violence as any action that gives pain to others, this broadens the definition so much that none of us is capable of real non-violence. Even if your intention is to help somebody, you may cause pain to that person by telling him a painful truth. So in those terms, it's very difficult to talk of pure non-violence.

In general what we mean by violence these days is physical violence. As long as your thoughts, emotions and words are not translated into physical action, people will more or less accept that your methods are non-violent. That, I think, can be put into practice. You can actually keep from performing acts that give physical pain to others. Then of course, there are those who will argue that mental pain is worse than physical pain...

AC: Yes, the Buddha has said this...

ASSK: So then you get into this argument about whether a physical act that inflicts pain on somebody is actually worse than some word or action that gives mental pain.

AC: I know that in Western countries it's been very easy for a lot of us to see the military machine as a body for violent aggression. In so doing we often polarize them from ourselves, judging them as the antithesis of *ahimsa* or non-violence. But I wonder if there is a way not to divide so sharply those who use weapons "justly" from those who would never use violent means under any circumstance?

ASSK: Take Burma for an example, during the time of the resistance against the Japanese. The Burmese Army was born out of the people and was part of it. And certainly, during the time of the Japanese resistance, the people did not think of the army as "them" and of themselves as "us." We were all one. Even after independence, as long as Burma was a democratic country, there was not this division between the military and the civilians. This "them and us" syndrome came in after the military took over power and became an elite. The privileged and the unprivileged. That's what it all amounts to. Privilege because they've got guns, money or power and the others don't have any of those.

AC: To continue with Nelson Mandela, I was particularly interested in his recounting of an ordeal with the American journalists from the *Washington Post* who went to interview him at Robben Island Prison. Apparently they tried to label him as a Communist and terrorist, as well as a non-Christian. They asserted that Martin Luther King never resorted to violence. He retorted that he was a Christian and even Christ who was a peacemaker, when left with no alternative used force to expel the moneylenders from the temple.

ASSK: Yes. He took out his whip, didn't he? I don't think one can afford to be dogmatic in politics. Dogmatism is one of the greatest dangers in politics.

AC: Another element of his book that impressed me was the power of the song, his stirring images when he was on trial with a courtroom packed with his ANC supporters singing and chanting. And the same when they were jailed in the earlier days of the movement. He explains how they all sang and chanted hymns throughout the night.

ASSK: That's very African though, isn't it?

AC: It is. But could you imagine hearing the thousands of people gathered at your weekend talks singing songs of freedom? Is there such a tradition of song and dance within the movement, as a means to nurture the unifying forces of love and determination?

ASSK: Actually, we don't have a tradition of community singing or dancing. It's not quite the same...

AC: Even during the marches led by Martin Luther King, song was a vital unifying aspect for the people in the movement. And in Hanoi, during America's bombing of the city, the tens of thousands of men, women and children sang as they hid in shelters deep in the earth. My point is that music and song ground the movement, take it out of the head, and place it in the soul.

ASSK: Well...during 1988 and 1989, some of the young people would sing democracy songs and this would be a great source of inspiration. Also, before the war, during the independence movement, our people would sing inspirational patriotic songs. But I don't think that it is the same as the African tradition where you just join hands and sing. Singing together as a form of community expression, even if it isn't a political song, is not a tradition among the Burmese. It may be different with some of the other ethnic groups in Burma. I know that we've always looked upon the Karens as particularly good singers. And I wonder if there isn't more of this kind of community singing and dancing among them.

AC: In watching you and your colleagues speak to the crowds on weekends I was thinking that a comparable expression to singing would be your use of humor. The people are constantly laughing...

ASSK: Yes, that might be particularly Burmese. They do have a sense of humor, and they're quick on the uptake. Like the jokes those comedians who were arrested soon after their performance in my compound last month told. Their jokes didn't really attack SLORC as such. But everybody knew exactly what they meant.

AC: I generally see you laughing with your colleagues and they've all told me how funny you are...

ASSK: Well, I have to admit that I have always had a sense of humor.

I can always see the ridiculous side of things and this helps me a lot, because I can laugh at my own situation. You know, I've found myself in situations some people have thought rather unpleasant. Of course, if you were really going to get uppity—they could be seen as unpleasant. But often, I've just seen them as rather funny. And I think I told you before, I don't think we've ever had a single meeting [with the NLD EC members] where there haven't been at least some laughs. Obviously, it's not a happy situation we're in, but the seriousness of the situation is something we can all joke about. In fact, lots of Burmese people joke about it; there are jokes about forced labor, about prison. This is very much part of our Burmese culture.

AC: Yes, I've come to see that. Just the other day several of us were listening to U Win Htein [Aung San Suu Kyi's assistant] describe his recent interrogation when the MI drilled him for twenty-seven hours non-stop. As he was unraveling his story everyone started laughing at the absurdity of SLORC's behavior, to the point of tears. He wasn't at all concerned with his own suffering. I think he did say that "it was rather unpleasant," but that's all...

ASSK: Actually, yes, it was the way they talked to him, their questions and views are quite absurd to us. Because they are so way out, really. They're not at all in touch with reality. What they think is so different from what is actually happening that it becomes absurd.

AC: Someone asked Václav Havel about the relationship of suffering and absurdity and he said that, "If one were required to increase the dramatic seriousness of his face in relation to the seriousness of the problems he had to confront, he would quickly petrify and become his own statue..."

ASSK: Yes, I think a sense of humor requires a certain amount of objectivity in the situation, which is why it's so healthy. If you see things as a whole, you can always see a humorous side of it. Which is why we laugh at situations which to some seem so serious. I mean, when U Win Htein and others were laughing at his account of the interrogation, if you see it as a whole it's quite ridiculous. But if you see it from just one angle it could be infuriating, humiliating, or even frightening for some people.

AC: Daw Suu, a simple question: what does love mean to you?

ASSK: I don't really think of love in an abstract way. When I first think of *metta*, I feel it within our movement, especially between my colleagues and myself. We work like a family—we are not just colleagues. We have a real concern and affection for each other, which is the basis of our relationships. I think this may have a lot to do with the fact that we have to work under such difficult conditions. It's only *metta* that is strong enough to keep together people who face such repression and who are in danger of being dragged away to prison at any moment. And the longer we work together the greater our bond of *metta* grows. From there these ties of friendship and affection have spread outward to include the families of colleagues. From there it spreads further, and with it the feeling of family grows. A family with a love of justice, a love of freedom, a love of peace and equality.

But let's go back to the more down-to-earth question of humor. If you're used to laughing at things, you start laughing at your own problems. You get used to seeing the absurd and funny side of things and you don't take your troubles that seriously any more. In the same way, if you are used to giving friendship and affection it's much easier to give it even to people who may think of themselves as your enemies.

AC: How are you able to feel affection towards tyrants?

ASSK: It just happens. I never imagine scenes where I'm oppressing them or getting my own back, or giving them a nasty time and making them miserable. Such thoughts give me no satisfaction, nor are they images that I see as particularly pleasant and desirable. What I do imagine is a time when all this animosity has been washed away and we can be friends.

AC: We discussed in an earlier conversation how insecurity was the root psychology of authoritarian regimes—a mistrust of one's own dignity, one's self-worth, and therefore a mistrust of others. In relationship to this I would like to ask you about finding power in vulnerability, rather than seeing it as a weakness. Indeed, many millions of women in the world today, after so many centuries of male repression, are calling out for us to wake up and see vulnerability as a virtue and a strength, a way into one's power and not a barrier to it. What do you think of this issue, and more specifically, from where does true power originate?

ASSK: The "power of the powerless" as Václav Havel said. I think power comes from within. If you have confidence in what you are doing and you are shored up by the belief that what you are doing is right, that in itself constitutes power, and this power is very important when you are trying to achieve something. If you don't believe in what you are doing your actions will lack credibility. However hard you try, inconsistencies will appear.

AC: And in regard to the issue of women I raised?

ASSK: Of course, women are consciously and unconsciously discriminated against. You'll find very few women in higher levels of administration, and obviously, it's not because they are less able than men.

AC: What about women's rights in Burma?

ASSK: People have often asked me about women's rights in Burma and I have always said very frankly, "Men do not have rights in Burma either." I do know that men are the privileged gender in Burma, as well as in many other parts of the world, but at the moment men are just as vulnerable to injustice and oppression. So first, let's give everybody their fundamental rights. Let's just try to stop men from being thrown into prison. This is not to say women are not thrown into prison too. But there are probably a hundred or even a thousand times more men political prisoners than women. So at this moment I find it very difficult to think of women in Burma as apart from the same movement in which men are involved. But I'm sure that the issue of women's rights will come out once we have democracy and everybody is enjoying their basic political rights.

AC: If I may, I'd like to return to the women's movement on a more global level. Would you speak of the positive signs of the women's movement?

ASSK: There's no doubt that thanks to the women's movement women have achieved greater equality in the realm of jobs and are being given more responsible positions. And there is also a lot more focus on their problems. Even in developing countries where women's issues are not given that much importance, people are beginning to be aware of the fact that they have got to do something to help their women. At the very least, make their lives easier physically. It should not be taken for granted that women must slave away just because they're women. In many rural communities they have to work physically harder than men. The men are there supposedly to protect them in case a lion or tiger comes or an invasion takes place, although such occurrences are becoming increasingly rare.

AC: It is time that men got over the belief that women want or even need men to protect them.

ASSK: Yes. I think it just gives men a chance, in some communities, to chat while they polish their bows and arrows.

AC: Do you see yourself as a feminist?

ASSK: No, I don't.

AC: You've written: "It is not enough merely to provide the poor with material assistance. They have to be sufficiently empowered to change their perception of themselves as helpless and ineffectual in an uncaring world." Fundamentally, what does empowerment mean to you?

ASSK: I think people must be given a reasonable control over their own destiny. They have to feel that they have some power over what happens to them. That is empowerment. But none of us can ultimately decide what will happen to us. There are too many factors involved.

AC: Nelson Mandela mentions in his memoirs that one of the things that he and his ANC colleagues talked a lot about during their many years in prison was how to sustain the awareness of the struggle in the minds of the people. I'd like to ask, how are you and your NLD colleagues attempting to ignite the people's desire for freedom to that level of momentum, as in South Africa, where it became an electrified movement that could not be stopped...

ASSK: What we have to make them understand is that the struggle is about them. That is what we always explain to the people. Democracy is about your job and your children's education; it's about the house you live in and the food you eat; it's about whether or not you have to get permission from somebody before you visit your relatives in the next village; it's about whether or not you can reap your own harvest and sell it to the person you want to sell it to. The struggle is about their everyday life. It's no use saying to a farmer that democracy is about better investment rules: that makes no sense to him at all. But democracy is about securing him the right to sow what he wants to, and to reap at the time he thinks the harvest is ready, and then to sell it to whomsoever he thinks will give him the best price. That's democracy. For a businessman, democracy is a system where there are sound commercial laws which are upheld by the institutions of the state, so he knows his rights and what he is allowed to do or not. He knows how to protect himself if anybody infringes those rights. For a student, democracy is the right to be able to study in good schools and in peace, and not to be dragged away to prison because you happen to be *laughing* with your friends over some funny characteristic of a minister. Democracy is the right to discuss your political views with your friends and to have the right to sit down at the tea shop on the campus and talk about whatever you want to, without wondering whether the MI are listening.

When Uncle U Kyi Maung was under detention, one of the Military Intelligence officers interrogating him asked, "Why did you decide to become a member of the National League for Democracy?" And he answered, "For your sake." That's what our struggle is about: everybody's everyday lives, including those of the MI.

Chapter 10

"Nobody can humiliate me but myself"

ALAN CLEMENTS: Daw Suu, what moves you to struggle for your people?

AUNG SAN SUU KYI: When I first decided to take part in the movement for democracy, it was more out of a sense of duty than anything else. On the other hand, my sense of duty was very closely linked to my love for my father. I could not separate it from the love for my country, and therefore, from the sense of responsibility towards my people. But as time went on, like a lot of others who've been incarcerated, we have discovered the value of loving-kindness. We've found that it's one's own feelings of hostility that generate fear. As I've explained before, I never felt frightened when I was surrounded by all those hostile troops. That is because I never felt hostility towards them. This made me realize that there are a number of fundamental principles common to many religions. As Burmese Buddhists, we put a great emphasis on *metta*. It is the same idea as in the biblical quotation: "Perfect love casts out fear." While I cannot claim to have discovered "perfect love," I think it's a fact that you are not frightened of people whom you do not hate. Of course, I did get angry occasionally with some of the things they did, but anger as a passing emotion is quite different from the feeling of sustained hatred or hostility.

AC: Of course, the potential for hatred to arise dramatically increases as violence is directed personally at someone, both psychologically and physically. Your country's prisons are filled with political prisoners; some, as I have learned, are routinely tortured by the military authorities.

ASSK: I'm not claiming any tremendous virtue for myself when I say that I feel no hostility towards soldiers. This is again a part of my heritage because I was brought up to think of soldiers as part of the family—as my father's sons. Because this kind of feeling was instilled into me from a young age, it's not something one can get rid of easily. But I easily understand why others who have been so ill-treated would not be able to develop a non-hostile attitude.

AC: Clearly, your vision of a democratic Burma includes a genuine reconciliation with your oppressors—SLORC. What do you think is required of the individual to confront his adversary and possibly win his friendship and understanding—not seeking to defeat him?

ASSK: Well, it has to begin with one's self, doesn't it? You have to develop inner spiritual strength, and those who have it do not feel hatred or hostility because they do not easily feel fear. It's all connected. If you can look upon someone with serenity you are able to cope with the feelings of hatred. But there cannot be serenity if there is fear. However, let me say, ordinary people like us, within the NLD, are nowhere near that level where we can look upon everybody with perfect love and serenity. But I think a lot of us within the organization have been given the opportunity to develop spiritual strength because we have been forced to spend long years by ourselves under detention and in prison. In a way, we owe it to those people who put us there.

AC: What is the core quality at the center of your movement?

ASSK: Inner strength. It's the spiritual steadiness that comes from the belief that what you are doing is right, even if it doesn't bring you immediate concrete benefits. It's the fact that you are doing something that helps to shore up your spiritual powers. It's very powerful.

AC: Martin Luther King used the phrase "divine dissatisfaction." He encouraged his people to grow weary and tired of injustice, to become "maladjusted," as he said it, to the racist system by which they were being oppressed. Now, on one level, you speak of genuine reconciliation, but at the same time, are you also speaking to the need of the population to grow uncomfortable and to steadily increase their dissatisfaction towards SLORC?

ASSK: It's not really the need to grow "uncomfortable." Nor are we trying to make the people become more dissatisfied. Our principal task is to encourage the need in people to question the situation and not just accept everything. Now, acceptance is not the same as serenity. Some people seem to think they go together. Not at all. Sometimes, the very fact that you accept what you do not want to accept and know that you should not accept, destroys the sense of serenity and inner peace, because you're in conflict with yourself.

AC: So the overcoming of complacency is the principal focus?

ASSK: Yes, complacency is very dangerous. What we want to do is to free people from feeling complacent. Actually, with a lot of people it's not a sense of complacency either. I think that many people just accept things out of either fear or inertia. This readiness to accept without question has to be removed. And it's very un-Buddhist. After all, the Buddha did not accept the status quo without questioning it.

AC: Yes, he radically questioned. It's the basis of his teachings.

ASSK: Yes, absolutely. In Buddhism, you know the four ingredients of success or victory: *chanda*—desire or will; *citta*—the right attitude; *viriya* or perseverance; and *panna*—wisdom. We feel that you have got to cultivate these four qualities in order to succeed. And the step prior even to these four steps, is questioning. From that you discover your real desires. Then you have got to develop *chanda*. *Chanda* is not really desire. How would you describe it?

AC: *Chanda* is normally translated as the "wish to do" or intention. Every action begins with it. Where there is a will there is a way.

ASSK: Yes. You must develop the intention to do something about the situation. From there you've got to develop the right attitude and then persevere with wisdom. Only then will there be success in your endeavor. Of course, the five basic moral precepts are essential, to keep you from straying as it were. With these we will get where we want to. We don't need anything else.

165

<u>AC:</u> So what you're doing is fostering a sense of individual courage to question, to analyze...

<u>ASSK:</u> And to act. I remind the people that *karma* is actually doing. It's not just sitting back. Some people think of *karma* as destiny or fate and that there's nothing they can do about it. It's simply what is going to happen because of their past deeds. This is the way in which *karma* is often interpreted in Burma. But *karma* is not that at all. It's doing, it's action. So you are creating your own *karma* all the time. Buddhism is a very dynamic philosophy and it's a great pity that some people forget that aspect of our religion.

<u>AC:</u> I've often noticed in Burmese Buddhist culture how people speak of the suffering they face in their present circumstances as simply the bitter fruit of past unwholesome *karmas* or actions. Such people will say: "I brought this suffering on myself through my own past ignorance and therefore I must bear it in the present."

<u>ASSK:</u> I think it's an excuse for doing nothing and it's completely contrary to our Buddhist views. If what is happening now is a result of what happened before, all the more reason why you should work harder now to change the situation...

<u>AC:</u> And, please correct me if I'm wrong, but such people often consider that the best way to change their unfavorable present circumstances is by performing *kusala* [wholesome deeds], such as giving donations to the monasteries, or making offerings to a pagoda or the building of a shrine and so on. This with the intention of generating wholesome *karma* that will hopefully improve their positions in a future life. Which obviously does nothing to change the more immediate source of their suffering, which is the SLORC.

<u>ASSK:</u> This is very much a common attitude. If something goes wrong, people tend to do something just for themselves, as it were. But I think you can also carry on working for others. Perhaps we should encourage this more; the idea that you can gain a lot of merit by working for others, as much as by working for yourself. In fact, I would like more of our Burmese Buddhists to understand this point.

<u>AC:</u> How much of your struggle is in fact, both about self-reliance

and the fact that our liberation is inextricably interwoven with that of other human beings?

ASSK: In our movement I use a very practical, simple argument. I always say, "I can't do it alone. If you want democracy, it is no use depending on either me or the NLD alone. What democracy means is government of the people, by the people, and for the people. If you want democracy, you'll have to work for it. You've got to join in. The more people are involved the quicker we'll reach our goal."

AC: You so frequently speak of the power of unity and the need for it. But the SLORC has you so hemmed in. Do you find it frustrating that you cannot yet really organize and unify the people?

ASSK: It's not frustrating because we do unite people. It's not at an obvious rate. But we do unify people, quite a lot. And we manage to sort out problems within our organization. The fact is that at the core of the NLD, we are very united. That is strengthening. We never have problems between us. The fact that A Aung Shwe and U Lwin were out [not imprisoned], and that U Tin U, U Win Htein, U Kyi Maung and I were in, hasn't affected our unity in any way. This is something that the authorities find very hard to believe. I do not think SLORC actually believes that we have absolute unity and make collective decisions. They think that one of us is dominating the other. Either I'm dominating them, or U Kyi Maung or U Tin U is influencing me, something like that. But in fact, it's nothing like that at all. I suppose they're looking at it from a military point of view, where the commander sends down orders and everybody else says, "Yes, yes, yes." Perhaps they find it unthinkable that there is such a thing as a collective decision.

AC: You said in an earlier interview that "everyone must stand up against the cruel injustices" of SLORC. This reminds me of Martin Luther King's words: "For every Negro that is violated, we have 1,000 more Negroes, who are willing to be violated. For every schoolteacher that is fired from his job, we have 4,000 more schoolteachers waiting to apply for that job. For every Negro's home that is bombed, we have 50,000 more homes that are willing to be bombed, for the vision and the future that we want." Are your people ready to stand up and say, we'll fill the prisons full in order to achieve our goal of justice and freedom?

ASSK: I don't think our movement is at quite that level. One of the reasons why the movement of black people in America was like that was because they visibly belonged to one side; whereas we are not marked out as belonging to one side or the other. I think it's always more difficult when the struggle is between people of one race and one religion. There is nothing that sets you apart except your principles and your goals.

AC: The apartheid of principles...

ASSK: What I mean is this: when Martin Luther King says that, "for every Negro's home that is bombed we have 50,000 more homes willing to be bombed," I don't know whether willingness comes into it. It's probably more the fact that there are 50,000 more black homes who know that they are just as vulnerable as the one that has been bombed.

AC: But, Daw Suu, I think the "willingness" was there. And that was the power of the struggle—dynamic unity. How much are you really willing to arouse that same spirit of dynamic unity that King did with the blacks, in your own people? The willingness to rise up against the injustices.

ASSK: Of course, one wants them to be united. But it's something that we have to work towards, steadily. It's not a job that will ever be finished. I don't think unity is ever complete—at least not in the human world. And although I realize and accept that our unity is not complete, that does not drive me to despair. You just have to keep working towards it all the time.

AC: One of the powers of King's movement was that he felt, as many blacks did, that no matter how cruel and violent the white people were to them in their non-violent marches, demonstrations, sit-ins and boycotts, ultimately, justice and goodness were on their side. "Cosmic companions" as King put it, or inherent qualities of the universe born from their conviction in the Christian religion. He said that this "knowing" presence of God as they faced brutality was a main factor in keeping the people unified. So no matter how dark it became they always knew that they had cosmic companionship. But this isn't true in Buddhism, is it? The universe doesn't take sides, but is always right because of the law of cause and effect?

ASSK: Yes. In Buddhism, as you know, we believe that you will pay for all the bad things that you have done, and that you will reap the rewards of all the good that you've done. And I think because of that, a lot of Buddhists think that because the authorities are cruel and unjust, you don't have to do anything at all, they will get their own desserts. I don't accept that. I don't think that one should just sit back and expect *karma* to catch up with everybody else. But I do think there is this underlying belief, not just among Christians or Buddhists, but among peoples all over the world, that in the end, right will prevail—the light will have to come. When I say this, I don't mean that everybody holds it, but that the majority of people do.

AC: I know it's a nice belief to hold, that "in the end, right will prevail." What evidence do you have to say, "The light will have to come"? It seems like just the opposite is closer to reality, for so many millions of people around the world.

ASSK: Whatever you may say, the world is better. Because in this day and age you can't just drag someone to a public place, chop off his head, and not have anyone say a word about it. Which government today would hang, draw and quarter somebody, in full view of the public, and think that he'd get away with it? We are less barbaric, people as a whole are more civilized. This is not to say that horrible tortures do not go on. They go on behind the scenes but at least people are beginning to learn that this is not acceptable. Take a place like England, which is supposed to be the mother of democracy. I'm sure there are lots of criticisms that you can make about England but if they had caught the Soviet spy, Kim Philby, and they had hung, drawn and quartered him in public, do you think the English people would have stood for it? Even though he was a traitor, those days are long gone. So people have progressed and not just in democratic countries but even in the old Soviet Union. Of course, they executed traitors but they certainly would not have taken them out into Red Square and chopped their heads off in full view of the public. So that's progress. It shows that people are beginning to understand that barbarism is not acceptable, that it's something to be ashamed of, something we must try to eliminate. You can't deny that there has been an increasing movement to control the savage instincts of man.

AC: I would like to immediately jump in there on the issue...

ASSK: Oh, go on!

AC: There have been more wars and murders in the twentieth century than all previous centuries combined. And Ken Saro-Wiwa, the Nigerian writer and environmental activist, was just hung in full public view of the entire world. Furthermore, CNN and the BBC covered the Bosnian nightmare, twenty-four hours a day, for forty-three months of "ethnic cleansing," in full view of the public. I need more evidence of how you determine your views.

ASSK: Let's put it this way. The values of civilization have become more dominant.

AC: As I said in one of our previous conversations, when European civilization spread, in most places it did so based on a policy of extermination of the indigenous populations. Perhaps from that perspective, there might be more dominant values of civilization today than before. But, I'm not sure at all that I'm convinced.

ASSK: Take Burma under the Burmese kings: those who were out of favor with the king were executed in very cruel ways. Now, Burma has been accused of many, many human rights violations. But do the authorities ever admit them? They do not. They will say, "No, we have not perpetrated these deeds." Whereas in the days of the old Burmese kings, there was no question of denying it. They would just do it. It was their prerogative and nobody would dare to question them. And they would not think there was any need for them to even pretend that they had not done these things. So that's progress.

AC: So are you saying that your country has become more civilized?

ASSK: Yes. It has become more civilized. As I said, think of the days of the Burmese kings when they really had power of life and death

170

over the people. I'm not saying that an authoritarian government does not have power of life or death over the people, but at least they know that it's not right to admit this. That's progress.

AC: That's calculated duplicity...

ASSK: That's progress. They're ashamed to admit atrocities, even though they commit them. At least they know that basically it's unacceptable to torture and to kill people wantonly. And they always deny that they do so. So that's a first step; a realization that what they do is not acceptable. The second step is to know that it's wrong.

AC: You're really cutting them a lot of slack...

ASSK: No. I'm not saying that their instincts are any better or worse than the old kings'. But the kings did not feel the need to temper their feelings of vengeance or cruelty. They felt that they had a perfect right to indulge in these feelings. At least the authorities here do not really think it is their right to torture and to kill. They can do it, and they do it. But they will not admit to it. If they are not ashamed of it and they think it's perfectly all right, then why don't they just say, "Yes, we torture. So what?" Now, has anybody in SLORC ever admitted to torture? They always deny it. They say, "No, torture doesn't exist in Burma." They go on denying it to a ridiculous extent. Recently the [SLORC's] representative to the General Assembly said, "There are no human rights violations in Burma." Why do they say that? If they think that it is all right to do the things that they do, they should just say: "Yes, we do that. So what? What's wrong with it?" Why won't they say it?

AC: Well, it's either sheer cowardice, pathological deceit, or the most breath-taking display of self-deception ever known. Or maybe they do recognize it is wrong and as you said, they do not admit it. Yesterday, in SLORC's newspaper, the Trade Minister was quoted as saying in a public speech: "As for the accusations on human rights violations, forced labor and so on in Myanmar, [let it be known that] Myanmar is firmly committed [to] and respectful of the United Nations Universal Declaration of Human Rights. And we, the government, are totally against human rights abuses."

171

ASSK: Why, this is what I mean...

AC: He goes on to say, "But, here I would like to state that the Eastern concept of human rights is not the same as the Western concept."

ASSK: Yes, but he's contradicting himself because he says that he respects fully the United Nations Convention on Human Rights. But of course, the authorities always contradict themselves and tie themselves up in knots.

AC: What is behind this belief that the Eastern concept of human rights is not the same as the Western concept?

ASSK: There's nothing in it. It's just because they know that they are violating human rights, and so it's self-defense. That's all.

AC: A mindless argument?

ASSK: Totally mindless! I remember at one time, during the early days, that one of the members of SLORC said, "Oh, those people who demand human rights, are they going to demand nudist camps next?" It's quite obvious that he had no idea what "human rights" means.

AC: So you really think they are that out of touch with reality?

ASSK: It's a very interesting question. We've often wondered about that ourselves. A while back, I mentioned Karl Popper's quotation: "There is no evil...only stupidity." And one really appreciates that remark very much.

AC: The SLORC Trade Minister ends his speech by saying: "And the people of Myanmar are living happily under freedom, human rights and democracy...free from any suppression of any kind." Daw Suu, you won, Burma is more civilized today than in times of old.

ASSK: Just look at that, it's just blatant. I don't know what to call it! Well, one's imagination boggles.

AC: Why do they spend the money to print this in English no less? Who's crazy enough to read it besides me?

ASSK: Perhaps they think we need a bit of laughter from time to time.

AC: But on the contrary, last week they stated quite boldly in their paper that they were in fact a "dictatorship." They don't seem to have any shame about that fact.

ASSK: Yes, they are one of the very few governments in the world that ever admitted officially that they were not a *de jure* government at all.

AC: In reflecting upon the issue of reconciliation between the NLD and SLORC, I was thinking today that it's going to require the authorities to reach deep into themselves for the courage to challenge their fear and admit their mistakes. Because, if there's going to be genuine dialogue and reconciliation, obviously they cannot just pull it out of their hats. They'll need a genuine change of heart. And for the first time, I actually feel some compassion for them. That's going to be a colossal challenge...

ASSK: Yes. I read somewhere that it is always more difficult for the perpetrator of a cruel deed to forgive the victim, than for the victim to forgive his tormentor. I found that very strange when I first read it, but I think it's true. The victim can forgive because he has the moral high ground as it were. He has nothing to be ashamed of. Of course he may be ashamed if he had behaved in a very bad way, or if he had groveled. Then he may acquire a hatred towards his tormentor, based not really on what the tormentor had done to him, but on what he had done to himself.

It was Shcharansky who said that when he was in prison he had to keep reminding himself, "Nobody can humiliate me but myself, nobody can humiliate me but myself." I think if you haven't done anything that is shameful then you can forgive your tormentor. But the tormentor finds it difficult to forgive the victim because he knows that he has committed an act of shame. And every time he sees his victim he is reminded of his shame. That makes it hard for him to forgive. I think it is the same with the victim who finds it difficult to forgive the tormentor. But the victim who has behaved well finds it quite easy to forgive the tormentor. Because every time he sees the tormentor, I'm sure he is empowered by the reminder of his own noble behavior—his courage. He might say: "I stood up against that man's tortures with dignity." And in a way, it makes it very easy for him to forgive his tormentor.

173

<u>AC:</u> You could actually see SLORC in this house, sitting down with you and saying, "Daw Suu, we're going to work this out together"?

<u>ASSK:</u> (*smiling*) Oh, very much so. I have no trouble envisaging such a thing. That might just be wishful thinking, in some people's interpretation, but it will have to happen some day. I don't know who will be involved, but it will happen...

<u>AC:</u> Are you confident about that?

<u>ASSK:</u> Oh, yes. That is the only way that countries do go. Mind you, the sooner they go, the less *dukkha* [suffering] there is for all the people concerned. Look at the former Yugoslavia. In the end, they had to talk about it. But look at the numbers of people who have suffered. That is why we say that "It all ends up at the table." But the sensible ones run to the table first, whereas the ones who are not sensible run to the guns.

<u>AC:</u> In your essay *In Quest of Democracy,** you've written: "Kindness is in a sense the courage to care." Would you say more about that?

<u>ASSK:</u> It's not really my own idea as such. I was discussing this with a doctor friend of mine a long time ago. I was saying that I had a rather idealistic view of doctors and nurses, because my mother was a very dedicated and compassionate nurse. All of her patients loved her, because she was so good at her work, and at the same time she was very gentle and caring. And this doctor said, "Well, doctors and nurses in general are not like that, because not too many of them have the courage to care deeply for all their patients. They have to take a rather unfeeling attitude, otherwise they couldn't cope with those who are suffering." He also said, "There are some, of course, who are truly compassionate and do everything they can for their patients. But those are in the minority, because not too many people have the courage to let themselves feel for their patients. It's too wearing, unless you are very strong and brave."

---

* This essay was written by Aung San Suu Kyi for a projected volume of essays on democracy and human rights which she had been hoping to dedicate to her father as *Essays in Honour of Bogyoke Aung San*. She was then placed under house arrest on 20 July 1989 and was unable to complete the project. Published in *Freedom from Fear* (Penguin Books, revised edition, 1995).

174

<u>AC:</u> The courage to let yourself feel?

<u>ASSK:</u> Yes, and to care. You have to have tremendous resources of compassion and strength, because you're giving it out all the time. And unless you have a lot of it, you run out of it all too quickly. You can't cope.

<u>AC:</u> Daw Suu, when it really comes right down to it, how do you cope?

<u>ASSK:</u> I think what really sustains us, is the sense that we are on the side of right, as it were, to use a very old-fashioned phrase. And the *metta* between us keeps us going.

<u>AC:</u> Are you old-fashioned?

<u>ASSK:</u> Well, talking about morality, right and wrong, love and kindness, is considered rather old-fashioned these days, isn't it? But after all, the world is spherical. Perhaps the whole thing will come around again, and maybe I'm ahead of the times.

Chapter 11

"We have only ourselves to rely on"

ALAN CLEMENTS: When you visualize a democratic Burma, in essence, what is it that you see?

AUNG SAN SUU KYI: When we visualize a democratic Burma, we do not visualize it in terms of great power and privileges for the NLD. We see it in terms of less suffering for the people. We're not starry-eyed about democracy. We don't think of it in terms of abstract institutions but in terms of what it can do to contribute towards the happiness and well-being of the people. We want a country where there is rule of law; where people are secure to the extent that one can be secure in this world; where they are encouraged and helped to acquire education, to broaden their horizons; where conditions conducive to ease of mind and body are fostered. That is why I would say that *metta* is the core of our movement—a desire to bring relief to human beings.

<u>AC:</u> How do you work within yourself with democracy as a vision, democracy as a process, and democracy as a state of mind? The reason I ask is that I've seen how the attachment to any goal often compromises, if not prevents one from actually achieving it.

<u>ASSK:</u> Well, the three have to be simultaneous. First of all it has to be a state of mind. You've got to act democracy. Then you have to work out the process towards the vision that you have. You can't really separate the three. They all go together. And this is very Buddhist, isn't it? Work, action and self-reliance. Both work and action come down to *karma*—action and doing. And of course, self-reliance is very Buddhist. We say, *"Atta hi attano natho."* "In the end we only have ourselves to rely on."

177

AC: Obviously, in your call for dialogue and reconciliation with SLORC some level of forgiveness is essential, balanced with some degree of justice. But what do you think is the core quality of forgiveness that allows one to genuinely forgive one's oppressors?

ASSK: To forgive, I think, basically means the ability to see the person apart from the deed and to recognize that although he has done that deed, it does not mean that he is irredeemable. There are aspects of him that are acceptable. To wholly identify a person with his deed is the sign of a real inability to forgive. For example, if you always think of a murderer in terms of the murder, you will never be able to forgive him. But if you think of the murderer objectively, as a person who has committed a murder, and there are other aspects to him besides that deed he has committed, then you're in a position to forgive him.

AC: But what quality of mind is required to look upon one's enemy and separate his cruel deeds from the other aspects of his being?

ASSK: It's just broadness of vision. Anybody who is broad-minded will know that a murderer is not wholly murder. He is a person who has committed murder, but there has to be a distinction between a murderer and the murder. Now mind you, there are murderers who have murdered so often that they are almost wholly murder. But I think there are few people like that. So ultimately, it's an ability to see around the subject, to see things as a whole by developing a breadth of vision.

AC: Your colleagues have made it perfectly clear to me that SLORC's disinterest in talking with you and the NLD is unequivocally rooted in fear. They've told me that it's their fear of losing power which translates down into a fear of "losing their security—property, wealth, privilege and status." They also said that "they fear for the safety of their families." And at the root of it all is their "fear of retribution." You continually encourage the powerless in your country to rise up against the injustices, but may I ask you for your views on SLORC having the courage to overcome their fears?

ASSK: In order to overcome your own fears you have to start first by showing compassion to others. Once you have started treating people with compassion, kindness and understanding, then your fears dissipate. It's that straightforward.

AC: What instigates the courage to cross the precipice of fear?

ASSK: That, I cannot say. I think there have been people who have been inspired by the teachings of great teachers. Or there are those who have been changed because somebody has shown them what it means to live without fear. And with some people, perhaps it's not one thing, but a combination of experiences that have led them to the conclusion that they have to change. But I don't think there is one solution for everybody. Each human being is different.

AC: What is the way to activate that compassion that you speak of?

ASSK: Sometimes, of course, it's not by activating compassion that you make people change. Sometimes people change because they find that there's no other way possible for their own good. When you take the old government in South Africa, the Latin-American military dictatorships, and other authoritarian governments in Eastern Europe, I think they accepted change because they realized that it was inevitable and it was best for them to go along with it. But what I'm speaking about is the real change that comes from inside through learning the value of compassion, justice and love.

AC: It's so sad that it takes so much blood and violence for real change to occur...

ASSK: Yes, this is very sad. I wonder why some people only see what they want to see. They're like a blinkered horse. Why do they not see the picture as a whole? Let's take the case of the elections in Burma. The authorities obviously thought that the NLD would not win such an overwhelming majority. As I understand it, there were a lot of people—including foreign observers and journalists—who had come to the conclusion that the NLD would probably win the greatest number of seats, but it would not get an absolute majority. What made them come to this conclusion? I can understand the foreign journalists getting the wrong impression of what was going on in the country. They were only allowed to come for a short time and were never allowed to talk freely to the people who would know.

But it's amazing that the authorities, with the whole machinery of government at their disposal, and all their people in the intelligence services running around spying on people everywhere, didn't realize that the results were going to turn out to be overwhelmingly in favor of the NLD.

AC: It shouldn't be that amazing, you've frequently used the word stupid to describe the SLORC. But could they have been really that stupid? Is it possible that it was a maniacal ruse? After all, the results have shown that most elected officials were jailed.

ASSK: I don't think it's that maniacal. And I think perhaps it's more about ignorance than stupidity. Because people are always afraid to tell a truth that would bring the anger of the dictators down upon them. And it is quite likely that their men at the grass-roots probably knew which way the elections would go but did not dare to tell the truth to their superiors.

AC: For SLORC to have held the elections in the first place seems to me, based solely on their dismissal of the results, to be one of their more colossal mistakes. Is it that SLORC doesn't know how to handle their miscalculation?

ASSK: It does seem to me that they really don't know how to handle the situation. They're not the only ones—I think few dictators really know how to handle a country in the long run. Because of the very nature of authoritarian governments and dictatorships they effectively prevent themselves from learning the truth, because people living under such regimes get into the habit of hiding it from them and from each other. Even those whose job is to find out what's happening in the country for the dictators acquire the habit of not telling the truth to their superiors. So everybody gets out of the habit of telling the truth, while some even get out of the habit of seeing the truth. They see what they want to see, or only what they think their superiors want them to see. Now, if you get into that habit, later you develop the habit of not daring to hear what you don't want to hear. So you end up not seeing, hearing, or saying the truth. And in the long run this blunts their intelligence.

AC: A total contortion of self and the blunting of creativity?

ASSK: Yes. Under authoritarian regimes, where you are only allowed to express certain things, the growth of talent becomes distorted. It can't flower. Like a tree that becomes distorted because it's trained to go just one way—the way that's acceptable to the authorities. So there can never be a genuine flowering or burst of talent and creativity.

AC: Why is diversity so disgusting to SLORC?

ASSK: Fear. Fear of losing their power. Fear of facing the truth. Fear of finding out that if they face the truth they will have to admit that they've been doing all sorts of things they should not have been doing.

AC: In a letter that Václav Havel wrote to the Czech President some years before the revolution, he described the regime as, "Entropic: a force that was gradually reducing the amount of energy and diversity of society to a state of dull, inert uniformity." In that same letter he concluded with the prediction that sooner or later, the regime would become the victim of its own "lethal principle," saying that "life cannot be destroyed for good." What is it in the human psyche—in the mindset of totalitarianism—that craves to imprison or crush freedom?

ASSK: I think it's because a despotic regime is afraid of different opinions and different attitudes from their own and would not allow them to flourish, let alone actions. That's real despotism.

AC: Why are people so afraid of each other that they cannot allow differences in thought? What's underneath it all?

ASSK: I suppose it's their own narrowness and their own limitations which make them fear the breadth of what is possible.

AC: You often use the phrase, "freedom from fear." If we reverse it to the fear of freedom, does it have any meaning to you?

ASSK: Of course, there is what Václav Havel calls the "shock of freedom." He spoke of all the problems that arose in the Czech Republic after it became a democracy. You have to adjust to a state of freedom when you come out from a state of captivity. Some people have no problem adjusting. Others do. This is true even for ex-prisoners, because in prison they get used to doing things according to a certain routine.

AC: I would like to hear your comments on a quote of Martin Luther King. He says, "Here is the true meaning and value of compassion and non-violence: when it helps us to see the enemy's point of view, to hear his questions, to know his assessment of ourselves. For from his view we may indeed see the basic weaknesses of our own condition, and if we are mature, we may learn to grow and profit from the wisdom of our brothers who are called the opposition."

ASSK: Well, it all boils down to the fact that you can benefit from criticism if you know how to take it properly. There are two ways of looking at criticism. If it is not justified, at least you learn something about the person who is criticizing you. For example, if your enemies are making totally unjustified criticisms, you learn about their values, their attitudes, their standards. But if the criticism is justified, all the better. You can learn to improve yourself.

AC: When you look back over the years from say 1988—the time of your entry into politics and assuming a leadership role in Burma's struggle for democracy—up to the present, in retrospect, have you made any mistakes that you are consciously aware of?

ASSK: I have asked myself that question. I'm sure I have made mistakes, but I cannot tell yet which mistakes I've made. In politics, only time will tell whether a step was a mistake or not. Something that you did accidentally may turn out to help the cause a lot. Yet something you did in all good will, very carefully, may turn out in the long run to be detrimental to your cause. It's difficult to say.

What have I done? I have to look over my political career. I've always called for dialogue. I do not think that could ever be termed a mistake. Then, there were those who said I criticized the government too freely. Was that a mistake or not? There are some who would argue that if I had not criticized them, they would have spoken to me. But they would not even consider speaking to U Aung Shwe [the present Chairman of the NLD], who has never criticized them and who has tried his best to be cooperative.

182

So, what was the result? The result was that a lot of people lost confidence in U Aung Shwe, before we were released and started working together again. And there are some who said this did not help the cause of the National League of Democracy, that he was too conciliatory. So what is right and what is wrong? We will not know until these times are past and we have achieved democracy. And even then, some of the answers will never emerge.

AC: What in essence does power mean to you?

ASSK: Power means responsibility to whomever has entrusted you with this power and to do your best for those people. That's a great responsibility. And if your best is not good enough, then it becomes a very great responsibility indeed. And I do think that anybody who's sensible should admit then, "I'm not good enough," and just step back. Unfortunately, this is not what power means to a lot of people who hold it or want it. For them power means privileges. But if you start off on the premise that power first means responsibility then you would be far less enamored of power.

AC: In reading about the lives of other freedom fighters like Mandela, Gandhi and King, I was struck by how each of them was incessantly confronted with personal struggles in acting responsibly along the fine line of staying true to their own convictions, while knowing their decisions affected millions of lives. Daw Suu, what is it like for you to hold the tension and the weight of that level of responsibility?

ASSK: It's just work for us. Day-to-day work. You don't sit back thinking: "Oh, I'm bearing this big burden of responsibility." You simply don't have the time.

AC: So you never feel such responsibility as a burden?

ASSK: No, not particularly. If I just sat and contemplated on the responsibility of people's hopes being centered on me, then I suppose it could become a great burden. But I don't have the time to sit and think about that in great detail. One just works and does one's best.

AC: You've been called "Burma's woman of destiny"...

ASSK: What do people mean by that?

AC: I was going to ask you the same question...

ASSK: Well, you know, I'm a Buddhist, so "destiny" is not something that means that much to me, because I believe in *karma*. And that means doing. You create your own *karma*. And in a sense, if I believe in destiny, it's something that I create for myself. That's the Buddhist way.

AC: Do you ever feel that you are living today in any way out of role to a life that you would have chosen to live?

ASSK: No, I don't think I'm leading a life which is completely different from the kind of life I would like to live. Of course, I would have liked to have had my family around me, especially I would have liked to have brought up my sons—seen them grow up. But that's only part of my life, my country also is part of my life. I think of life as very broad and open. And there are many things that can be embraced within its compass. So, I do not feel that I am living an unnatural life. I also know that you have to make choices in life and give up some things. It's only the immature who think that they can have everything they want in life.

AC: Does the notion of hope have any meaning to you?

ASSK: Oh yes, but I think hope has to be accompanied by endeavor. Hope is different from wishful thinking. Just sitting and saying, "Oh, I wish this or that would happen." That sort of attitude is too wishy-washy to deserve the term hope. If you are working for something, you have the right to hope that you'll be successful. But if you're not doing anything, then I don't think you have the right to say, "I'm hoping for democracy." That's just sheer wishful thinking.

AC: So many of your people look to you as a symbol of their hope, the one who will bring them freedom. How do you unveil them from this belief?

ASSK: By convincing them that they too can do something. A lot of people tend to take the view that, "Oh, there is nothing we can do." Or, "We would if we could, but..." That's nonsense. Everyone

184

can do something in order to help out, whether small or large, if they set their minds to it. Everyone has a role to play.

Opportunities that can further the cause of democracy are coming up all the time. For example saying "no" to somebody who's attempting to force you to do something you shouldn't do. Or helping somebody who is doing something for democracy. They can speak up for justice and speak out for human rights. If they witness some gross violation of human rights, they can pick up a pen and write about it, and try to get that letter to somebody who will be able to do something about it.

<u>AC:</u> How is it that some of the greatest leaders of our era, some of them renowned for their noble values, go about getting the love they need in ways that are self-deceptive? And more specifically, how can a great leader best put a check on his or her own potential self-deception?

<u>ASSK:</u> What do you mean by "a check on self-deception"?

<u>AC:</u> Every one of us has some level of ignorance that shrouds us from reality. By a check on self-deception I mean: what safeguards can be developed by even the most prominent, well-respected leaders to support their ethical judgment and not be unconsciously lured into self-deceptive activities?

<u>ASSK:</u> I don't know what safeguards there are. As I've said before, I think people just have to go on trying. I don't think anybody can afford to sit back and say, "That's it, I'm perfect; I don't have to try any more." It's a simple answer. A constant self-awareness. That's very Buddhist and I don't find any great mystery in that. Which is not to say that all those who try to develop awareness succeed to the extent to which they aspire. I think even monks have to practice this all the time. Constant effort is always required.

<u>AC:</u> I do know as a meditator that awareness is essential. But isn't self-deception a very subtle and insidious veil? The corruption of consciousness can take place in a split second. How to be aware of what one doesn't see about oneself?

<u>ASSK:</u> I think self-deception is something everybody practices, not

only those who have power. Some say, "There's nothing we can do about the situation and we just have to accept it." That in itself is self-deception. If someone really wants to get involved there is always something to do. So I do not think self-deception is the prerogative of the powerful. It's just a human failing to which we are all prone. And the best defense against it is the awareness of what you're doing, even if you're trying to deceive yourself. If you have really developed awareness, you know that you're trying to deceive yourself, or you should know it anyway.

AC: Why is it so hard to admit one's limitations and mistakes?

ASSK: Because I suppose people feel vulnerable—that they will be laughed at or criticized. Nobody likes to be criticized. It's very human. Human beings like to be appreciated. They like to feel good. And I suppose most criticism makes them feel bad. Or perhaps it's the way in which the criticism is made. There are those who are capable of making criticisms in such a way that the person who is criticized does not feel bad. I think that's a great gift and only some people have it. But very few.

AC: During your weekend public talks you frequently criticize SLORC's actions, but never attack any of them personally. I know that the basic purpose of your criticisms is to change the system, but how does one make the distinction between being politically more loving towards the adversary as a means of change, and that of criticizing actions?

ASSK: Politically, you criticize the actions of whoever it may be. It doesn't have to be an adversary as such. Sometimes, within the NLD, we have to criticize what some of our members are doing because it affects the work of our party. So criticism is not something that we level just at SLORC. But when SLORC first took power, they said they would maintain a neutral position and not take sides. They would just make sure that there were free and fair elections. But as time went on, it became obvious that they were doing nothing of the kind. They were trying to crush the NLD. They were attacking us in every way they could. Then we started criticizing SLORC. It became necessary. So, of course I criticize SLORC when I speak on Saturday and Sunday. Because I'm reading out the letters of the people who are putting forward what they see as injustices.

AC: I'm sorry to keep bringing this up, but it's just my way of trying to understand you as a leader. Do you love your enemy into transformation, or do you criticize them into that transformation?

ASSK: I think I've said to you before that I have not gotten to the stage when I can claim that I feel *metta* towards everybody. And I do not think I can claim that I have these overwhelming waves of *metta* going out from me towards SLORC. But it is the truth that I don't feel hostile towards any of them. I would be very happy to be on friendly terms with them. And I can say with absolute truth that I have never used abusive terms in speaking about them. I don't mean just in public but even in private. The strongest things I have said against them is either that they are very stupid or that they are acting like fools.

AC: Do you ever question your approach in your struggle?

ASSK: Of course I do. It does not mean that because you believe in *metta* you keep from criticizing where there is need for criticism.

AC: I agree. But isn't the main issue here about the most effective way to bring change—to soften the hearts of your oppressors and relieve the entire population from their suffering?

ASSK: We've learned from experience that the *metta* approach is misinterpreted by the authorities. They see it as a weakness.

AC: How do they interpret loving-kindness as a weakness?

ASSK: Well, let's take it in the political context. During my six years under house arrest, and while Uncle U Kyi Maung and Uncle U Tin U were in prison, Uncle U Aung Shwe [the NLD Chairman] tried very hard to keep the NLD together as well as trying to establish a harmonious relationship with SLORC. He never said anything to which they could object. During those six years the NLD behaved in such a gentlemanly way that some people accused it of sheer cowardice and the lack of will to act. And what was the result? They [SLORC] just came down heavier and heavier on the NLD.

AC: So there came a point in the struggle that the *metta* approach was determined not as effective as your present approach?

ASSK: We have not given up the *metta* approach. Because basically, we are always ready to work with them on the basis of mutual understanding and goodwill. But that does not mean that we're going to sit and wait. We believe in action. That's active *metta*, doing what is necessary at any certain point.

AC: Recently you held a three-day conference of the elected MPs within your compound. What was the main purpose of the conference?

ASSK: As you know, 27 May was the sixth anniversary of the 1990 elections, the results of which showed clearly that the people of Burma wanted a democratic government. But those results have not been honored by the SLORC. Nevertheless, we believe very strongly that elected representatives have responsibilities towards the people who elected them. So we decided to convene a conference to discuss future policies and to see what we could do to help the people. Of course we did gather the elected members who were not jailed, driven into exile or killed.

AC: What decisions were made at the conference?

ASSK: Besides deciding to step up the fight for democracy and calling for a future Burma which would be ruled by a civilian Parliament as elected in 1990, the conference authorized the executive committee to draw up a new constitution.

AC: What are your impressions of SLORC's reaction to the conference?

ASSK: They panicked, thinking that we were going to convene a parliament and create trouble. Actually it's interesting because they keep saying that elected members of the NLD are nobody and yet the idea of these people gathering together to hold a meeting seems to have made them extremely nervous indeed. So in a sense the SLORC's reaction was an acknowledgment of our public support.

AC: A lot of people have been arrested. Do you know how many are still detained by SLORC and do you know the status of your personal assistant U Win Htein and your international media coordinator U Aye Win?

<u>ASSK:</u> We know that 150 of those detained have now been released. Personally we have heard that there have been about 300 arrests. We are not sure what has happened to the remaining one hundred or so. But we know for sure that at least four elected members are still held in Rangoon. Plus thirteen non-elected delegates who were taken away before the conference. So in Rangoon alone there are about twenty to twenty-four who were taken away before the conference and not heard of since. U Win Htein and U Aye Win are in the hands of the Military Intelligence. And those people will not have any defense rights. As you know, SLORC does not abide by the existing laws and what they are doing is contrary to the existing laws. They keep saying when they want to attack us that they won't tolerate any action contrary to the existing laws. But they are the ones to constantly flout the law.

<u>AC:</u> Why do you think SLORC allows your weekend talks to continue after strictly warning you to stop them? And will you continue them come what may, barring your rearrest or them barricading your street the way they did on New Year's Day?

<u>ASSK:</u> The authorities have never wanted to stop us before. Actually, in August of last year, a couple of journalists asked a very important man in the government why they were allowing those talks to take place and the reply was "Let's see how long the people will keep on coming!" They seem to have taken for granted that the people would soon lose interest and that the crowds would be slipping away. But what happened, as you've seen, is that after we left the National Convention in November the crowds in fact grew bigger. And after our National Convention last week, and the arrests, the crowds were enormous [10,000], with a lot of new faces, despite the danger. The people wanted to show us their approval for the fact that we were doing our work in spite of all the repression and intimidation that we have to face. This is a demonstration of public support. The authorities have only now made it known that they did not want those talks to continue. There might be problems tomorrow, but we do not think they have the right to say not to

continue them especially when they themselves are holding what they call "spontaneous" demonstrations of people in support of the SLORC and those people are allowed to meet publicly. The fact that the crowds grew bigger after we left the National Convention shows two things: one is that people in general did not like the National Convention and they took in the fact that the NLD would not attend until meaningful talks had taken place; secondly, the people rally to us in times of trouble. They thought we would be in great trouble after we had left the convention and they were showing that they were behind us. I think it is the same which has happened when we convened the party conference which turned into a party congress rather than a conference. All the elected members had been arrested except eighteen.

AC: Is there any kind of dialogue presently going on behind the scenes between the NLD and the SLORC?

ASSK: None whatsoever.

AC: Why doesn't the SLORC simply put you on an airplane and expel you from the country? What do you think is preventing them from taking such an easy, simple measure instead of allowing you to continue your activities?

ASSK: They can't expel me! I am a citizen of Burma and no country would accept me unless I ask for political asylum which I certainly won't do.

AC: If in fact SLORC were to allow a parliament to convene based on the results of their free and fair elections in 1990, what do you envision would occur?

ASSK: Whatever we do we will do it with a view to national reconciliation. If SLORC were to convene a parliament according to the results of 1990 we would certainly show appreciation for the gesture and we would certainly like SLORC included in the process of national reconciliation.

AC: It's been some months since we discussed the issue but do you really think it's possible to achieve democracy in Burma without international economic sanctions? And if not, why aren't you calling for sanctions against SLORC?

ASSK: We do not think that economic sanctions are the only way to bring democracy to Burma. There are many factors involved and you can never tell in advance what it is that is going to make the crucial change. I think a united effort from the international community is very useful. We do believe in the importance of the international community. As you know, our main support is here inside Burma. We depend on the support of our people to achieve democracy. But we are also aware of the great importance of the international community. SLORC is saying that it does not care what other countries think and that it can do what it wants. But of course, as you are aware, SLORC is trying very hard to get economic cooperation and economic aid from other countries. In this day and age nobody can be indifferent to what the rest of the world thinks. So we are not indifferent to world opinion. But we do not like to think too easily of economic sanctions and whatever is done we want to make sure that it is really going to help our country move towards democracy. Sometimes it is true that some measures involve short-term suffering. Although I do not believe that people in Burma would suffer so much from economic sanctions since the majority of the people, the masses, are benefiting very little out of economic opportunities that have arisen since SLORC took power.

AC: At this critical point in the struggle, especially in light of SLORC's dramatically escalating repression, are you calling for all foreign investors to immediately divest their business interests in Burma?

ASSK: No, we are not doing that yet. What we are saying is that there should be no more further investments in Burma until such time as there is progress towards democracy. Also, we are asking those who have already invested in Burma to assess or to reassess the situation and to rethink their commitments.

AC: If democracy is achieved, what will happen to the investments that are jointly held by foreign companies and SLORC? Would these investments be nationalized under a democratic Burma? Or would they be modified, the money lost or returned to the investors?

ASSK: We would look at each case individually and we would like

191

to make sure that whatever is done is done justly and with the benefits to the people in mind. We would not like investors to suffer
unnecessarily. We would not like SLORC to suffer unnecessarily.
We do not believe in imposing something on the others just as a
way of saying or showing that we are in a position to do it.

Chapter 12

"The courage to face yourself"

ALAN CLEMENTS: One of the most basic, and yet essential questions: what does being human mean to you?

AUNG SAN SUU KYI: As a Buddhist, if you really want to consider what we, as human beings, are here for it's quite simple: we are trying to achieve enlightenment and to use the wisdom that is gained to serve others, so that they too might be free from suffering. While we can't all be Buddhas, I feel a responsibility to do as much as I can to realize enlightenment to the degree that I can, and to use it to relieve the suffering of others.

AC: People the world over acknowledge the significant sacrifice you made having remained under house arrest and away from your family, rather than taking SLORC's offer to leave Burma and go into exile. But you've made it clear that it was a "choice" to stay and "not a sacrifice." Is it fair to say that your choice to stay was in part based on an expansion of your concept of family, which embraced your NLD colleagues and the whole of the people of your country?

ASSK: Yes and no. I have to admit that I have not consciously made an effort to expand my concept of family. It's just that my colleagues have become my family because they're warm-hearted and affectionate. We share the same goal, trust each other, and have a sense of unity. With our shared sense of purpose, it has created a family-like feeling. Also, I should add, that perhaps because they know that I'm alone, they care for me in a way in which a family would do.

AC: You've said that you're trying to educate the people in your country to help themselves, to have a voice in the matter, to have the courage to speak up, to question and challenge injustice and repressive authority. I would like to take the issue beyond Burma, and ask you as a mother to share your thoughts on how parents can foster the qualities of free and open inquiry in their children?

ASSK: Well, I encouraged free inquiry simply by answering as many of my children's questions as I could. As a child, Alexander especially [her eldest son] used to ask a lot of questions. And I would try to answer every one of them. I would never brush it aside as unimportant. And if his question had to do with something that I didn't know or that I couldn't answer, I would look it up in a book, and then try to answer him. Now, my mother was very good about that. She never once told me not to ask questions. Every evening when she returned from work, she used to lie down on the bed because she was rather tired. And then I would walk round and round her bed, and every time I got to the foot of her bed, I would ask one question. You can imagine, it doesn't take that long to walk around a bed. And never once did she say, "I'm too tired, don't go on asking me these questions." Mind you, she couldn't answer a lot of my questions. I remember asking her, "Why is water called water?" Now, it's very difficult to find an answer. But she would never say, "Don't ask me such nonsensical questions." She would try to answer or she would simply say, "I don't know." I respected her for that.

AC: How can one instill and nurture the seeds of greatness and love which lead a young adult to seek the betterment of humankind?

ASSK: You first have to make a distinction between ambition and the desire to do something for the world in which you live. A lot of young people today are ambitious or want to be great without knowing what it really means. Many of them want to be famous, privileged and treated as a star. That's not the same as wanting to serve the world. Nevertheless, it's difficult to say how one fosters greatness in young people. I think you have to begin at a young age. And it's just not enough for parents to try to instill these values in you. I think you have to be in an environment where you see that such values are respected. One of the main reasons why it was easy for my mother to instill the idea of service in me was that I knew that my parents were respected for the service they had rendered to the nation. I felt that service was something desirable to work towards. But in many societies today, both in the West and, I'm afraid, increasingly in the East, the drive is towards material achievement. Often in an environment like that it's difficult for the parents alone to try to instill a sense of service. But you have to keep on trying. Of course, one has to be careful not to be too heavy-handed with the young in trying to advise them, because they don't usually take very happily to heavy-handed suggestions.

AC: Daw Suu, what would you say are the main characteristics of the Burmese people—an amazingly diverse culture with over sixty-four indigenous races and 200 different languages and dialects?

ASSK: I can't talk as far as the ethnic peoples are concerned, that would be a presumption on my part. I can only talk about the ethnic Burman majority, because that's what I am. There are a great number of ethnic groups in Burma and the Burman are just one of them—the biggest group, we are of Tibeto-Burman stock. I have not studied the cultures of the other ethnic peoples of Burma deeply enough to comment on them, apart from the fact that my mother always taught me to think of them as very close to us, emphasizing how loyal they were. She always spoke of them with great respect and warmth.

About the Burmese in Burma, the first thing that comes to mind is the fact that they are Buddhists. But also the fact that not every Burmese is a good Buddhist. Another aspect of the Burmese is that they are a colorful people. I see them in Technicolor, as it were. I think the Burmese do go in not just for colorful clothes but also colorful emotions.

AC: Fourteen of the fifteen armed ethnic minorities in Burma that have been fighting against SLORC have cut "ceasefire" deals with them. Two questions: what are your impressions of these deals, and when you achieve democracy how will the NLD go about working with these groups to unify and bring them into a democratic country?

ASSK: These are not real ceasefires. These groups have continued to hold on to their arms. So it is quite clear that these ceasefires are not permanent peace settlements. What we would like to achieve is a permanent peace settlement that will apply to the whole of the country. The only way we can bring this about is to create a framework within which all the ethnic minorities can voice their hopes, their aspirations, their dissatisfactions without fear. Within a legal framework they must be allowed to express all their feelings, and by doing that we shall be able to come to an understanding. We do not think that this union can be built by the Burmese alone—it has to be built by all the ethnic groups. We want all of them to be involved in the building of the union. We want a genuine national convention that allows all the ethnic people to participate freely and fully and from that convention we hope to come up with a constitution that is truly accountable to the people of Burma. On such a solid foundation we want to build a true relationship with the ethnic people of Burma.

AC: I think many people in the West tend to have a stereotypical notion of South-East Asian countries, especially the less developed nations like Laos, Cambodia, Vietnam and Burma, as mysterious, alien nations 10,000 miles from our shores. While others often generalize these countries as lands drenched in decades of horror and blood: the wars in Vietnam and Laos, Pol Pot's genocide in Cambodia, Ne Win's thirty-odd-year brutal dictatorship in your own country and, of course, SLORC's ongoing repression. And you, as a Burmese having lived in Western countries for twenty-eight years, what do you think the common bonds between Burma and Western countries are?

ASSK: Well, our colonial legacy cannot be denied, whether we like it or not. The great majority of existing laws in Burma as well as our educational system were introduced and influenced by the colonial government. The schools, hospitals and railways—all these trappings of colonialism came to Burma through a Western power. Apart from that, I think the Burmese in general are by nature a tolerant race and also very open to other cultures and ideas. But we have been made intolerant by the authoritarian system which has been imposed upon us.

AC: Months before your wedding on 1 January 1972, you had written to Michael, "I only ask one thing, that should my people need me, you would help me do my duty by them. How probable it is I do not know, but the possibility exists." You obviously felt a very strong sense of duty to your people, as far back as the age of twenty-six, perhaps longer. Would you share your impressions on how your sense of duty has evolved over the years, to the point where it's become the entire focus of your life since your return to Burma in 1988?

ASSK: I don't know if you would call it a process of evolution. I think it was instilled in me as a child. It was always there, and it came to the surface when there was a need for it.

AC: A seed nurtured from childhood that rooted when the environment was right? Or was it innate?

ASSK: I think that the sense of duty can be innate. Some people have a stronger sense of duty than others. And of course your upbringing decides whom you think you owe this duty to. I was taught by my mother that I owed this duty to my people.

AC: But why?

ASSK: By what she told me about my father, and of course there must be something in my genes that inclines me towards a sense of duty.

AC: In a previous conversation you said, "Truth is power. The power of truth is very great indeed. And I think this is very frightening to some people." When I asked you what truth was, you replied that in essence it was "sincerity." But what is it about sincerity—the authenticity of spirit—that is so frightening to some people?

ASSK: Basically, sincerity is the desire not to deceive anyone. That's why sincerity is truth, because sincerity means you're not attempting to deceive anybody. Unless of course you're deceiving yourself. If that be the case, then you have to start by being sincere with yourself, before you can be sincere with others. But some people think that it is necessary for them to deceive others and perhaps even to deceive themselves, in order to feel comfortable with what they are doing.

AC: So in some ways, sincerity is like a bright, clean mirror that makes the insincere mind feel a bit too uncomfortable with itself?

ASSK: Yes. A bright, clean mirror can show up a lot of things that you would rather not see.

AC: Where does the concept of sincerity fit into the Buddhist moral code of precepts?

ASSK: I suppose it would go under avoiding *musavada*—avoiding what is not true—non-deception. And sincerity doesn't just simply mean not trying to deceive, but it also means trying to reach out to others.

AC: So active sincerity is a concern for the welfare of others?

ASSK: Yes. Of course there are people who want to reach out to others to win over their good opinion, but not in a sincere way. They put on an act or say what's not true in order to gain people's good will or support. Sincerity is linked with the desire to reach out to people honestly and openly.

AC: The misuse and abuse of power has been an issue of perennial debate. May I ask you for your thoughts on what are some of the safeguards to protect one from corruption through the acquisition of power?

ASSK: I suppose what you need is the courage to face yourself. I think that's the best safeguard against corruption. If you're brave enough to face yourself, I mean, to really look in the mirror and see yourself, warts and all, then I think you would not be liable to corruption. As a Buddhist, I cannot help thinking that if one really understood the meaning of *anicca* [impermanence] one wouldn't chase power and wealth at the expense of one's moral being.

AC: So one's moral judgment is distorted without an understanding of *anicca*? Would you explain the interconnection?

ASSK: I think it's probably, in part, my Buddhist background which makes me feel that everything will pass away, but my deeds and their effects will stay with me. So while all the trappings of wealth and power will pass, the effects of my actions will remain with me until they have been fully worked out.

AC: Staying with the issue of the abuse of power, it seems that many leaders have cultivated the dark art of mass manipulation, a type of charisma, or some kind of spellbinding energy. Hitler is an example...

ASSK: The word "charisma" comes from the root meaning grace, doesn't it? So how would you call Hitler charismatic?

AC: Only in the sense that he had the ability to move his nation to such a level of absolute perversity. Perhaps I'm abusing the word, but let me ask you, how is it that some people have the ability to move people so powerfully?

ASSK: I think that one must make a distinction between the charisma of a particular individual and the spell cast by his power. I think that you will find in general that people in powerful positions seem to cast a spell wherever they go. That is because people are impressed, awed or frightened by power.

AC: Awed into darkness like in the case of the Aum cultists in Japan and their sarin gassing in a Tokyo subway?

ASSK: Yes, but who are these people?

AC: This is the question. What can one do to find his way through the intoxicating dogmas and self-distortions based on psychological projection and get to the truth of another person's real intention?

ASSK: Well, I think you've got to be used to facing the truth. It all comes back to that, doesn't it? Most people don't go around exposing themselves to everybody. No normal person would do that. That does not mean that there are not some people who are quite aware of their own faults and weaknesses. And that's part of facing the truth. But there are some people who simply cannot face the truth, not just about themselves, but even about those who are near and dear to them. I was discussing this with some friends the other day: there are people who always think that their children are lovely and have no faults, when in fact, everybody can see that their children are not like that at all. If these people cannot even see the faults in their own children, how can they see any faults in themselves?

There is another type of person who is quite aware of their faults and weaknesses, as well as those of people near and dear to him. That does not mean that they will go around criticizing their family or themselves. But there is an awareness. And if you are aware of your own faults, you will be aware of the faults of others as well. This is not to say that you'll be harsh with those people. I think that those who are aware of their own faults generally tend to be less harsh on others than those who are not aware of their own faults.

AC: So it all comes down to self-awareness and the developing of an ability to examine one's awe towards those individuals in positions of power, and from there, having the courage to question authority?

ASSK: Well, sometimes it's sheer laziness, I think. A lot of people get into habits out of sheer laziness.

AC: Questioning is too burdensome?

ASSK: Yes. Mentally. Or sometimes morally. Sometimes you just don't want to sit up and question yourself, "Is it right for me to be serving this sort of person?" Life is often a moral dilemma. But I think some people prefer not to look at it that way because it's just too exhausting.

AC: The human predicament...

ASSK: Life is a moral dilemma, but it's more of a moral dilemma in some cases than in others. I noticed that especially when I went from Japan to India. When I was in Japan, which of course is a very rich country, I had no qualms about eating and dressing as I pleased. It did not worry me that I was wearing a warm coat because everybody else was wearing a warm coat. It didn't worry me that I ate well, because everybody else was eating well. The only person I saw in Japan whom I might have described as poor was a man who was drunk, but he might not have been poor at all. He might have been looking shabby and disheveled only because he was drunk. From Japan I went straight to India. And then I was aware of this moral dilemma, of living in a society where there was less equality. And

I suppose that the less equality in a society, the greater your moral dilemma becomes.

Now in India, whenever we went into the town I lived there would be beggars on the way. And it was always a moral dilemma: do I give or do I not? It was not because I did not want to spend the money but because I had heard from a lot of people that there was such a thing as wealthy beggars, who beg as a profession. In a sense, they were just having you on. I found myself asking this question to begin with: do I give or not to these beggars? If I give, am I helping them or am I just promoting deceit? In the end I came to the conclusion that if I give something to them it should be out of a sense of generosity and for no other reason. So life is a moral dilemma, all the time. And of course, in societies where there is gross injustice that can be a moral dilemma too. But sometimes I think in this case it can be less of a dilemma, because you simply opt for the side that stands for justice at the risk of danger to yourself.

<u>AC:</u> What is the single most difficult moral dilemma that you have ever faced in your life?

<u>ASSK:</u> *(long pause)* I wouldn't say there is a single most difficult moral dilemma. I think one faces moral dilemmas all the time, especially if you are involved in politics. One should always remember that politics is about people. If you start forgetting that, then you turn out to be like Stalin or Hitler, just manipulating people. But the moment you acknowledge that politics is about people, it means that you have to take into consideration their human weaknesses and feelings. Sometimes of course that interferes with the efficiency of the work. And that is a constant dilemma.

<u>AC:</u> What has been the most difficult decision you have had to make starting from the time you first entered politics in 1988?

<u>ASSK:</u> There's one that I remember. This was in connection with the arrangements to help found the National Party for Democracy. There were so many varying opinions about who should be in the party and who should not. And at first I found that very worrying, because if I backed a particular set of candidates it would mean some would be displeased. Now, this was something I should have seen

straight away, but sometimes one does not see the obvious. Suddenly it occurred to me, "What's all this worry about?" I should simply back the candidates whom I thought were most suitable. It was the only honest and right thing to do. Which I did. In fact, the ones I thought best were the ones whom others in general thought best too. There was no problem. But that taught me a lesson. Sometimes I think we worry for nothing at all. It's like that business with the beggars. In the end, I decided that it's your generosity that is important; a real generosity that is sincere and from the heart.

AC: Do you ever feel a sense of dilemma about your duty to your people, so many millions of people in need of security, living in states of malnutrition, in varying degrees of fear, if not terror? Do you ever feel that you just can't give enough?

ASSK: No. I can only give as much as I can. Nor do I have this megalomaniac sense of me giving to everybody who needs it. I have always been very frank about the fact that there is a limit to what I can do. I'll try my best, but beyond that it's not possible. This does not mean that I sit back and say, "Well, that's it." I want to try to raise the standard of my best as far as I can.

AC: When you reflect upon your people's suffering, what is it that first comes to mind and stirs your heart?

ASSK: That we ought to do something about it, whatever we can. That is always my reaction when I see something that should not be. It's no use standing there wringing your hands and saying, "My goodness, my goodness, this is terrible." You must try to do what you can. I believe in action.

AC: I would like to ask you for your thoughts regarding the issue of free speech and free expression? And is there ever a limit?

ASSK: I think it's important to honor the connection between free speech and respect for other people. You can't just go on and say anything you want about anybody. There has to be consideration for other people. But I do not think that one should curb free speech on the grounds that you are criticizing someone or something. That's not right. On the other hand, free speech does not mean that you can stand in the middle of the road and hurl obscenities at anybody who walks by. This is just an exploitation of your right to free speech.

<u>AC:</u> What about freedom in art and music, say in the West, we have so many varied expressions—from gangster-rap music, to Robert Mapplethorpe's highly provocative photography, to Oliver Stone's controversial film, *Natural Born Killers*. Do you feel that limits should be imposed on artistic expression?

<u>ASSK:</u> I have to confess that I am not talented musically and because of that, I would say that my understanding of the needs of the musically talented is limited. And I have not really studied the arguments of those who support the view that you can do anything as long as it justifies your musical and artistic need.

How do they justify this view that you can say any lyrics that you want? I can't quite follow it. Can you say anything in a song that you would not be allowed to say, for example, in a public speech?

<u>AC:</u> It might not be published or produced, and even if it did, it might not get any air-time, but why not remain free to express your truth?

<u>ASSK:</u> Well, I don't think that's acceptable.

<u>AC:</u> Why?

<u>ASSK:</u> It's not just in the Western world. I think that everywhere people do try to take advantage and misuse their rights. I have always said that once we get democracy, there will be people who misuse their democratic rights and use them just for their own pleasure or personal gain. Probably there will be people who use the right of association in order to found the kind of organizations that will be used to attack democracy itself. It happens all the time. Democracy is far from perfect. One always has to question. There it is again— the questioning mind. The questioning mind has its pluses and minuses. You have to question all the time whether by forbidding a certain speech, song or film, that you are in fact interfering with democratic rights, or whether you are protecting those who need to be protected. This is why I say life is a moral dilemma. But I don't agree with everything that's happening in the West, which is why I say that I would like our democracy to be a better, more com-

passionate and more caring one. That is not to say we have fewer freedoms. But that we will use these freedoms more responsibly and with the well-being of others in mind.

AC: And the main element of Western democracies that troubles you?

ASSK: It all comes down to violence. The kind of songs and music and films that you are talking about deal with violence in some form or other. There's a violent streak in human nature and I don't think it's peculiar to the West. Perhaps what has happened is that in affluent countries people somehow don't know quite how to cope with this violent streak. Is it that they lose their ability to cope with violence because the affluent society imposes certain conditions that do not provide an escape valve?

AC: Like authentic spiritual values? But violence is everywhere.

ASSK: Yes, violence is everywhere. In America, there is violence on the streets, there is violence in films and songs and music and so on. But then in a place like Rwanda, there was this violence on the battlefield. The violence is in the streets in the form of racial struggle. And what about the former Yugoslavia? There, violence was everywhere. There is violence in Burma: violence committed by the authorities against the people. It is the same in other authoritarian states. So yes, there is violence all over the world. There is something in human nature which seems to require people to erupt into violence from time to time.

AC: What do you think it is in people that indulges itself pleasurably in the viewing of violent art, television or film, that finds violence entertaining?

ASSK: I don't know because I have never enjoyed such films. I like films that are interesting and beautifully made. I think that again is part of my training. My mother always used to say, "I don't believe in paying to make myself miserable." And I strictly endorse that point of view.

AC: What about from the point of view of Václav Havel saying that the intellectual is essentially a provocateur, one who constantly disturbs? Do those forms of art and music and film interest you?

ASSK: Yes, to be provocative of course I think is acceptable, to provoke change or reaction. But it depends on what you are trying to provoke.

AC: So, it really all comes back to one's intention?

ASSK: Indeed!

AC: You mentioned in a previous conversation that of all human traits it was "hypocrisy" that ignited your temper the most. Has SLORC's hypocrisy made you at all cynical? Do you struggle with that?

ASSK: I don't quite understand what cynicism means. One has to recognize the fact that people do not always act as they speak. This goes on all the time. And that doesn't mean that everybody is like that. There are people who do what they say and say what they think.

AC: Let me say it more specifically. Western countries, America in particular, have an obsession with building weapons of all kinds. As a matter of "free enterprise," we broker these weapons all over the world. Even here in Rangoon I have seen SLORC generals traveling in their motorcades, sandwiched between soldiers, with their fingers on the triggers of their Uzis. Isn't it time to address the weapons industry in the West and, of course, the East too? China is a worry.

ASSK: There are sellers only because there are buyers. It's not just a matter of the countries which are producing the arms. It's also a matter of the countries which want to buy these arms. This is a reflection of the fact that the human race is far from learning to live without violence.

AC: As a leader dedicated to non-violence, would you be for the abolishment of all weapons of mass destruction?

ASSK: At this point in time it's idealistic, but I wonder whether a time will ever come when it's no longer a simple idea but something that could be put into effect practically. I wonder if we could remove all instincts of violence from the human race.

AC: Can you imagine yourself as the leader of a free and democratic Burma, having to make a decision to use violence against humans, to use force that you know will kill people?

ASSK: All members of governments may have to do that under certain circumstances.

AC: So the "skillful" use of weapons and violence as a politician comes with the territory, so to speak?

ASSK: It's an occupational hazard.

Chapter 13

"To learn the power of the powerless"

ALAN CLEMENTS: When I was in university, I had a growing angst that I couldn't identify except by its outermost appearance. I thought that if I pursued the system I would most likely be swallowed up by the "American Dream," and somewhere down the road find myself with a house, two cars and a family, and probably consider myself happy. This realization scared me so much that it jolted me from what I thought I should do in order to become successful, on to a path that was based on my passion and my instinct. Which eventually led me to your country and inspired me to become a Buddhist monk. I have two questions in relationship to this. First, what does mediocrity mean to you? And secondly, what would be your definition of greatness?

AUNG SAN SUU KYI: I don't think there's anything wrong with people finding happiness in a house, two cars and a family. If it is a really happy family, they are going to generate happiness around them, so there's nothing wrong with it. And I think modesty in one's desires is not a crime, neither is it something to be ashamed of. In fact, I rather admire people who are modest in their desires and do not give in to them all the time. That is very much in line with Buddhist thinking.

But if you think of a house and two cars as the be-all and the end-all of your existence, and you will do anything to get this house and two cars, even if it means trampling on other people, of course that's wrong. Whereas if it's just your modest ambition that you will work steadily and along the right way, without hurting others, towards this modest existence of a house, two cars and a happy family, I don't think there's anything wrong with it. A lot of people who seem very ordinary from the outside have very great minds and spiritual values that we know nothing about.

As to greatness; there are so many different sorts. I mean, what makes a composer great for example? His music. He may not have a terribly attractive or inspiring personality but if he writes beautiful music, then he's a great composer. Someone who plays beautiful music is also a great musician. So it is very difficult to define the word "great."

I have read somewhere that in politics greatness is defined as the capacity to inspire other people to join in a great cause. And I suppose, to a certain extent, this is the same with religious leaders too. You would call a religious leader great if he inspired a lot of people to join in his spiritual quest. But I wonder whether greatness is something that you can speak of out of the context of your relationship with others around you. I mean, can you talk about somebody sitting alone on an island, who has no contact with others, as a great person?

In general you speak of greatness in the context of your relationship with others; what you do for others; what you inspire in others. If there's nobody to listen to a musician's music, nobody will think of him as great, until the day that somehow his music reaches the ears of those who are made happy or inspired by it. It's the same with a book. A great book is always a great book, whether or not the author is still alive. But nobody will think of the author as great until somebody has read his works. So this great mind will exist by itself, whether or not there are others to appreciate it. And in that way, I think, if anybody has a seed of greatness in him, it will be there whether or not there are others to appreciate it. But whether this seed can be made to grow and flower so that the world recognizes it is another matter. That can only be done, I think, in the context of this person's relationship with the rest of society.

AC: Many people associate your name with a voice that speaks for the voiceless, a power that stands up for the powerless—the simple people, the ordinary folks, and the disenfranchised. That's the vast majority of people not only in your own country but the world over. How might you apply the concept of greatness in the life of such people as a beggar, a refugee or a political prisoner?

<u>ASSK:</u> Individual aspirations differ all the time. But I suppose one seeks greatness through taming one's passions. And isn't there a saying that "it is far more difficult to conquer yourself than to conquer the rest of the world"? So, I think the taming of one's own passions, in the Buddhist way of thinking, is the chief way to greatness, no matter what the circumstances may be. For example, a lot of our people [political prisoners] meditate when they're in prison, partly because they have the time, and partly because it's a very sensible thing to do. That is to say that if you have no contact with the outside world, and you can't do anything for it, then you do what you can with the world inside you in order to bring it under proper control.

<u>AC:</u> If I were to sum up the struggle of your people and the overall crisis in Burma, I would say that it's the "courage to feel genuine emotions." For those in the democracy struggle, it's the courage to feel self-esteem, self-worth and dignity—the courage for action. And for the authorities it's the courage to feel shame and remorse; the courage to love and the courage to humble themselves to people. But what is it that is distorting all these people from feeling their right feeling, so to speak? Is it as simple as the fear of feeling?

<u>ASSK:</u> I think it also has a lot to do with the training to be objective. And it's awareness that leads to objectivity. The more aware you are, the more objective you become. This is very Buddhist, isn't it? And I think that those who have no sense of awareness of what's going on around them and inside them cannot have these feelings which are so important for doing the right thing in this world. If you are not aware that what you are doing is wrong, then you will not feel ashamed of it. One is living in pure fantasy—a type of madness and a total lack of objectivity. Which all comes down to an inability to face the truth. If you are living in a world where everything you do is justified by such things as "patriotism" or "the good of the country," then you will not be able to take the next step of being ashamed and wanting to correct yourself.

<u>AC:</u> Do you think this is simply a matter of training? Or such poor training that deluded fantasies become a bad habit, a way of life?

209

ASSK: Yes, it is a matter of training. I have come across a lot of parents who always stand by their children, whether or not they are in the right. I do not think that would help these children to grow up and to become objective and fair-minded. When we were living in Simla I came across one case like that. A little boy had been rather obstreperous. He had been running around in a crowded place and he could have caused a traffic accident. A man there stopped him, put him under control and told him to stand at the side of the road. Now when he met the boy's mother, he explained that the boy had been running wild and he had to take him aside because he might have gotten himself killed or caused an accident. And you know, the mother was not grateful at all. She was furious! I was totally astonished. If I had been in her position, I would have been, first, very grateful to the man for what he had done. And secondly, I would have been very apologetic. I would have said, "I'm sorry my son has been causing all this trouble, and I'm so grateful to you for having put a stop to this." But that mother was absolutely furious with that man for saying her son had been naughty. These things happen all the time. And if you grow up in a family where everything you do, as opposed to what other people outside do, is justified, then you won't grow up to be objective. You will always think that whatever you do is right and justified, whereas what other people do is wrong if it opposes your desires. So, training comes a lot into it. But I think there is also nature. I think people are born with certain characteristics. In these days you would say it's genetic. But how well you are nourished will also make a difference. So your training and your upbringing can help you to a certain extent, but not all the way.

AC: How did this repressive band of generals—SLORC—emerge from the mystical parenting of an ancient Buddhist culture?

ASSK: Well, one might as well ask how the Khmer Rouge emerged out of Cambodia. It does not mean that just because you have a good, caring religion, everybody practices it. A lot of people give lip-service to their religion. They can recite the prayers, attend the ceremonies, perform all the rites, but they may not really absorb anything into their hearts. You must have known many people who meditated not just for days but for months, even for years, but whose attitudes towards the world did not substantially change, or whose attitudes never changed. Have you come across many like that?

<u>AC:</u> Yes, in both cases, change does seem to come slowly, if at all. But let me ask you. Some people in the world have an urge for wholeness, while others seem to have a fascination with darkness. But in order to be whole or move towards that wholeness, one must awaken to and integrate darkness. Perhaps I'm wrong but it seems to me that in your own inner process of awakening you've been forced to confront many outside events that I would consider dark. Would you share what you have learned about yourself from darkness?

<u>ASSK:</u> Well, I have never thought that I had entered the darkness. I think that people outside see the whole thing in a much more dramatic way than those inside do. I suppose it would be a lot more dramatic if one were taken from one's home and put into a prison cell and the doors went clang. But it was not like that with me. On the first day I was put under house arrest a lot of people came and turned the house upside down and took away a lot of stuff. And after the upheaval, which went on through the night, I just stayed on under house arrest, and it didn't seem particularly dramatic.

<u>AC:</u> Yes, but so many people come to you every day to explain the hardships they face. Colleagues of yours are imprisoned, some even tortured, and you've suffered to some extent. What have you learned from these daily encounters with suffering?

<u>ASSK:</u> You learn about both the best and the worst in human nature. Of course, you learn about the worst in human nature from those who inflict the torture and the suffering. And you learn about the best from those who are able to stand up to that suffering without being broken in spirit.

<u>AC:</u> I think it's fair to say that many people in the world have an instinct or urge to serve others—a calling to give something back to life, and not just consume. How can one nurture this instinct to give? For some it ignites, then flickers and fades quickly...

<u>ASSK:</u> Some people are born with the instinct to give and others are

not. You will see little children who love sharing their sweets and toys and other little children who don't. That is nature. But of course, there are parents who let their little children go on being selfish and there are parents who say, you've got to share. My mother was one of those parents who always said you had got to share. And in her opinion selfishness was one of the worst sins that anybody could be capable of. She always used to say, "So-and-so is so selfish!" I heard this as a tremendous condemnation. So I would say I learned a lot from my mother. She believed in serving others and in gaining satisfaction and happiness from giving, rather than from taking.

AC: Were there other important values that she instilled in you?

ASSK: She also taught me to admire and respect the values for which my father stood. She emphasized that fear was not something you should encourage. In fact, she would get very angry with me if I was frightened. She did not like cowardice at all. And she would get very angry about the fact that I used to be afraid of the dark. She would not encourage such namby-pamby feelings. She thought very highly of courage, responsibility, spiritual service, and sharing. My mother was an extremely upright woman.

AC: The most salient feature of the Buddha's teaching is awareness: awareness of the moment, the here and now; the ability to be alive and present. May I ask for your reflections on the importance of living in the present moment, rather than indulging the past or anticipating the future?

ASSK: Well, I think people who do not have some work that really interests them or which really occupies their mind and spirit are people who do not think in terms of the present. U Win Htein and somebody else were talking the other day and the other person said to him, "Oh, I'm feeling frustrated. How about you?" And he said, "I'm just too busy to feel frustrated." I think this is it! If you have a lot of work to do and you believe in the work you are doing, you do live in the present. There is no question of learning how to live in the present, you just do it. You have no time to live in the past, and you know that the future comes out of what is done in the present. I think people who are happily occupied are joyful, and those

Aung San Suu Kyi outside her front gate
on the day of her release from house arrest,
July 10, 1995. STUART ISETT

With the international media during a photo session at her residence a few days
after her release from house arrest in July 1995. YAMAMOTO MUNESUKE

Crowds greet Aung San Suu Kyi the day after her release. STUART ISETT

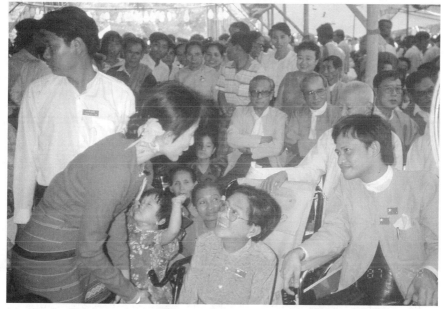

Aung San Suu Kyi during an Independence Day celebration at her residence January 4, 1996.
The man and woman she is talking to were partially paralyzed as a result of having been tortured while
incarcerated by SLORC authorities. ALAN CLEMENTS/THE BURMA PROJECT USA

Deputy Chairman of the
NLD, U Tin U.
ALAN CLEMENTS/THE BURMA
PROJECT USA

Aung San Suu Kyi having an informal lunch at home with NLD delegates, December 1995.
YAMAMOTO MUNESUKE

Paying respects to Thamanya Sayadaw in Karen State, Burma, October, 1995.
COLLECTION OF THE BURMA PROJECT USA

Aung San Suu Kyi with U Kyi Maung at her residence.
LESLIE KEAN/THE BURMA PROJECT USA

With Madeleine Albright, 1995. Then U.S. Ambassador to the United Nations, Albright traveled to Rangoon to meet with Aung San Suu Kyi. She also met with Khin Nyunt, Secretary-1 of the SLORC.
COLLECTION OF THE BURMA PROJECT USA

Giving a speech from the gate of her residence, with NLD youth security guards in the foreground, in early 1996. Later that year her regular weekend speeches were banned by the SLORC.
ALAN CLEMENTS/THE BURMA PROJECT USA

SLORC Secretary-1 Lt. General Khin Nyunt, Head of Military Intelligence, February 1996.
ALAN CLEMENTS/THE BURMA PROJECT USA

The NLD Executive Committee, 1996. Front row (l. to r): U Lwin, U Kyi Maung, U Aung Shwe, U Tin U, Aung San Suu Kyi. COLLECTION OF THE BURMA PROJECT USA

Family photo taken on 19 December 1995, in Rangoon. Left to right: Alexander, Kim, Aung San Suu Kyi, Michael Aris. AKIRA TAZAKI

who are not happily occupied are frustrated, bored or resentful.

<u>AC:</u> Many journalists have asked you questions specifically about your safety and the possibility of assassination. There are many examples throughout history of people who courageously stood above the status quo and spoke about truth, freedom and justice and in so doing were killed; King, Gandhi, Kennedy and of course your father are but a few examples. My question is, if it's explicable, why is it that when one challenges existing norms and has a fair degree of power behind you, society wants to take you down, crush or kill you?

<u>ASSK:</u> I think there is something that makes people feel very strong emotions towards those who are prominent. John Lennon was not killed because he was working for human rights or speaking up for democracy. I think there is something in human nature that attracts one to prominent people, and the attraction is not always of the right kind. It can be of the negative kind, that makes them want to destroy and kill. So, I think, it doesn't particularly have anything to do with truth-speaking, as it were. On the other hand, of course, in political situations, if you tell the truth it may be painful to some people. My father once said in one of his speeches that he had been told by one of his colleagues that he had a knack for speaking the painful truth. The truth is painful to some. And when people are in pain, they can often lash out. It depends on what they are like. There are those who, when they feel pain, analyze the source of the pain. They handle it in a rational, intelligent way, while others simply lash out and hit anybody who is around, regardless of whether the pain was caused by themselves or by others.

<u>AC:</u> Your struggle in Burma is very often compared with the movement against apartheid in South Africa, led by Nelson Mandela. How has the struggle in South Africa affected your own ideas or values? And secondly, could you speak about how Nelson Mandela has perhaps influenced you as a person, in your approach to politics and in your vision of democracy?

<u>ASSK:</u> South Africa and Nelson Mandela are not the only influences on my view of the democratic struggle in Burma. Of course, we think of South Africa because it is the most immediate example of a nation

which has totally turned its back on an obviously unjust system. That's not to say that everything is going smoothly in South Africa and nobody ever thought this would happen. Everybody knew that South Africa, even under a democratic, mixed government, would have to face many problems which have proliferated under an apartheid government for so many decades. South Africa is an example of reason getting the better of prejudice because the whole system of apartheid is based purely on prejudice; on the view that blacks are not as human as whites. It's the same in Burma. The feelings of those against democracy towards those who want it is sheer prejudice. We would like reason to overcome prejudice. And of course the injustice of a system that allows people of one color to dominate another is no worse an injustice than that in a system that allows the people of one organization to dominate the rest of the country. These are the parallels, and because of that we like to study the situation in South Africa.

But there are many differences as well. Among themselves, the white South African government did practice democracy. They were not like the military regime. Their attitude towards the blacks was totally negative and unjust, but among themselves they did have respect for the democratic process within their limited circle. If you read anything about Helen Suzman, you will find that although she was opposing the regime, she had full rights as an elected member of Parliament. So there was respect for the parliamentary system.

On the other hand, the attitude of the whites towards the blacks was one of convinced superiority. The whites—not all of them, mind you, but a lot of them—were really convinced that they were genetically superior to the blacks. It was not anything that could be eradicated or leveled by education, upbringing or environment. I do not think this is an attitude that is held by the military regime in Burma, although they do try to assert that they are superior in patriotism. But sometimes one feels that they are protesting a bit too much, and one wonders, in fact one is rather convinced, that it's just talk.

AC: I know that you have a high regard for President Václav Havel of Czechoslovakia. May I ask how he has influenced you as a leader?

ASSK: Well, I've read his writings of course. He has really affected me indirectly, in the sense that it's what he wrote about how it was in Czechoslovakia that influenced me. And then of course, things like the "power of the powerless," and so on. But what impressed me most about Czechoslovakia was the intellectual honesty that some of the best people maintained. They would rather be plumbers, road-workers, street-cleaners and bricklayers than compromise their intellectual integrity by joining a university or the government. They accepted the superiority of the mind over the body and placed the importance of intellectual integrity far above that of material comfort. That has inspired me a great deal, and I think this is a wonderful example of what you can achieve when you try to maintain your spiritual and intellectual integrity.

AC: SLORC's infamous "Visit Myanmar Year 1996" campaign is a major concern of the generals. Are you advocating would-be travelers and tourists to stay away from your country?

ASSK: No, we are not doing anything like that. What we are asking for is a boycott of "Visit Myanmar Year 1996." This begins in early November 1996 and it goes on, I believe, until the end of April 1997, since this is considered as the height of the tourist season. We are asking for this boycott first of all as a demonstration of solidarity with the democratic movement in Burma. We do not expect tourists to stay away from Burma forever. And anyway we have got nothing against foreigners. It is just that SLORC is using "Visit Myanmar Year 1996" as a propaganda weapon to show that they have been able to achieve what they wanted although they have not been able to do so. The reason we would like tourists to keep away from Burma particularly during that Visit Myanmar Year 1996 is to show that they understand that a lot of conveniences, such as roads, hotels and tourist sights have been achieved at the expense of the people of Burma. The people of Burma have suffered a lot. As you know, they have been forced to take part in the building of roads and bridges. People have been moved away from their homes, entire villages have been destroyed in order to clear up the places for the tourists. So we would like potential visitors to Burma to show that they are not going to buy their pleasure at the expense of the ordinary people.

223

AC: New hotels are going up all over Rangoon as well as other parts of the country. Tourists will be coming, how many no one can be sure, but they're coming. What advice can you give to the tourists, especially to those who might respond to your call for sensitivity?

ASSK: First of all they should ask themselves why they are coming. It's not possible to give advice to everybody. I do not know why people come. Some people come on package tours, simply because they just want to take back photographs and say they've been there—the "I've been there" syndrome. And some people come because they are genuinely interested in the culture. But how would I advise tourists who come to Burma? I would say, "Please ask yourself—why do you want to come to this country? Do you think by coming you are going to do the country any good? Or is it in order simply to satisfy some vanity or curiosity in yourself?"

AC: Perhaps many people who read your words will want to know how they can assist you and your people to achieve democracy. What can someone do to help?

ASSK: It's like apartheid in South Africa. If only a few people in the world had refused to buy products from South Africa, it would not have had an effect. But there were many, many people, who refused to buy anything from South Africa. In fact, I never bought anything from South Africa because there was apartheid. I was one of those who felt that we morally could not support what the South African government was doing.

There is much that those who wish to help Burma achieve democracy can do, such as refusing to support those businesses that are helping prop up an unjust system in Burma.

AC: So anybody in the world who has a regard for freedom...

ASSK: Can do his bit. Everybody can do his bit if he is really interested. Everybody in Burma. Everybody in the world outside Burma.

AC: Can foreigners who sympathize with your movement financially assist you and the NLD in your efforts?

ASSK: No. Under current regulations we are not allowed to accept donations from foreign sources and we are very careful not to do so. We are very strict about this.

AC: Were you able to receive the money from the Nobel Peace Prize?

ASSK: I never accepted that money or any other prize money for myself. I have used those funds to set up a Burma Trust for Education and this is kept abroad. We use that to help educate young Burmese who are in Thailand and so on. Those foreigners who would like to help Burma and cannot help us directly could contribute to that trust fund and we would be grateful.

AC: What will it take to bring your people's struggle for freedom and democracy to a greater level of global appeal? Is more suffering needed?

ASSK: I don't think you can find an easy answer to that. It's different from one country to another. People shouldn't forget that it took many years before the world started taking an interest in Nelson Mandela, and it had to do not just with the fact that he had been imprisoned a long time, but also with the fact that the world itself became more interested in such things as human rights. I think that with the development of communications technology, people are taking more interest in what is going on in other parts of the world. And I think it reflects something about human interest. The fact that the black people of South Africa have been terribly oppressed for far longer than twenty-five years did not seem to strike them as much as the fact that one person, Nelson Mandela, had been in prison for twenty-five years. He was not the only one, either, mind you. There were others as well. But this is human nature. People like to be able to identify with others. It was because so many people could identify with Nelson Mandela as a husband and as a father. By that time he was, I think, a grandfather who had been totally removed from his family and who was prepared to put up with those twenty-five years of imprisonment for the sake of his principles. That moved people greatly. So something that moves people to identify themselves with what is happening in Burma will raise the level of their consciousness. And you can never tell what it is.

AC: A three-part question: one, how confident are you that democracy will be achieved in Burma? Two, what are the most essential factors needed for that goal to be achieved? And thirdly, is there a possibility of giving a time-frame for when you feel that democracy will be achieved?

ASSK: I can answer the last question first. No, I don't believe in trying to predict when. And also I think it's dangerous to try to predict these things when one can never tell. The first one, yes, I am confident that we will achieve democracy. And the second, what is needed is for the people to understand that they are not powerless. They've got to learn the power of the powerless. There is a lot that they can do to achieve what they want. They should not see themselves as helpless and totally in the hands of the powers that be.

AC: It has been about eleven months since your release. How would you assess the struggle at this point?

ASSK: The members of our party are getting much more active and they're beginning to work again. As you know, we've formed a legal aid committee, giving our members and supporters practical help and showing them that there are ways in which we can protect ourselves and our rights. We are not just saying, "You can protect your rights," but actually saying, "You can protect your rights like this. We will come and protect them for you in accordance with the existing laws. You can say to those who try to arrest you unlawfully they have no right to arrest you because you did not break any of the existing laws." I think it has to be done by practical demonstration. We have to show them how these things can be done. Some people are so afraid that they don't even dare to take the help that is offered to them. But then there are others who accept the help. When those who are not so brave see that others do accept the help, they are encouraged. So it goes on like that.

We do it by practical means. We just don't go to people and say, come on, do something for yourself. We do things. They see that we protect our own people—we send out our lawyers to defend them. We put together this legal aid committee and we work. Then they start thinking that these things can and do happen.

We are going to increase our practical projects in ways to help the families of political prisoners. It's not just giving them money.

We want to help them to help themselves. Our decision to hold a conference of our elected representatives on the sixth anniversary of the 1990 elections was an indication of the progress we had made in the reorganization and reconsolidation of the NLD. As many people know that decision had wide-ranging repercussions that proved how strong the public support for the NLD is.

<u>AC:</u> The cold war has ended, but here we stand with a planet full of problems: nuclear bombs and nuclear waste, pollution of all kinds, over-population, over-consumption, global warming and defor-estation. What do you see for the future of the planet and do you have hope for the survival of the human race?

<u>ASSK:</u> Yes, I do have hope because I'm working. I'm doing my bit to try to make the world a better place, so I naturally have hope for it. But obviously, those who are doing nothing to improve the world have no hope for it. Why should they? They're not doing anything to improve it in any way. But I think there are many, many people who are working really hard to improve the situation. I don't mean by this politicians or leaders of social or religious movements. I mean ordinary people who feel what nowadays might be termed an old-fashioned sense of duty towards the society in which they live, even if it is just their street or apartment block. And those who are working to bring about positive changes are always more powerful than those who are sitting and letting things take their course.

<u>AC:</u> I'd like to read the final few lines from your essay, *Towards a True Refuge:** "...'the darkness had always been there but the light was new.' Because it is new it has to be tended with care and diligence. Even the smallest light cannot be extinguished by all the darkness in the world because darkness is merely the absence of light. But a small light cannot dispel acres of encircling gloom. It needs to grow stronger, and people need to accustom their eyes to the light to see it as benediction rather than pain. We are so much in need of a brighter world which will offer adequate refuge to all its inhabitants." What does the light refer to?

---

* See chapter 6, note #1 for details.

ASSK: Light means that you see a lot of things that you don't want to see, as well as things that you want to see. If there's light, obviously you see everything, so you have to face a lot of things that are both undesirable and desirable. You have to learn to live and cope with the light, with seeing rather than not seeing. A lot of people who commit injustices don't see what they don't want to see. They're blind to the injustice of their own actions. They only see what justifies them in doing what they have done, refusing to see what reflects badly on them. It's the story of SLORC...not daring to face the complete picture, that people are fed up with the situation, they are tired of poverty, corruption, aimlessness, and stupidity. But the authorities don't want to see the truth.

AC: On the chance that you are re-arrested and held incommunicado, may I invite you to speak to those of us in the world who wish to support you and your people's aspirations for democracy and freedom.

ASSK: It's very simple. You must not forget that the people of Burma want democracy. Whatever the authorities may say, it is a fact that the people want democracy and they do not want an authoritarian regime that deprives them of their basic human rights. The world should do everything possible to bring about the kind of political system that the majority of the people of Burma want and for which so many people have sacrificed themselves.

Burma should be helped at a time when help is needed. And one day we hope to be ourselves in a position to help others in need.

Appendix A

A Conversation with U Kyi Maung

Deputy Chairman of the National League for Democracy U Kyi Maung is regarded as the man most singly responsible for leading the National League for Democracy to overwhelming victory in the elections that took place in Burma in May 1990, while Daw Aung San Suu Kyi and U Tin U were in detention. In his youth he joined the struggle for independence from Britain, suffering head injuries during a demonstration in 1938. At the outbreak of war he joined the Burma Independence Army and later rose to the rank of colonel. He was strongly opposed to the military takeover of 1962 and was therefore forced to retire in 1963 from control of the South-Western Command. He was twice imprisoned, for a total of seven years, and in 1988 on the outbreak of the democracy movement he was imprisoned for a third time but released after a month. In September of that year he became one of the twelve members of the Executive Council of the NLD and it was in that capacity that he led the party to victory in the 1990 elections after the leadership of the party had been arrested. In September of that year he was tried by a military tribunal and sentenced to twenty years in prison. However, he was released in March 1995 and soon resumed his work for democracy as Deputy Chairman of the NLD. A cultivated man with a great love for literature and music, he is known by many for his immense courage and his commitment to the freedom of his country.

ALAN CLEMENTS: How did you first meet Aung San Suu Kyi and what were your impressions of her?

U KYI MAUNG: Well, by chance, at the home of a mutual friend

here in Rangoon. It was back in 1986. But let me tell you it was completely uneventful. We spoke for only a few minutes. My most lasting impression was how shy and reticent she was. She seemed like
a decent girl who had no interest in frivolous talk or gossip. In fact,
I remember thinking how peculiar it was that I never saw her laugh
at that time, or it could have been that she didn't want to communicate with strangers (*laughing*). Anyway the point is that she did-
n't impress me at all. Except by how young she looked. She must
have been about forty-two at the time but she could have passed
as a girl of seventeen.

AC: And from there?

UKM: Then about a year later my friend U Htwe Myint came to
see me. He's now in prison. But at that time he was a close associate of Suu's. He said, "Aung San Suu Kyi is interested in getting
involved in politics. She wants to know if you're willing to con-
sult with her." I told him that I had no interest at all. None. I had
no plans to get involved in politics. Twice he returned with the
same request and twice I gave him the same reply. So the subject
stopped there.

AC: Was it because re-entering politics meant a most certain return
to prison?

UKM: No, not at all. Under a totalitarian regime, whether you are
in politics or not doesn't matter, there is always the possibility of
arrest. You might call it an occupational hazard. There's no law here.
When the authorities don't enjoy their meal they snap someone up
just like that. So I don't base decisions on whether I would be re-
arrested. I couldn't care less. I operate on the assumption that I could
be nabbed at any moment. That's life with SLORC. However, I
always consider myself a free man. I've been in prison four times
for a total of about eleven years and I don't consider it a special matter to waste my energies on.

AC: Were you surprised that Daw Suu was interested in entering
the cauldron of Burmese politics?

UKM: Well, she had a lot going for her. Of course, she was the daughter of *Bogyoke* Aung San—a "warrior-statesman" as she might put it—our national hero. Furthermore, Suu was a Burmese citizen. If entering politics was her interest, so be it, that was her right. But I was surprised she was taking an interest in me. That is to say, we were total strangers. I didn't know her nor did I know her capabilities. But about a year later, at the end of July 1988, I was hauled off to prison for the third time. I was taken in with nine others and kept for twenty-eight days because of my long-time association with Aung Gyi, a veteran politician who wrote a lengthy letter to Ne Win, our resident dictator, asking the old man to step down. But an hour or two after my release, U Htwe Myint came to my house again and said, "Aung San Suu Kyi would like to see you." So I thought to myself, well, let's see what this lady is up to...now is the time, a revolution was stirring. So I drove over to see her. The essence of the meeting was this: I said "Suu, if you're prepared to enter Burmese politics and to go the distance, you must be tolerant and be prepared for the worst." She listened attentively.

AC: What was Daw Suu's interest in you?

UKM: I was a veteran jail bird (laughing) and well over twenty years her senior. Later on I learned that she was watching people, looking in all directions for people who could be trusted—candidates you know, for the struggle. She was born with revolution in her blood but she needed all the help possible to see it through. So from then on we began to meet frequently, until later that year we all formed the National League for Democracy. This is a concise version of the facts.

AC: So Daw Suu trusted you as a veteran of the opposition voice?

UKM: She showed me respect and was fond of me, I think. She trusted that I could be relied upon. I was given the task of writing the NLD party manifesto, which I did, and after presenting it to the party it was accepted. Also, Suu trusted that I could be sensible and talk sensibly. Whatever thoughts, impressions and attitudes she might have, she could gauge them against my own. In other words it was a good working relationship.

You see the whole concept of us forming the NLD was simple.

There was a massive vacuum in Burma with this one-party system, and all we did was fill the hole. After some reshuffling, U Tin U became our Chairman, Suu our General Secretary and I took charge of research. But when U Tin U and Suu were arrested on 20 July 1989, I became the spokesman for the NLD, talking to foreign journalists, handling the press, that sort of thing.

AC: It's curious that you of all people were not imprisoned along with Aung San Suu Kyi and U Tin U. You were the man articulating the views of the NLD to the world, the voice of Burma's struggle.

UKM: Well, they did make a mistake. They underestimated my capacity for making myself a nuisance to them. Then I became the *de facto* Chairman of the NLD until the elections were held on 27 May 1990. On 6 September I was hauled away to jail.

AC: But how did you manage to avoid prison for nearly fourteen months after Aung San Suu Kyi and U Tin U had been arrested?

UKM: You see, I was constantly followed and harassed. But I didn't make any fiery speeches. I didn't harangue people overtly for one thing. It's not my nature to throw my weight around, you know. I'm quite happy to live anonymously. I keep reminding myself I'm nobody. Maybe that is my asset, I think, maybe my only one (*laughing*)...

AC: There must be others. You seem free of political ambition...

UKM: Yes, I'm prepared to leave politics at any time—on the spot. I always say if any member of my party is dissatisfied with my work, I'm prepared to quit without conditions. I said to my colleagues: "Look, it's a game and we're players in the game. So let's play it without so much ego—without nonsense." If you don't like my decision and you are not in favor of it—if you are dissatisfied with it—if you want me to leave, well then, I'll leave the League. I'm prepared to leave the whole business to you. I think my colleagues are convinced of this. And since my house is a few minutes' walking distance from Suu's, well, I'll just walk home without a fuss. I consider this attitude an asset.

AC: Sir, a simple question: why did SLORC hold their free and fair

232

multi-party elections for the establishing of a democratic nation when in fact as the results came in they imprisoned the majority of elected MPs, tortured to death a few, forced others into silence...

UKM: They thought they were going to win.

AC: That's shocking. SLORC had just massacred thousands of unarmed pro-democracy demonstrators and created a "terror state" using such means as institutionalized torture to control people, and you say they actually thought they would win.

UKM: SLORC thought we as a party were broken. They went as far as to say, "Now that the head is chopped off, the limbs are useless." Now you can deduce for yourself the kind of people we are dealing with.

AC: They miscalculated? Let me ask you, sir, isn't it possible that SLORC's real intention was to weed out from society all people with popularity and political ability and to eliminate once and for all the democratic apparatus from Burma? Isn't it possible that Ne Win himself concocted this whole multi-party democracy business as a diabolical ruse to further his dictatorship? To continue your image, not only to decapitate the democracy movement, but to dismember it piece by piece.

UKM: Well, they were shocked and angry when they realized that they had lost in their own places—in all the military areas. They were so utterly sure that their own people at least would vote for them. You see, we were told that SLORC's Military Intelligence made a rough secret survey to determine how the voting pattern might turn out, and they didn't realize until it was too late that the majority of people would be voting for the NLD. They were really shocked when the results turned out to be so contrary to their own expectations.

AC: There's something very devious about the whole affair...

UKM: There's a lot of credibility to your hypothesis but I did hear reports that some of the ex-BSPP people, higher-ups, actually broke down and wept when they heard the results. We heard that in some places banquets were even prepared to celebrate victory. We heard this from many sources. They're not very good actors, you know, so these reports are credible.

AC: But still, from what I've learned about Ne Win he only broaches his schemes to a few. Anyway, with the election results coming in and the elected MPs being imprisoned, you must have considered that your hours were numbered.

UKM: I was prepared for anything because the MI were following me everywhere. But I've never considered that my freedom is theirs to give or to deny. I just do my business with that knowledge, always.

AC: Then on 7 September 1990 they came and took you away—may I respectfully ask you, sir, to share your impressions of that moment?

UKM: It was after midnight. They always come after midnight for me. They came to the gate and were shouting like anything to open it up. I got up and dressed, all the while knowing that, "Here comes Insein." I already had a rather lengthy prison record, I'm what you might call the habitual offender (*laughing*). My wife and I looked out of the window and saw they had jumped the fence. Perhaps a platoon or more of armed soldiers had surrounded the house. Then a major from Military Intelligence reported to me with a warrant for my arrest. After that they started ransacking our cupboards and drawers. They searched the whole house, turned everything upside down, just like in the movies. This took quite some time. I think they were looking for guns or heroin or it might have been pornography...

AC: Did they even bother with a trial?

UKM: Oh, of course. That's just where the party begins. Everyone was brought to court, charged and sentenced. Mind you, they don't just go through the motions. They take their non-judicial system quite seriously. They paraded me before some brass with seventeen others; all were chained together except me, with handcuffs no less. In the party were engineers, lawyers, artists—democracy folks. Then a SLORC superstar witness stood up and said, "We raided the NLD headquarters some time ago and seized this document." Ironically, it was an excerpt from a small booklet outlining the negotiating principles of how to achieve mutual agreement between opponents.

234

They bungled through a stream of witnesses—policemen and other MI goons—trustworthy types. By this time I was getting a bit bored so I asked the judge, "Would you allow me to cross-question them?" The judge was not the least bit amused. He snarled at me like I had spit on him. So I sat down and smiled. He asked me, "Are you guilty or not guilty?" "Not guilty," I replied. One by one we pleaded "Not guilty." One by one each of us was told to stand up to be sentenced. One by one the SLORC judge gave us ten years for those lined up in front and seven years for those behind. Then I was whisked away to my solitary abode to continue the struggle from within.

AC: One wonders how these people sleep at night...

UKM: Oh, let me tell you a short story. We had some visitors over at Suu's house this morning who had come down from the Karen State. The Karen elder proceeded to tell us his story of incarceration. During his trial for his non-offense the judge called him up close to his desk and said, "Brother, you have done nothing. You are absolutely innocent. But my superiors have ordered me to give you a seven-year sentence. However, I will reduce your sentence to only three years." Now the Karen elder told us how pleased he was to hear that, especially after having already waited well over a year for his non-trial. He thought to himself, well, I only have to serve less than two years more. After the sentencing was over and he was on his way back to his cell the judge came over to him and said, "I'm sorry about what I just did. They just sacked me and sentenced me too." "Why?" the elder asked. The gentleman replied, "Because I gave you three years instead of seven which the higher authorities had ordered." So Suu, hearing this, asked the elder, "Please, sir, could you give us the name of that ex-judge? We must find this man and look after him. We must treat him as a very special person."

AC: You know Aung San Suu Kyi as well as anyone. How would you characterize her?

UKM: One of the great things about Suu is that what you see is what you get. She's genuine, she never play-acts. She's not a pretender. She speaks her mind straight and frank. Another wonderful quality in Suu is that she genuinely loves people. She flourishes from her contact with people. She listens to them, learns from them and she's patient. You see her on weekends, look at the rapport she has with her audience. They're her family. Also, Suu is funny. She has an abundant sense of humor. When we're together as a group, say in meetings, she is always telling jokes. Always. We all do. There's always a genuine feeling of love among us, we are all a family. This is the atmosphere we work in.

Now Suu is always Suu, in private or in public. But one thing is that she's not one for suffering fools. You have seen her at the center of a number of big press conferences. If a journalist asks her a crude or pointless question, she puts it right back in his lap. Suu responds to sincerity and whether someone is intelligent or feeble, doesn't matter to her.

Also, she's a fanatic in carrying out her duty to her country. Look at her work schedule. She starts at 8:00 or 8:30 a.m. and sometimes will not stop until 7:00 or so in the evening. It's one long talk-fest. People from all over the country come to see her, from all walks of life—farmers, students, laborers, rickshaw drivers—Suu wants to know! She wants the truth, the facts. She wants to hear how people feel, to know what's going on—their day-to-day lives, their hopes and concerns, their struggles, the cruelties, the inhuman behavior of SLORC. We all know that politics are about people, so with that in mind, it is really quite simple—Suu makes people her priority. However, Suu has got a devotion bordering on fanaticism, to the point of fault, I think. She is a real workaholic. Now, I have some influence with her in these matters so I will say it, and she would readily admit it. As you know there is a near-endless stream of journalists coming to see her from all over the world. For example, during one pool interview there were a lot of cameras focused on her and hot blinding lights blazing down on her. Then came the questions—a barrage of them being asked simultaneously. She was fielding them as fast as they were fired. I felt pity for her. It was punishment. It was an inquisition, not an interview. I just stood by and observed. But at the end of the session, I told her I wouldn't allow such a thing to happen again. See, Suu is like a daughter to me. I didn't appoint myself as such. She has a high regard for my wife and I and we consider it an honor.

AC: It's really touching to feel your care for her...

UKM: Suu needs all the help she can get. For instance, when Suu was under house arrest she took no provisions from the authorities. She sold much of her furniture just to survive. There were times when she had barely enough to eat, and was so weak she could barely walk or get out of bed. Her hair was falling out. And she pretty much refuses to talk about this—it's not her way. And I respect that—we all respect her way of handling hardship.

Now when she was released, there was no medical care. None at all. So we arranged for someone whom we could trust. Others would help her too. The main point here is that Suu needs a lot of help.

AC: For seven years now SLORC has criticized and slandered Aung San Suu Kyi in every way imaginable. Their two most consistently used criticisms are that she doesn't understand her own people through having lived abroad for over twenty years and that she is married to a British citizen. May I ask for your objective impressions of these?

UKM: It's really silly. No, it's downright pathetic. The SLORC's criticisms of Suu come from one of five motivations, all of which depend on how much fear and insecurity they feel on any particular morning: it's jealousy, envy, anger, greed, or childish stupidity. In SLORC-speak these are known as the Buddha's five moral precepts. Suu is intelligent and brilliantly conversant in her mother tongue, Burmese. She has studied classical Burmese literature and poetry. So when her enemies criticize her as an absentee citizen or a carpet-bagger, I feel sorry for them. Obviously, she was absent from Burma for a long time, but look at the people who were here for all those decaying years under the dictatorship. What did they do for the country? They must really ask themselves this question.

Clearly, Suu's years abroad were a great gift to her as well as to her country. It was her time of education. To live and learn and to absorb democracy. To get freedom into her blood so to speak, to get it flowing through her veins. She had the rare and wonderful opportunity of serving at the United Nations under one of Burma's great statesmen, Secretary-General U Thant. She's lived in so many different cultures—America, England, Nepal, Bhutan, India, Japan; she knows diversity. Suu's absence from Burma was not an absence at all. It groomed her, matured her into adulthood, into womanhood, so that she could come back and serve her people, to help them to help themselves to challenge the deadening cruelty of authoritarianism. At least that's my way of seeing things. Perhaps I'm trying to interpret her destiny. But the situation speaks for itself.

Even her critics are dumbfounded at how she delivers her talks as she does without talking over the heads of people. I have learned from her in this way. Suu speaks practically in everyday language. I have seen her talk to farmers in the delta, rickshaw drivers, laborers, the ordinary people—and they fall in love with her. Suu is always making friends. That's her spirit, her power—she loves people.

Nor does she play the role of a saint either (*laughing*). There is nothing saintly in Suu. She would readily admit that as a child she was afraid of the dark and ghosts and that she has no exceptional courage in her, only that her sense of duty drives her. "Even though you may be afraid," she says, "you have to face it, get over it, and do your work." That's Suu's simple message and she delivers it every time. And as for Suu having married a foreigner—he's a very nice man.

AC: Sir, on 16 July 1989, the SLORC announced regulations allowing military officers to "arrest political protesters at will," and administer one of three sentences on the spot: three years' hard labor, life imprisonment, or execution. Then on 20 July, the SLORC "arrested" Aung San Suu Kyi. Would you take us back to the moment?

UKM: Oh it was nothing special, really. Yet another of SLORC's absurdities. But we expected Suu's arrest. She knew it—we all knew it. Nor was their show of force the least bit surprising. The prisons were filling up faster than there was space. SLORC was on the hunt and the voice of freedom was their prey.

As for Suu's arrest, well, I'll explain. Around 6:30 or so that morning, many armed SLORC troops surrounded Suu's compound. When I arrived it was the oddest sight...all these soldiers poised like robots with their guns pointing at her house. They were still; frozen in a state of siege. And all for what? Just one lady! Arrest was imminent, it was obvious. Oddly the commander, a SLORC officer, let me into the compound. Now, by the time of my arrival all of our NLD Executive Committee Members were there except U Tin U. Troops had also surrounded his compound. For a moment I thought they were going to imprison us all. But we carried on, had a casual lunch and joked a lot. See, none of us is the least bit concerned, nor the slightest bit intimidated by SLORC. So, we just laughed the day in.

AC: A casual lunch, with laughter and joking? You describe a party atmosphere more than a state of siege. You were all about to go to prison. How is it possible to be so jovial under such conditions of oppression?

UKM: Oh, there's no secret about it. I know it sounds strange to you that we were joking and having fun with all those soldiers surrounding Suu's compound, but you have to realize that Suu is really funny. Ask U Aung Shwe and U Lwin (NLD EC Members). We were cracking jokes the whole time. Of course, we did a few practical things like deciding who would fill the vacant places of the NLD's Executive Committee and made a short agenda to carry on into the future.

AC: It's refreshing to feel the flesh on a myth rather than to keep it imprisoned inside a sacred dream.

UKM: Well, that's good, isn't it? Ideals can keep you wondering, you know. They might keep you full of hope but hope is contrary to our policy of action. We're much more down to earth about such things. Politics are about work and pragmatism. Democracy is an earth-based endeavor. So all this business of ideals and hopes has to be put into action. But let me come back to Suu's arrest. No doubt, it was an ugly moment. But it was inevitable and we accepted it...that is what I'm saying. It wasn't as tragic or grave as many people might assume it was...there was no melodrama in other words.

AC: Sir, you had been to prison three times by this point—a total of seven years. You knew well how notorious Insein Prison was, with torture and sub-human living conditions. However, Aung San Suu Kyi had never been imprisoned. Did you counsel her in any way about how to handle prison life or deal with solitary confinement?

UKM: Well, in all seriousness a lot of our discussion was about Suu's arrest. I did think she would be taken to Insein—house arrest was not on the cards. But there was nothing mentioned, at least to my recollection, about how she should handle prison life. You have to understand, Suu is determined, she can handle herself. Of course, we knew the soldiers would walk in at any minute. Remember that we had been surrounded by soldiers for months by this point. So having them outside Suu's compound was simply SLORC's logical next step. So at about 2:30 or so we said, "All right...they must be getting impatient outside waiting for our meeting to adjourn." So we said our goodbyes, and we all left. That's all...

AC: What about the arrest itself?

UKM: Oddly, the soldiers didn't enter Suu's compound until 4:00 or 4:30 that evening. Ten hours hardened like statues. Well, they may have waited so long because there were a lot of our NLD youth activists in her compound—twenty or so. They were Suu's security. In fact, the whole day they played Suu's speeches and democracy songs loudly over the speakers. Let me interject here that as a matter of policy, we believe that the most effective weapon to unveil ignorance and repression is a non-violent education. So our NLD youth gave the soldiers an all-day scolding with freedom songs and Suu's words on courage and human dignity. All those things they love to hear.

Well, when they finally raided her compound, which was our NLD headquarters, of course, they placed Suu under arrest. Also, they took our typewriters, cameras, video equipment, tape-recorders and all our NLD registration cards—files that listed the names and addresses with photographs of every NLD member nationwide. Now put this in context and you get a clear picture of the absurdity of it all. All this occurred during SLORC's "free and fair multi-party democratic election campaign process." After Suu and U Tin U's arrest, U Aung Shwe and I carried on the work.

AC: Sir, you were the last person to see Daw Suu on the day of her detention and from what I am told, the first person that she asked to see upon her release. It must have been quite a special moment to see your dear friend and colleague after such a long separation. The struggle resumed?

UKM: Well, it never stopped you know. But yes, we too were happy that Suu was free. I'll take you there. It was Monday, 10 July 1995. There's one SLORC security man—a chap who has been at Suu's gate for several years now. Well, this same officer came to my house that afternoon. My two dogs started to howl. I was in my study doing political research, reading a crumbling old book on the collapse of some fascist regime or other when my wife calmly walked in and said, "There's an intelligence officer at the door." We looked at each other with that uncertain kind of silence. Well, I put down my book and went to the door and I asked the obvious, "What is it?" He replied with a very straight face, "Daw Aung San Suu Kyi wants to see you." Well, my immediate thought was that something had happened to her. "Is she seriously ill?" I asked. "No, she's not ill," he replied. That's all he would say. I still had no idea that she was released. So I deferred myself to his hospitality, "Are you here to give me a lift?" "No," he responded, "come in your own car." Only then did I know it wasn't a re-arrest. Then he said, "Daw Aung San Suu Kyi would like to see your wife, too."

We arrived at about 5:00 in the afternoon. SLORC guards let us in, and as we drove up to Suu who was standing on her doorstep she quipped, "Uncle, what took you so long, six years to drive a mile?" Only then did we know Suu was free, that she had been released. So we went inside, the three of us. We exchanged stories, filling in the blanks, so to speak. Suu was unscathed, untouched, her mind as free as a bird. I had never doubted it and seeing her again after six years just confirmed my instincts. We laughed and joked at the absurdity of it all. I know from my own incarceration that prison never weakened my spirit; rather, it strengthened my resolve. The same with Suu. Her convictions had always been strong but nothing like what I saw that day. She was Suu with a free heart, an iron will and a lightning-bolt mind.

But just as we were about to leave U Tin U arrived with his wife. The news had spread like wildfire. He said that outside Suu's front gate was a swarm of camera-crews and journalists. Then our current NLD Chairman U Aung Shwe arrived. Now the party was warming up, we had tears in our eyes from laughing so much. Then by nine that night the front gate was fully packed with foreign journalists and photographers. The main point I would like to make is that the struggle had never ceased for any of us. Nor was it dormant. We all had a lot of time to think during our detention and now that we were all united again the energy together was stronger than ever. But it was time to settle down and get on with practical work. One party was over, and another one was about to begin.

AC: How does one maintain freedom in prison and not succumb to anger, bitterness and thoughts of revenge?

UKM: Freedom in a sense means absence of fetters which restrain you physically and mentally. A person thrown into prison immediately feels the impact of loss. It's difficult to pin it down to any single factor as it comes out of so many factors, such as: the loss of contact with one's family and friends; termination of the normal daily life that one is accustomed to; denial of access to books and radio and companionship with people living in one's close proximity; having to contend with difficulties just to carry out simple chores beneficial to yourself and others who are in more dire circumstances than yourself, etcetera.

I was put in prison for the first time at the end of May 1965. On the third day of my incarceration I overcame the feeling of loss in a flash, and quite unexpectedly at that. It was as if someone advised me to stop thinking about anything at all.

Later on I paraphrased that idea at length to guide my conduct throughout the eleven years' duration of my life in Insein Prison. It says: "In your present state of isolation you are denied all data to serve as premises for your thinking, and based on which you have to draw appropriate conclusions. So go on thinking about anything if you are determined to make your life miserable." Ever since, I believe I have been able to manage my life, to live with a degree of success on a path free from excessive anger and frustration.

AC: I know that arbitrary arrests are commonplace in Burma. May I ask you for your thoughts about this SLORC tactic?

UKM: Arbitrary arrests are mean, irresponsible measures designed to crush political opposition and therefore are much to be deplored. These arrests are ruinous to political organizations working for democratic change in a number of ways. In a one-party state such as we have been accustomed to in our country for over three decades, arrests of political activists in the capital cities create ripples all over the country. Lower echelon security men in district towns—eager-beaver types—might initiate arrests on their own, even without specific instructions from their headquarters. Families of political activists are the worst hit because, more often than not, they lose their principal breadwinners. Impositions of extremely harsh sentences by the surreal courts have been the standard custom throughout this period. Treatment meted out to political prisoners since the inception of the SLORC regime is noted for its extreme brutality.

AC: The numbers of people attending your weekend public talks are noticeably increasing week by week. Do you ever anticipate armed SLORC soldiers advancing on the crowds and arresting the whole group in a major crackdown?

UKM: Several things to consider. One is that reconciliation could come about at any moment. They are allowing the weekend talks for a reason. We can only speculate why. Suu, Tin U and I—all of us at the NLD—really hope, what I mean to say is that we really want to believe that there is an opening here. Maybe allowing our talks to continue indicates something genuine in them. If so, it's a start. Maybe they are learning something from our words. Maybe it is that they feel the *metta* among the people. Maybe they yearn to have that *metta* directed towards them rather than it being forced or coerced from people. It could be that this metta that is being generated among the people is having an effect on them. *Metta* does that you know. Maybe it is opening them to a new way of treating people, seeing them as human beings to be honored and served rather than oppressed and robbed. It could be that they are moved by the people's courage. People who are not only willing to defy them but who are also ready and waiting to forgive them. It's all possible.

Secondly, we wish we could provide decent accommodations

for our people that come and listen. As it is now they are forced to sit on newspapers or plastic bags or directly on the dirty asphalt. And it's sweltering, without shade. We know the risk they are taking. This is unpleasant for us to see. Troops could come in at any moment, block the sides and say, "Don't move." But the people are following their conscience. They're committed to freedom. That is special. Call it dignity in action. The courage to live freely and not wait for freedom to be delivered. So I'm not worried. Nor am I worried for the people. We are in this together.

Now one day, perhaps soon, I don't know—we never know, do we?—I'll be incapable of taking a few steps outside. I'll be infirm and feeble. At that point I'll just lie down on my bed and die. I don't have any illusions about my worth, you know. Someone younger and stronger will replace me. I encourage that. But for now this work is my duty, and no one is imposing it on me. I too am following my conscience. So as long as I am needed I will stand and speak. I don't have any fears or worries, nothing at all.

Thirdly, I'll answer your question. I believe that at this point the SLORC would not want to arrest the weekend crowds. Their international image is being scrutinized and this intolerable act would surely be counter-productive. And all the foreign journalists with their video cameras would be thrilled to shoot SLORC soldiers for posterity. The sad spectacle could then be seen worldwide on CNN and BBC. That would be ample evidence of the kind of people we have to deal with.

AC: Several months down the road there could be ten thousand people attending your talks. How do you think SLORC will respond to this?

UKM: Well, we've learned that the authorities are quite disturbed about our "happy hour." But some of them must be enjoying them or they wouldn't be happening. But you see, they want us to behave like subjects in the old days of monarchs and Burmese kings. To kowtow like frogs. This is their mentality. Perhaps they see us as beggars in defiance of their almighty throne of superiority, and we're like "things" to be used and abused at their whim. They can't stand the fact that we're happy—those of us at the core of the NLD. But of course, at any time they're welcome to join the party, so to speak.

<u>AC:</u> Just how repressed is free speech in Burma today?

<u>UKM:</u> You can answer that yourself. Practically. I suggest that you put my words to the test, if you have the courage to do it. Go into the city to a corner teashop and stand on a box and say a few words about democracy. Now see what would happen. You would no sooner get the word "justice" out of your mouth than you would be grabbed and put on the next plane out of here. And for a Burmese to do that, it's a one-way truck-ride to Insein. This is why I say Suu's compound is the only liberated area in Burma. From there we say all sorts of things. We joke about the SLORC and tell them how much happier everyone would be, themselves included, if they would just talk to us. Suu was telling the crowd last weekend that "One day if you look back at these long days of struggle and fear— when you reminisce on the situation—you and us—who are gathered together in this place, you behind the barbed wire, and we peering over the gate, you will laugh at the absurdity of it all. Yes, it is really inconvenient, though one day, that day might come— that day must come. That is one privilege that dissidents all over the world have had so far. When they reflect back upon their courage in the struggle they feel elated. And you too, all of you will surely feel that way one day. The time is near, it's coming."

<u>AC:</u> But why are the authorities allowing the weekly talks despite having banned them?

<u>UKM:</u> Call it what you will—a concession or a tactical maneuver— we believe that this action of the SLORC is not without pluses for them. Just to list a few: the scene of the weekend talks over time has fast changed itself into a tourist attraction. This is good for "Visit Myanmar Year 1996." Also, it could very well help soften the perception of people whose knowledge of SLORC acquired through the Western media had the SLORC projected as being a brutal and repressive regime. Furthermore, SLORC benefits from the letters to Suu written by her followers about what current gripes there are against the SLORC which need to be attended to. And lastly, these talks enable SLORC to maintain continuous assessment

of the state of mind of the NLD leadership whom they consider their adversaries.

AC: And the benefits for the NLD?

UKM: Well, viewed from our angle, these weekly talks offer the NLD leadership an opportunity to dispense their views on the current political situation for the benefit of its followers with whom communication by means of printed matter is impossible [printing rights having been denied to the NLD since July 1990]. Under present conditions, this is the only place in the country where dissidents can counsel, confer, express, exchange and propagate their convictions among themselves with a degree of impunity. One cannot help but include a third factor into this bargain. By this, I mean the crowds who, braving SLORC's disdain, congregate regularly at Suu's gate to listen to her talks. The police and security details regularly raid their homes by night to check the night-visitors' list. [If anyone is staying overnight the law requires that the matter be reported to the Local Law and Order office early in the evening, or the host risks being fined or even imprisoned.] The ward security men then ask people to stay away from the weekend talks to keep themselves out of possible trouble. Half a dozen [SLORC] photographers take pictures of the people in assembly for identification purposes. Yet, undaunted, people come crowding back week after week.

AC: Are you a religious man?

UKM: It is a difficult question for me to answer. I live by a few precepts taught by the Buddha. If I were to tell you what these precepts are, I'm afraid you might be confused; so I'd rather not elaborate. Be it sufficient just to say that whatever they are, these few precepts have enabled me to get on well with my life.

For example, you were quite surprised when I told you how much we laughed together on the day of Suu's arrest or again in some grim episodes that we covered together. It can be explained by the fact that the narrator had no regrets at all for what had happened in the past. The "I" and the "me" of the past are dead and gone. By the same token, the narrator of the present is not worried about what might happen to "him" of the future. In fact, "he" is not status-conscious at all. What I strive for is to live a life of complete awareness from moment to moment and to provide the best service I possibly can to all living beings without discrimination and with a detached mind. Does religion serve politics? I do not speculate. I just try to do my best.

AC: Sir, you follow the teachings of the Buddha which is the path of non-attachment. May I ask, how does your understanding influence your leadership in your people's struggle for democratic freedoms?

UKM: Drive around the city streets and you are bound to come across big red billboards at road junctions on which are written slogans reflecting the current thoughts of the authorities. These billboards are representatives of the forces we have to contend with. Someone once wrote that "the kindest of men had to watch their words."

One of the things that Buddha taught us was to step outside ourselves and see our own stupidity—as often as we can. We regard the teachings of the Buddha as an inner compass to keep ourselves on course. Actions geared to the mood of the moment and not related to the overall strategy could prove to be disastrous.

AC: Sir, before your resignation from the Burma Army you were a respected commander. You were in combat, you've faced bullets and I suspect that you've killed people—the enemy. As a Buddhist can you kill with love in your heart?

UKM: Yes, I have killed men in war—the enemy. But with love in my heart? You can't lie truthfully, can you? So no, I wouldn't call it love in the real sense. I'll explain briefly. I was not fighting out of hatred for the enemy who was attempting to crush us. It's just honest combat. I had a job to do and I was doing it.

AC: Would you as a leader of the democracy struggle instigate an armed struggle against the SLORC if you had weapons?

UKM: No. I don't believe in armed struggle to bring about political change.

AC: You fought against fascism in the '40s, so why not fight it in the '90s?

<u>UKM:</u> Don't get me wrong. The only reason I joined the army was to fight for independence. That's it. If this war had not come to Burma I would have been more than content to pursue my real interest which is music and drama. I love the arts. But you see, we were kids. Just like leaves lying by the roadside, when the strong wind of revolution came we were swept away. My involvement in the army was quite incidental and not by design. We had no choice but to fight for independence. You don't doubt such choices…you just do it. But given a choice, I would never have opted for arms. All right, have I cleared myself?

<u>AC:</u> No, sir, you haven't. I'm just trying to understand your views on non-violent activism as a principal leader of the freedom struggle.

<u>UKM:</u> As for that non-violence business, I don't condemn it, but I'm not a Gandhi. If I see the need for force, I would tackle it head-on, without hesitation, if that is the only means available to me.

I was trained to fight and if somebody attempted to manhandle you, I wouldn't tuck my tail between my legs and run away, listening to you scream with my back to you. That's cowardice. It's despicable. Nor would I sit there in meditation, trusting that my *metta* would dissolve the ordeal. I'm no saint. I would try and defend you. Now I don't like the use of force, but I could never tell you that I would completely abstain from it. But Gandhi said that too.

<u>AC:</u> Will the struggle for democracy in your country be successful without much stronger support from the United States and Europe?

<u>UKM:</u> We are not relying on external support alone. It's a people's movement. That is our focus and our strength.

<u>AC:</u> So it's just an issue of patience and non-violent perseverance?

<u>UKM:</u> Yes, patience. We don't need to run away. If they imprison me again, fine—I'll go to prison. I am as free in prison as I am in my own home. But putting me back in prison doesn't solve anything.

You see, another thing is that they [SLORC] think they cannot talk with Suu on a one-to-one basis. But a street-cleaner can talk with Suu on a one-to-one basis. Why do they doubt that a big general could have his say? So as you see I may be living in a fool's paradise but I'm happy where I am. I am not worried. The problems they [SLORC] are dealing with are of such magnitude that unless they cooperate with us they won't be able to secure the cooperation of the entire population.

<u>AC:</u> I remember a story that St. Augustine describes. I am not sure where I read it. Alexander the Great caught a pirate and asked him, "How dare you molest the sea?" The pirate retorted, "How dare you molest the whole world? I have a small boat, so I'm called a thief and a pirate. You have a navy. So you're called an emperor."

Here in Burma, SLORC takes the perversion one step further. They subjugate the whole country and for this they call themselves magnanimous leaders and the upholders of justice. While you at the NLD lead a non-violent "revolution of the spirit" and are labeled "subversives," essentially political terrorists.

Now SLORC has cut deals with Burma's armed insurgents, and more recently with Khun Sa, the world's most notorious heroin druglord, but ironically SLORC won't talk with the NLD. Perhaps you could clarify these so called "ceasefires" once and for all?

<u>UKM:</u> First of all, these fifteen insurgent groups should be called by their true names. They are ethnic minorities who have taken up arms against SLORC. These people—men, women and children—are citizens of Burma. They are human beings. That is the first point.

Secondly, these ceasefires are in no way an end to ethnic problems in Burma. In my view, they are nothing more than an R&R device. Take just one example, that of the Wa people of Shan state, in the Golden Triangle area. The ceasefire is nothing more than a cooling-off period for them to regroup and train even more of their population. In Wa villages every household must produce one male to undergo military training.

Now, this applies to the Kachins too. It applies to every one of the fifteen groups. They've all retained their weapons and what is called a ceasefire is just a retraining and regrouping period. So it's fair to say that these ceasefires cannot guarantee long-term peace.

And there's another problem. The SLORC every now and again announces a period of public money laundering. They even publi-

cize it in their newspaper: 75 percent return on undeclared cash—
no questions asked. So it's no leap of the imagination to understand
why heroin production has radically increased in Burma since
SLORC seized power. There is clear, hard evidence for this. Of
course, the black money then goes directly into real estate. Some
of the finest land in Rangoon and Mandalay has been purchased by
black money. Mansions with swimming pools are built and in some
cases left empty. The black money is getting into the tourist business through hotel constructions. It's going into jade, sapphire and
ruby mining.

AC: Sir, there is a twist of irony to the fact that George Orwell was
a police chief in one of Burma's major cities during the 1920s and
then to hear you at Sunday's public talk explain and decode a few
Orwellian concepts from his book, *1984*. As you had said, "all under
the watchful eye of Big Brother." Were you inferring that Orwell's
1984 was similar to SLORC's "1996"?

UKM: Of course, all the elements of *1984* are here in Burma today.
Perhaps slightly watered down, but they are here. Thought-control is the bulwark of a totalitarian regime, although not confined
to that system alone. It can operate even in democratic societies,
at more subtle but equally effective levels. The manipulation of the
public mind through propaganda and disinformation is a vast, fas-
cinating topic. It's important for us all to understand how control
occurs; control of the masses through tortured terminology and
abstruse concepts used by governments, PR firms, advertising agen-
cies and hidden censorship. There's control through educational systems and within religions. We have to learn to question...to learn
ways of protecting ourselves and to be vigilant in peeling away the
layers of distortion. Not to be imprisoned, in other words, by propaganda. But let's stay here in Burma with our SLORC's brand of
Big Brother.

AC: Would you explain how Big Brother operates in Burma and also
explain who this Big Brother is, SLORC?

UKM: SLORC is a clique of twenty-one generals. That's it. With a
bunch of subordinates who dare not defy the brass. These gener-

als control every aspect of life in this country. Totalitarianism by function is Big Brother. So all these Orwellian terms, "thought-control, brainwash, Newspeak, the Ministry of Truth, the Ministry of Love," all of them, exist in variations within all systems of control. They are not as sophisticated as Orwell depicted them, but nevertheless they are here, and for the same reason—to deny life!

AC: How does "Big Brother SLORC" enforce their will upon political dissent or even ordinary Burmese citizens?

UKM: SLORC has shown repeatedly that they will use any means within their grasp to crush dissent and even the suspicion of dissent. They go about this in a variety of ways. Harassment is a mandate, so it seems by the frequency with which it occurs; they axe a person's work, confiscate land and property, public beatings, force the young and old to build roads, bridges, dams, without compensation. They'll snatch people in the middle of the night. Suu said it before her arrest seven years ago, she says it now, we all say it— "Nothing has changed, let the world know, under this regime we are prisoners in our own country."

AC: Does that mean that this "Big Brother SLORC" is so maniacal, so cunning, so perverse, that for some yet-to-be-known reason they are allowing you, Daw Suu and U Tin U to speak publicly on weekends to serve their own devious self-interest? Or are they truly opening to a new way of being, a micro-step towards authentic reformation?

UKM: A new way of being? Authenticity? These concepts are not within SLORC's vocabulary as of yet, that is unless they study our weekend talks. And yes, anything is possible. Anything could occur—even the dinosaurs became extinct. All I am saying is that their repressive habits are so fossilized that I seriously doubt that their thought is thawing or that they are on the road to an authentic democracy.

Now as for them allowing our public talks. This is yet another Orwellianism. At our public talks, you see, we have SLORC's version of the two-way television system. There are SLORC MI men out there mingling with the crowds. Watch those Burmese who video row after row of people. Why? We all know that Big Brother SLORC will be watching us close up within an hour or so. And since Suu frequently criticizes SLORC's repressive tactics brought to our attention by individuals who write to her, some must be using the information to maintain a grip on others within their own ranks. That's the nature of fear-based regimes: no one is safe, no one can be trusted...even if you happen to be at the very top. That is except Big Brother himself. Whoever that fiction is.

AC: Václav Havel has written about the effects of the secret police in Czechoslovakia. He called them, "That hideous spider whose invisible web runs right through society...[creating] a dull, existential fear that seeped into every crack and crevice of daily life...and made one think twice about everything one said and did." Is this the general atmosphere created by the SLORC's MI?

UKM: Yes. The clan of the spider is watching us right now. MI are at the corner of my street. They are outside the gate. On the main road. Wherever I go they follow. They have cellular phones and transmit information instantaneously to headquarters. The whole country is webbed and wired. And you can be sure they followed you here. They are at your hotel. They have most likely searched your room and tapped your telephone.

AC: You're not the least bit concerned about the "hideous spider"?

UKM: No, I'm not. Not in the slightest. In fact, the more the SLORC observes and listens the more they will be able to trust us, because our intentions are sincere. After all our struggle for democracy doesn't exclude them, it includes them. And all this MI business, well, they use it as fodder for character assassinations and all that SLORC-speak.

AC: I have to admit, for research purposes I have forced myself to watch SLORC-television and read their newspaper. What a chore, and rarely a day goes by without a malicious and slanderous half page commentary about Aung San Suu Kyi, U Tin U and yourself. But who reads this? Who are they appealing to? Does anyone believe what they print? Do you ever read the newspaper or watch television, perhaps for no other reason than to become more acquainted with your enemy to perhaps give you further insight into how their minds work in order to bring you closer to dialogue and hopefully reconciliation?

UKM: Listen, the irony is that they don't believe any of it themselves. They know it's all nonsense. We know that. The whole country knows it. Everything they say and print is trash. It's rubbish. Even if you tried reading it, most of the stuff they print is unreadable. It's written in such a long and rambling style with so much distortion that you can barely locate the point. It's like trying to watch television when it's out of focus. We have a boy scout version of Big Brother.

AC: I understand that you're a playwright banned by the regime? Do you still write underground?

UKM: No, no, no…that's not accurate. I am nowhere near a Václav Havel, if that's what you mean. I just happen to love good drama; a good story in other words. Even if I could write, it's no use my writing because if the authorities saw my name my work would immediately be burned or used for toilet paper. There's absolutely zero chance of my work being published. None.

AC: Does SLORC tolerate even the slightest whisper of political satire, say, buried deep within the pablum of a magazine article, or hidden on page 911 in the nightmare of the novel's protagonist? Are they that scrupulous?

UKM: Everything original, provocative and intelligent, anything with an inspired dimension to it is censored by SLORC. Almost every writer in our organization refuses to write or create, or is forced out of the profession. Now if any of us published something, the authorities would immediately find out who the author was and would ban it. Or the writer would be harassed or detained. All our artists, musicians, writers, actors, anyone belonging to our side—the NLD—it's blanket treatment. We're banned. So a great resource of intelligent and creative talent has been absolutely removed from society. Except the puppet show SLORC puts on, which is bad comedy.

AC: Would you give a few examples of how SLORC censorship operates?

UKM: There was a theater piece that was performed at the recent 75th Film Diamond Jubilee here in Rangoon. One actor came out on to the stage after the curtain fell and pointed a finger in the direction of SLORC's MI Chief [Khin Nyunt] repeating the final words that he as the Burmese hero of the play said during the final scene of the show: "You, sir, think that because you have the guns, you are superior." Something to that effect. Of course, the MI Chief couldn't bear the free publicity and sauntered out of the audience in disgust. Soon thereafter the actor was banned from acting for three years, or maybe it was five.

Then on Independence Day, we held a celebration for our NLD members within Suu's compound. You were there. Well, that theater piece mid-way through the celebration was a brilliantly executed, witty and intelligent piece of political satire. There was nothing base about it at all. In fact, the actors were just repeating old jokes—some had even been used in the shows on SLORC television. Well, those actors and musicians, eleven of them, were arrested on their return home to Mandalay. All but four were released after several weeks of interrogation. The two main actors will likely be sentenced and imprisoned [they were both sentenced to seven years' hard labor.] This is the price of free speech under SLORC. But you see, those actors knew the score beforehand. One had been imprisoned a few years before and they knew it could very well happen again. Nevertheless, they stood up, delivered their jokes, and performed boldly and courageously. This is why I said to you, Big Brother SLORC is always watching.

I'll give you another example. A well known young musician recently produced a tape titled *Power 54*, which was in reference to his 54th recorded song or something like that. He put the piece up to the SLORC censorship board and they passed it. Immediately it received wide distribution because of his fame, that is until the SLORC thought that 54 was in reference to Suu's house number, which is 54 University Avenue. The authorities hit the roof and removed every tape from every store in the country within days. Are the SLORC scared of Suu?

Sometimes fifteen, twenty, or even forty or more pages may be torn out of a one-hundred-page magazine. This could create problems. The stories are numerous. This censorship board has been in operation for three decades or more. Dictators loathed free thought. Their idea of society was tailored after places like East Germany.

AC: When a dialogue does occur with SLORC, may I ask, what will be the first item of business on your agenda?

UKM: The first thing we want to do is listen. We would like to hear what it is they want. It is my belief that every time you talk with your enemy it must be your genuine wish not to destroy him. It's a mutual deal, a reciprocity, a give and take. It can't be one-sided. As you advance your interests so too must you advance the interests of your enemy. Sincerity is the key and sincerity takes courage. Why? Because to be sincere requires openness—a genuine willingness to listen, to be willing to reflect upon opposing views to those of your own. I believe that within everyone, buried beneath the distorting layers of pride and fear is a heart of goodness, it's the natural state of humankind. All this egoistic subterfuge—greed, arrogance, insecurity, racism, domination, all of it blocks the living daylight out of the intrinsic sincerity of the human heart.

In reality, I don't see SLORC as the enemy, really. Sure, on a conventional level of speaking I use the word. I use strong words to describe my disdain for them because of their behavior. I say, call a spade a spade. We're grown-ups talking. But under it all they're human—they bathe, eat and sweat like the rest of us. Equally, they have hearts. They have goodwill. It's in them, I'm sure of that. We just want more of it. So much more that they make it the predominant expression of their speech and actions.

Now they publicly state that they are working non-stop for the benefit of all the people and with magnanimous intentions. Well, if it's genuine, then put it across to us. If it's real then we'll do our best to greet their sincerity with our own. In that spirit, I have no doubt that we can work it out, happily.

We do not want to hurt them, humiliate them, nothing, that is if they cooperate with us in the endeavor. I say let us stop wasting time. People are suffering. So they should put their heads together and count back from ten. When they get to one they should say one nation for the people, by the people, and make haste to University

255

Avenue with the good news. We're waiting for their invitation but we can't write it for them. They must show some genuine goodwill.

AC: How do you think the NLD and SLORC could start working together?

UKM: It would be important to confirm the results of the May 1990 elections as a first step. Let me explain why. The military's anti-democratic sentiment seen during the mass demonstrations of 1988 and in its aftermath had focused on the National League for Democracy. Its intensity had grown in proportion to the NLD's popularity with the people and found expression when it decided to place U Tin U and Suu under house arrest on 20 July 1989. When the NLD won 392 electoral seats out of the total of 452 seats in the election held on 27 May 1990, the SLORC issued an edict on 28 July 1990, known as Notification 1/90, obviously to obfuscate and delay the process of democratization. Prompt rejection of Notification 1/90 by the NLD leadership and its call for the SLORC to convene the first Parliament in September, 1990, further aggravated the situation.

In the first week of September, the SLORC decided to launch a major campaign to annihilate the NLD organization. Mass arrests of NLD activists and elected MPs were carried out throughout the country and various charges were made against them resulting in long-term prison sentences. In the meantime fresh directives were given to the NLD to stop recruitment of new members. We were not allowed to replace those organizers who had been removed by death or disability. And if the numbers in any organizational unit fell below five, that office had to be shut down.

In January, 1992, the SLORC ultimately embarked upon the process of holding a National Convention under their own direction and tight surveillance, setting their own agenda and hand-picking non-MP members whose strength approximated a 6 to 1 ratio with elected MPs forming the minority. The NLD tagged along with the SLORC while insisting from time to time upon its objections to various irregularities in the conduct of the National Convention. The breaking point came on 29 October 1995 when the Chairman of the National Convention Convening Committee [a

SLORC general] decided to ignore an important request made to him by the Chairman of the NLD [U Aung Shwe].

I believe that so much misery, suffering and wretchedness imposed upon the people of Burma had their genesis in the military's denial to respect the will of the people as illustrated in the result of the election held under their auspices in 1990. By tracing this history I mean to show the linkage between the excesses that have developed from one source: namely, the military's misguided concept of democracy. To untangle the problem, I suggest that they accept the result of the election held on 27 May 1990 as the first priority.

AC: Sir, it is not easy for me to ask you this question. Military Intelligence observes every move you make. Does re-arrest concern you?

UKM: You don't seem to understand that imprisonment is not a concern of mine. The spider, that "hideous old spider," so what? His web is dirty and dusty, filled with the empty shells of his victims. But I am not afraid. Of course, re-arrest is possible. It's there at any moment of the day or night. Burma is lawless. Without justice. Everything's arbitrary. So what I am saying is that the seriousness of the situation is balanced by the absurdity of it. I defend myself with irony and humor. That poor old spider, despite his nasty ways, is trapped in his own web. And I'm happy while he's confined to hunting. Now imagine the mind of a hunter, always looking, suspicious of every sound. Always at odds with his environment. He wants to conquer and kill. That is a very, very, sad state of mind. It's pathetic. I'm in no hurry. My freedom is not tomorrow, it's today.

AC: Peace accords and settlements are occurring in Bosnia, the Middle East and possibly in Northern Ireland—once bitter enemies are talking, in some cases, after decades of horror and bloodshed, even genocide. But why not in Burma? After all you are all Burmese, you're family, really. Furthermore, SLORC has a magnificent chance in the palms of their hands, the most precious of opportunities. I use the word with hesitation, but they can redeem themselves, gain worldwide respect, and more importantly gain the respect they so desperately crave from their own people. Arafat, De Klerk, even Kissinger have won the Nobel Peace Prize. Is Khin Nyunt next?

UKM: Good question. That's exactly what we want to know. Why? Why is it that they are waiting? Why are they so angry with us? Why wait? Tell us face to face. We can handle it! But Khin Nyunt as a Nobel Laureate? Well, in the way that you put it, who knows?

AC: But, sir, surely you must have some idea of why they are waiting?

UKM: Maybe they're not waiting. I told our people this morning that actually we are in a dialogue with SLORC. I'll explain. Read SLORC editorials about us in their newspaper, the *New Light of Myanmar*. They're talking to us. Are they not? Then, we talk to them through our weekend talks at the gates of Suu's house. SLORC videotapes the talks. The only problem is, we are talking back to back (*laughing*). What we need is someone to come and help them by saying, "Come on boys, you face this way" and they'll listen. But this is a dialogue. They call us clowns, subversives, heaping insult upon insult. That is no way to put food in the mouths of malnourished people. That's not the way to unlock the cells of political prisoners. That's not the way to honor the results of the 1990 elections. But who can say that it's not a beginning? Maybe it is their way of opening to us. My mind-set is different from theirs. They're so unpredictable. Except, that is, for their policy of repression. That's consistent.

AC: Let me ask the same question in another way. You have made it quite clear that SLORC's desperation roots in one thing—fear of losing power. What does that mean in reality?

UKM: Fine, I'll tell you. What's biting them is fear. Fear of revenge. Fear of persecution. Fear of losing face. Fear of losing their property, their mansions, their cars, their motorcades, all these privileges—it's the fear of losing power. These generals know they have done wrong. They fear for their security, they fear for their own families, for their sons and daughters. But I can assure them. Listen. The past is the past. What is done is done. We will not take up this matter any more than to the extent that it is permissible to the majority of the people.

Almost everyone is aware of the indictments and legal proceedings going on against South Korea's two former presidents. Almost everyone is aware that in South Africa Desmond Tutu is heading a Commission for Truth and Reconciliation. Some people will not be able to escape blame for deeds done nearly two decades before. But our Burmese people are by nature compassionate and I think the people will forgive them. That is my belief. Forgiveness will win. This will strengthen our nation and not weaken it. The generals must understand this. And if they want to talk to us, we're ready, now!

AC: Sounds like a message worth repeating at next weekend's talk.

UKM: Such words we will reserve for our initial talks. You see, they don't believe us. They don't believe that the people are forgiving. Even if Suu had such a mind-set, I could correct it. "Well Suu, that won't serve the purpose of benefiting the people of Burma." But that's not the case. We don't operate from a policy of revenge or vindictiveness. We want truth and reconciliation, not deceit and persecution. Forgiveness will be the bedrock of Burma's democracy. But each day that SLORC delays means yet another day of suffering for a lot of people.

AC: Perhaps what's needed is an appropriate mediator to get SLORC to the dialogue table; President Carter comes to mind. Or perhaps a mutually agreed upon team of mediators; people from both sides.

UKM: I think this is a fabulous idea. Please help us to turn SLORC's face towards someone who really inspires faith from both our sides. If there was an outsider that SLORC selected to mediate between us it would be a godsend.

AC: Do you think the SLORC would be open to this as a possibility?

UKM: No, not at the moment. They don't trust anyone to be impartial.

AC: There're ways to remedy that. Perhaps they need an incentive, like loans from the World Bank or International Monetary Fund, or aid from the US or the European Union...

UKM: Anyone who could help nudge SLORC to the conference table would be just fine. We will give them our full guarantee that they can be abusive, they can say anything to us, as long as they sit down with us face to face. If they really need to scold us, go ahead, howl if they want to. As long as they don't do us physical harm, that's all.

AC: Speaking of physical harm, how could these generals ever trust that they will go free?

UKM: Many people who have suffered. I mean really suffered much more than myself...more than U Tin U...more than Suu, are laughing and joking about their experiences as we do. You look a bit shocked...

AC: Yes, I am. It is hard to understand your humor and laughter in the face of such overwhelming suffering. I've talked with Daw Suu about this very point. But I'm beginning to see the value of turning the whole ordeal around and making it work in one's favor. Otherwise, as Václav Havel said, "One tends to petrify into one's own statue." A very uncomfortable image. But please, back to you...

UKM: Well, that's a good point and it relates to what I'm saying. If we harbor hatred towards our oppressors we instantly turn into that statue. Which is the opposite of compassion and forgiveness. Now, if need be I'll go out into the streets to persuade people who have really suffered. I'll ask them personally to show their mercy, to align themselves with our way of thinking. I'll speak from my own experiences—I've survived prison, many times—and here I am. It should go without mention but I'll say it. Certainly some grieving is needed. A loss has occurred and grieving is human. It's needed for some people. But dragging up all the evils of SLORC and others won't give us any real relief at all. Now I'm confident that the vast majority of our Burmese people want freedom, not revenge.

AC: I certainly respect your confidence and convictions nor am I one who espouses absolute justice. But sir, it is true that causes have effects. When cruelty has been inflicted upon people mustn't some form of justice prevail? What is democracy without the rule of law?

UKM: That is why Suu said, and we all agree with her, that we will be quite happy if some responsible people on their side would just say yes, we have done such-and-such and we are sorry and we'll see to it that others belonging to our side do not repeat such things. We would be quite happy to hear something like this. We won't cut off their salaries or imprison them. This is our attitude.

AC: Do you envision some role for the SLORC in a democratic Burma?

UKM: They need re-orientation. They are completely uneducated in matters of democracy. These men cut their political teeth under a totalitarian regime. What is the political concept behind that? Follow the leader...

AC: I would like to ask you a personal question if I may. You live on the radical edge of uncertainty moment to moment, never knowing when or if you will be taken away at any time of the day or night. How does this "great unknown" affect your marriage?

UKM: No...please ask anything you would like. In fact, I am glad you asked the question. My wife is my friend, my best friend, and in so many ways. She too is dedicated to the struggle. In so doing we are both under constant intimidation and scrutiny. Now I've said quite enough about the MI outside our compound. They follow us everywhere we go. These things do affect us, but my wife seems to have gotten used to it. I heard her talking to friends the other day about the possibility of my re-arrest and she said, "From the moment when Suu asked us to come see her on the day of her release, we knew that we would be liable for re-arrest again." She is aware of the situation. But she too jokes about it. Little things like, "Well, you know eleven years are missing from our marriage," or that "We have to stop meeting this way," meaning when she would visit me in prison. That is this reality in SLORC-controlled Burma. Democracy, marriage and imprisonment all walk hand-in-hand. I think for all of us in the struggle our idea of marriage has expanded to include separation from our family and loved ones as inevitable. We accept that fully. It's a choice we've all made.

AC: Sir, if in fact you were re-arrested, what would you say to the people of the country, should this be your last opportunity? What message would you like to leave with them to carry on the struggle?

<u>UKM:</u> For the coming generations I would encourage them to empha-size two most important things; education, and to enrich themselves with a sense of history. Knowledge is essential. They should learn about Burma, our history, our people, our own world, as well as the world at large. This will assist them in shaping their own lives, freely.

To grasp history is to grasp the importance of interrelatedness; where, why and how, the causes, conditions and the consequences of thought and action and how they affect the development or demise of civilization—human existence at large. Everyone plays a part and the gift of life is to play that part with profound respon-sibility. Furthermore, the twentieth century has taught us great lessons in all aspects of human involvement. There have been some advances which humankind could never have imagined. In this cen-tury we have seen the folly of ideologies, such as Fascism and Com-munism, that are inconsistent with creativity and the flourishing of the spirit. From the nineteenth century came the rise of the British Empire that sent a plague of exploitation around the world. Yet it too was humbled. We have witnessed all types of war from urban violence to global wars, from bolt-action rifles to the nuclear bomb, typewriters to cyberspace, a revolution in music and dance, there's just so much, and within it all have come a few good men and women with vision, that remarkable gift to see our tomorrow today. Gifts that are shifting our thinking about the future of the planet, our survival as a species. It's all about interrelatedness. So I would like to encourage all generations to explore this fully. From this I believe there will be the flourishing of civilization, and not its untimely demise—I hope.

<u>AC:</u> How would you encourage specifically the present generation in Burma and their children, and their children's children, if need be, to further your vision of a free and democratic Burmese society?

<u>UKM:</u> Do everything humanly possible not to live in fear. That's all.

<u>AC:</u> On the possibility that this book—your words—might find its way into the Burmese language and smuggled into one of Burma's many prisons, would you care to say a few words to the many pris-oners of conscience?

UKM: I would like them to remember that the collapse of the Soviet Union was unpredictable and that once the deterioration started, it continued at lightning speed. While our democracy forces are strong, gaining momentum day by day, the people will not rest until freedom is secured. Know that.

AC: Sir, if I may, I would like to ask you a personal question. How would you like to be remembered after you pass from this life?

UKM: Oh...I don't want to leave anything behind, nothing at all, no landmark, no gravestone, no books, nothing—just like a bird flies out from the water, traceless. I would want to be burnt. I want to be buried in an unmarked grave. Nor do I wish to leave any message for you or for anyone. But I will say, when you look at your life, it's ridiculous, really. And to build a monument over one's bones is even more ridiculous. I don't believe in monuments. Look at the amount of brass they wasted for Stalin's statues...

AC: You seem absolutely immune to SLORC intimidation, nor do you have any fear of re-arrest or imprisonment. But you're human. Doesn't it get to you sometimes?

UKM: I couldn't care less. What I do care about and practice off and on throughout the day is to be aware. That's all. To be aware. See, I have pieces of paper in my pockets which I carry with me, quotes, inspiring reminders. They refocus my mind on the here and now. That is the most important thing to me. To be present. Awake. Aware. Because you know, my life in prison was not a bed of roses. But I used the time to my advantage. I never forget that what I am seeing now—that pale green line streaking across the pond, or the shadow of the tree across your leg—all these things disappear the moment I turn my face to the other side. This is life's simplicity. Just the here and now. Aware that nothing is permanent, and all of it, as empty as a shadow. That barbed-wire fence across the back of Suu's compound that we see, why worry about the presence of such an irritant. It's insignificant. Now if I worry about anything, it's that I might lose this sense of awareness. So I guard it as something precious. Things pass...that I have seen. Life is what you make it, now. Nothing profound, very basic, you see. So let us put our energies into life. In this way I try not to lose my perspective.

AC: Do you ever contemplate your own death?

UKM: Yes...when I stand up there speaking to the people on Sunday, I sometimes visualize myself with a projectile piercing my heart, the blood, and my fall to the ground. But I don't worry. I'm not worried at all. I don't care. If it is coming, let it come. But what I do fear is that I would be so weak that I would choose the easiest way out, lie around in bed all day and read some book on the collapse of yet another totalitarian regime...

Appendix B

A Conversation with U Tin U
Deputy Chairman of the National League for Democracy

U Tin U joined the Burma Independence Army in 1943 aged only sixteen. After independence he was given a commission in the reorganized Burma Army and was twice decorated for courage in action against the Kuomintang. He rose rapidly through the ranks and in 1974 was appointed Chief of Defense Services and Minister of Defense. During popular demonstrations against military rule in 1974 and 1976 he was hailed as a champion of the people. This had much to do with his dismissal from the armed forces in 1976. That same year he was sentenced to seven years' imprisonment. Released under an amnesty in 1980, he entered a monastery and lived as a monk for two years. On returning to lay life he studied law at Rangoon University and gained the LL.B. degree. In 1988 he quickly joined the democracy movement as one of its leaders, becoming Deputy Chairman in September of that year. In July 1989 he was arrested and later tried by a military tribunal and sentenced to three years' imprisonment. Having served almost his full term he was retried and sentenced again, this time for seven years. He was released in 1995 and resumed his former post as Deputy Chairman of the NLD. U Tin U is seen by many to combine in his unique personality the best qualities of soldier, Buddhist scholar, lawyer and politician.

ALAN CLEMENTS: Just how far back do your Buddhist roots go?

U TIN U: From the time of my birth. My parents were devout Buddhists and they would bring me to the village monastery quite often. I was, I think, around eight years old when the abbot taught me the basics about Buddhism. And I still remember how much he stressed the four *brahma viharas*—the qualities of loving-kindness, compassion, sympathetic joy and equanimity. My life began in the sweet environment of *dhamma*. But some years later my father died. This saddened me greatly. I became disappointed with life and I told my mother I wanted to be a monk. She kindly gave me her permission. But after my second year as a novice, I went back to school. When I was in the tenth standard, General Aung San, Daw Aung San Suu Kyi's father, called on the youth to join his army in Burma's struggle for independence. My friends and I were filled with patriotic fervor. He told us: "The struggle for independence means that you must take hold of a great vision, you will meet many obstacles, you must even face the possibility of death. It will not be easy but if you are inspired, let us join hands and face whatever we must face to gain our national freedom." His words made sense, so I explained to my mother that I wanted to be a soldier with General Aung San. At first she refused, tearfully. But then she agreed. Her last words were, "If you join the soldiers to fight for freedom, then fight gallantly—without fear." So I joined the struggle and did my very best to gain our liberation.

AC: And the struggle continues fifty years later. When do you think it could end?

UTU: Soon. Very soon our country will be as lawful as the *dhamma*, a place of peace and justice where our people can enjoy their basic freedoms. But like meditation practice, we must work hard.

AC: On my way into your compound today, I noticed the ominous presence of SLORC policemen and MI personnel in front of your home. Then when your wife greeted me at the gate she stated that you were "upstairs gathering medicines and a bed-roll in anticipation of re-arrest." You've been to Insein Prison three times, a total of nine years in solitary confinement. Doesn't the SLORC understand that imprisoning the leadership of the NLD, you, Aung San Suu Kyi and U Kyi Maung, strengthens the NLD's resolve for democracy and freedom rather than crushes it?

UTU: Honestly, it's quite difficult to know what SLORC knows and what they don't know. They change all the time. They may very well want to re-arrest us but I think at this point they don't dare. They have already alienated the entire population and to re-arrest us would just make matters worse. But even so Daw Aung San Suu Kyi feels the need to deepen people's understanding of democracy. The more that the people understand democracy, the less helpless they will feel whenever a crisis develops. We at the NLD feel that in time we will have built such a strong organization that such difficulties as our potential re-arrest would be easily overcome. We represent the people and in so doing we want to educate them to also represent themselves. This is a mass democracy movement, a people's struggle.

AC: You, Aung San Suu Kyi, and U Kyi Maung live under the constant pressure of SLORC intimidation and threat of imprisonment. You are followed everywhere you go by MI, your telephone is tapped, letters opened, nothing is safe or private. You live on the edge of uncertainty at every moment, always unsure about whether they'll come in the night and take you back to prison. Nevertheless, you consistently maintain a genuine warmth and lightness of spirit. How do you succeed in acting so?

UTU: *Anicca*, as we say in Buddhism; all things are impermanent. Why should I be concerned with things that are out of my control? I'm fully prepared to be taken away day or night. I'm aware that I am at the SLORC's physical mercy. We are all aware of this reality. But the momentum for democratic change has been started and going back to prison would do nothing to stop it, in fact, it would only serve the cause. This is perhaps the main reason why SLORC doesn't dare to re-arrest us. Meanwhile, we work together as a family. This brings me a sense of great joy. I could say, in fact I will say, this is the happiest time of my life. Because I know that democracy will be achieved in the end. It will take work, by everyone, but it will be achieved.

AC: If any of you are imprisoned again, how do you think the people of Burma will react? Will there be demonstrations or a nationwide strike? If so, do you think the SLORC would respond with violence?

UTU: Sporadic protests could happen in various parts of Burma, but not on the scale of 1988. And SLORC would very likely take harsh repressive actions in the wake of such protests. But such actions would meet with severe international condemnation. We feel that the United Nations would be compelled at that point to isolate the SLORC fully as the pariah state it really is.

AC: Despite your release from prison last year SLORC has escalated their repression of the entire population; Burma is a nation under siege. Why did the authorities release you and Aung San Suu Kyi to begin with? What was their motive? Is it a cruel ruse to agitate disturbances through their MI men and blame it on the NLD so that they can imprison you for good?

UTU: It's possible. Totalitarian regimes operate in that way. But in our view negative world opinion against SLORC has dramatically increased since 1990 due to SLORC's defiant abuse of human rights, as well as the imprisonment of our NLD leadership and of course many thousands of other political prisoners. SLORC wants money and foreign investment. In fact, SLORC is somewhat crazed in its need for money. In light of this obsession, Daw Aung San Suu Kyi's release brought about a degree of relief in pressure exerted by the international community even though the growth in investment shows no remarkable change. Her release was probably a miscalculation on SLORC's part. Or I should say...a good move for the wrong reasons.

On the other hand, the SLORC might have assumed that since Daw Aung San Suu Kyi had been severed from her leadership role for six years, she would not be in a position to reassert the prestige she had acquired prior to her arrest. Of course, just the opposite has happened. She is stronger than ever and we at the NLD are even more unified than ever. Like you just said, incarceration didn't impede our struggle, it enhanced it. And if they re-arrest us it will only enhance it even more. I do think SLORC will come to understand that they must talk with us, because we're not going to run away. All of us at the NLD are here to stay and talking with us would be the best way.

AC: Let's start from the beginning. You, sir, an ex-army general, along with Aung San Suu Kyi, stand together with your NLD colleagues and lead a non-violent revolution for the restoration of justice and freedom in your country. How was it that you first became involved in the struggle?

UTU: During the pro-democracy upheavals of 1988, my colleagues urged me to address the public. At first I declined. I wanted to continue living quietly practicing *vipassana* [insight] meditation. I think I was a bit attached to the tranquillity and peace of the practice. But my colleagues would not give up, and after many discussions we all agreed to form a league which we named the All-Burma Patriotic Old Comrades' League. Nearly all the retired officers from all over the country came to our headquarters, which was my house, to offer their services.

Daw Aung San Suu Kyi addressed the public on 26 August 1988. U Aung Gyi had given an address on the 25th. So everybody forced me, you see, to join in. I was compelled. They told me, "You were once the Chief of Staff. Now you must return to service and help the people who are suffering and struggling for the restoration of democracy." So on behalf of our newly formed league, I addressed the public in the Rangoon General Hospital compound. There was a huge, energetic crowd, and I spoke for about thirty minutes. But after this, we felt that although we had formed a league, it was not enough. We needed a leader, a strong leader who could lead the whole show. And although our group was large, consisting of military personnel and some portion of the population, I knew that I could not lead the entire country along with the ethnic races. We needed somebody who understood democracy, someone who had really lived it, and we thought Daw Aung San Suu Kyi was the one to do it. Of course, as the daughter of General Aung San, she had become very popular and the people perceived her as a leader. And although we didn't say it personally, we thought that she was quite brilliant.

AC: What were your impressions of Daw Suu when you heard her speak?

UTU: When I first heard her voice, listening to a recording of her Shwedagon address, I was very impressed. Her words were strong and clear, and there was no hitch at all. Some people who live abroad a long time can hardly speak Burmese when they come back to Burma. They are no longer fully conversant. But she spoke fluently and with daily Burmese usage. Some of the jokes she cracked were very consistent with the present situation. She was clearly a very rare person. And with about 500,000 people gathered around her for her first public address, I realized that the people were eager for democracy, and that they were thinking that she was the unifying force that could lead the movement. We didn't say "leader"— she was the lady who could try, who could attempt to guide our people towards what they desire so much. Soon thereafter, my colleagues and I decided to seek unity among all parties who were trying to restore the people's legitimate rights. Some of the veteran politicians wanted our league in particular to join with her, because as former military personnel, we could provide a protective force around her. We agreed that I would meet her, and I would go alone. Which I did.

AC: What did you know about Daw Suu before meeting her? Did you know anything other than that she was *Bogyoke* Aung San's daughter?

UTU: I knew that she was usually abroad. That was my only knowledge about her. And that she used to come back yearly in order to lay the wreath at the Martyrs' Mausoleum—the place where her father is buried. At these times I would see her name in the newspaper—a young woman—named Ma Aung San Suu Kyi. That's all.

AC: And your first meeting with Daw Suu; would you take us there?

UTU: When I came to her house she was sitting on the corner of the sofa in the main room. She was alone. I paid my respects to her by addressing her as "Daw Aung San Suu Kyi." I used her full address, because I respected our beloved leader Aung San very much. At that time, I never addressed her as "Daw Suu Kyi" or anything else, but as "Daw Aung San Suu Kyi," giving her my full honor and my respect.

AC: I'm curious, sir, as to why you call her "Daw Aung San Suu Kyi" and not "Suu" like U Kyi Maung does? Or "Suu Suu," as his wife calls her?

UTU: No, I never call her Suu. Ever since our first meeting, I have not changed how I address her. Her name is a composite of her grandmother, "Suu," her mother, "Kyi," and her father, "Aung San." When I use her name, I give respect to her family. Even though she is younger than me by nearly nineteen years, I never call her "Ma Suu" or "Daw Suu." I call her Daw Aung San Suu Kyi. Out of respect for these family names, I affix Daw, which means "lady," or "Madam."

AC: When you first met Daw Suu, what were your impressions of her?

UTU: It really struck me that the way she talked, her complexion, her features and gestures were strikingly similar to those of her father. She resembled him in almost every way. I thought that she was a female replica. So inspired, I thought she was the lady who could carry on his work. Also, she had a very clear mind and a very strong head. Her way of speaking and dealing with me was efficient and kind. Of course, we exchanged a few pleasantries. Then I said, "I listened to your first public speech. We cannot make it alone. We need unity within the struggle for human rights and democracy." She agreed. "All right," she said, "fine, let's go forward and work together." That's all.

But as I was leaving she did ask me, "Did you meet my father? Did you know him?" "Yes, of course I knew him well," I said. "How?" she asked. I told her that I had known him from my days as a cadet and an officer in his Patriotic Forces. I said, "The last time I met your father was at Maymyo, he was the Deputy Chairman of the Governor's Executive Council, and I, a Lieutenant. At that time your father was visiting with the Chief of Yawngshwe State and one of the Chiefs of Shan State together. And I saw your mother too. That was the last time I saw your father alive."

So she asked, "Did you notice at that time a small girl being carried by somebody?" "No," I said. "That was me, that was me," she told me. Then I told her that General Aung San was a great leader, who inspired us all in the struggle for Burmese independence. But, very unfortunately and very sadly, he wasn't able to witness the independence for which he personally gave so much. After leading such a great struggle, he didn't see its fruits. "And now his sons and daughters do not have the opportunity to enjoy the independence of which your father was the architect," I told her. "It strikes me that now I have to serve and cooperate with you, so that you, his only daughter, may enjoy the great fruits of Burma's independence."

AC: Few people have gained the respect and trust that Aung San Suu Kyi has for you. As her close colleague you work with Daw Suu on a daily basis and share the podium with her every Sunday at your public talk. May I ask you for your most candid impressions of what makes Aung San Suu Kyi who she is today? And what is it about her that you most respect?

UTU: Leadership and her qualifications in terms of her knowledge and intellect. Her mind is highly developed. Mentally she is very absorbed, just like her father was. And she was well brought up and well disciplined. Also, she is straightforward, frank and direct. People trust her because she speaks the truth. And she does it in a simple way, but it's powerful. When she speaks to the people she says, "Do not think that I will be able to give you democracy. I will tell you frankly, I am not a magician. I do not possess any special power that will allow me to bring you democracy. I can say frankly that democracy will be achieved only by you, by all of you. By the will, perseverance, discipline and courage of the people. As long as you possess these qualities, democracy will be achieved by you. I can only show you the path to democracy. That I can explain to you, from my experience learned from abroad and through research of my father's works done during his day. I can only give you the knowledge and the method. Democracy can only be achieved through the effort of our entire population." This is the Daw Aung San Suu Kyi that I respect. The lady speaks frankly and the people like it.

Also, she took pains and rendered brilliantly her political role at the time of the national crisis in 1988 and 1989. Despite the enormous hardships imposed upon her, she traveled relentlessly throughout the country to hear, to see, and to share the people's political, economic, and social struggles with great patience. She possesses the qualities of loving-kindness and compassion. And even though she seems to be weak in appearance, her inner will is very strong and determined. She always has a sympathetic feeling for those who are suffering and helpless. Her experience abroad makes her very effective at dealing with international institutions for our cause. Her nearly six-year house arrest matured her way of political, economic and social thinking. All the nationalities in Burma trust her honesty, as they did her father's. She would be the sole leader who could unify all the indigenous races in Burma. I shall have to say, she is not an ordinary lady. She has become a most qualified leader, whose abilities the people trust for the restoration of peace, justice and democracy in Burma.

AC: How has she most influenced you?

UTU: I used to be a general with an aggressive motive, you see. But she has calmed me down, softened my belligerence. She can quiet my aggressiveness with her gentleness. It's quite remarkable, even by observing her movements and gestures, she is so graceful. Of course, her respect and affection for me is an honor. Now when I met her I told myself I must behave. I must not be too aggressive. I have gradually learned and trained myself to be more kind.

From the age of seventeen until nearly fifty, my life was a struggle. I had a very rough life. I had to stay many years in dense jungles during the war. I've been wounded in battle numerous times. As I said, I lost my father, and my son died at a young age. After being promoted to Chief of Staff I was betrayed, sacked and imprisoned. I lacked politeness, and felt aggressive. And when I addressed the public I spoke my mind, even though it was often detrimental to others. And by her influence, I came to understand that I must behave as a gentleman, a civilized man. So, my aggressive tendency has, I think, been tamed by her. I respect her, and she also respects me.

AC: Has SLORC ever tried to coerce you to break your association with Daw Suu?

UTU: Yes. They used to spread rumors among my friends that I was associating with her for the wrong reasons. Of course, I didn't pay any attention to them. But while I was imprisoned this last time a SLORC intelligence officer during an interrogation session pointed a finger and with raised voice said, "You were a General and the Minister of Defense. You were mature in your duties. So why are you working for Aung San Suu Kyi? She has no experience whatsoever of Burma's politics. All she has is her father's name behind her. Why do you work with a woman who is so inexperienced?"

Honestly, I felt sorry for this man. So I told him, "If you meet her, you too will join the movement. She has a brilliant and talented mind. Eventually you will realize this, because Daw Aung San Suu Kyi is struggling not only for the people but for you too."

AC: You have been with Aung San Suu Kyi on numerous occasions, some of them life and death situations. Sir, may I ask you to recall a story or two with her, experiences that have most influenced you?

UTU: On the 15 or 16 August 1988, bad news reached Daw Aung San Suu Kyi and me. A huge unruly crowd had run amok with the Military Security personnel at the Central Trade Corporation office in the downtown area. I hurriedly went to the scene to quiet things. I could control the situation to a certain extent. I begged the people to demonstrate peacefully. Yet I realized that I could not stay any longer to maintain the tranquillity. The situation was getting too far out of control. I felt that some sort of violent action was going to occur. People would surely die. Immediately, I returned to Daw Aung San Suu Kyi's house, explained the situation, and instantly she asked me to accompany her to the scene. I tried to explain that it was not a good idea, that there would be firing, that it was not advisable to proceed to that area. She explained that we do not turn our backs on violence. So at her insistence we went, quickly. We traveled together in a car with some escorts behind us. Upon arrival, the crowd had burned down the Trade Building. It was in flames. We saw looting and destruction of vehicles. The crowd was frantic and quickly we were engulfed, unable to move in any direction. I felt that danger was imminent. The escort boy shouted to the people, who had gone wild, to give way for Daw Aung San Suu Kyi who had come to see the situation. As soon as the people realized that Daw Aung San Suu Kyi was present, they restrained their agony and calmed down. They politely helped us through. And their faces changed from anguish to awe at seeing her personally at the scene. Yet, Daw Aung San Suu Kyi showed balance and clear intent. In my eyes she was proving her integrity and discipline in the face of danger. I learned something that day from her. It's far better to face danger than run from it.

AC: Were there other such moments that left a lasting mark on you?

UTU: Many. But I'll tell you just one more. This incident happened on the way to Hlawkar village, just beyond Mingaladon, near to the airport. Ko Win Htein, Daw Aung San Suu Kyi's personal secretary, was traveling with her in her car, and I was just behind them. Our convoy was forcibly stopped somewhere near Hlawkar village and Ko Win Htein got out and explained our program to the security police.

Suddenly, a burst of automatic gunfire was fired from a certain distance, with the intent of intimidation, to dissuade us from proceeding further. I was stunned at the firing. I jumped out of my car and stood in front of hers to face any consequences. Instead of being the least bit frightened she got out of the car and calmly asked what had happened. I shouted at the armed police on the small hill, why were they shooting randomly? As soon as the leader recognized that Daw Aung San Suu Kyi was present he explained that it was an accident. Furthermore, he politely apologized for the mishap and we were allowed to proceed. As we traveled on in silence I thought to myself how calmly she had acted and by virtue of just asking the most polite question, "Why? Why are you shooting?" She was genuinely interested rather than being upset, as I was. I think that's one of her strengths. She always wants to know why, whether friend or foe. She questions principles, whereas I would have reacted to the person.

AC: On 20 July 1989 both you and Aung San Suu Kyi were incarcerated and placed under house arrest, charged as it were, for "endangering the security of the state." Of course, a few months later you were placed on trial, sentenced, and imprisoned. Sir, would you take us through those historic events, from your arrest up to imprisonment?

UTU: In the early morning on the day of my house arrest, a hundred or so armed military personnel surrounded my house. Why they didn't immediately enter the compound I don't know, but those extra hours gave my wife and other family members the time to tear up and flush down the toilet every NLD document, letter, and address that was in my office. I prepared myself mentally and emotionally for my arrest by sitting in meditation. Several hours later when they raided the compound the authorities ransacked the whole house, taking away all remaining documents, books, and some medicines. Communication lines were cut. Of course they told me that I was now under house arrest.

Armed guards were posted around my house. Barricades were placed at the junction of the road and at my gates. Even my wife had to ask permission to leave the compound to shop for food, which was given only hours or sometimes days later. But the most unpleasant thing was that my house arrest forced my tenants who lived in our small rental house on the property to move. This was my only source of income since my pensions and gratuities had been cut off in 1976—the year I was first imprisoned under the Ne Win regime. Of course, living without income is not easy but we simplified our life and adjusted.

AC: Of course, soon thereafter the situation greatly intensified.

UTU: Yes. On 22 December 1989 I was hauled before SLORC's Martial Law Court and charged with numerous offenses. I can only remember three; that I had correspondence with foreign democratic leaders; my actions constituted "sedition" against the state. And during my tenure as Chief of Defense Services, they claimed that I conspired to overthrow the government. I denied all charges and steadfastly pleaded not guilty. One prosecution witness testified against me. But I wasn't allowed to cross-examine him, nor was I allowed to produce defense witnesses. Of course, this was a severe violation of human rights. The judge said, "Is there anything you would like to say for the mitigation of your punishment?" Before I could answer the military officer in charge of the trial read out my sentence. "We sentence you to three years' rigorous imprisonment."

AC: What was your reaction?

<u>UTU:</u> On hearing the sentence, I stood up and turned around to those senior military officers who were witnessing the court proceedings. There were perhaps twenty or so men in the back of the room, most of whom I in fact had trained during my time as Defense Chief years before. They were children at the time. I was general of the army. It was these men that I wanted to speak to and not the SLORC judge.

I said, "I did not attempt to split the army. I joined the army at the age of sixteen for one reason, to struggle alongside of *Bogyoke* Aung San for our national independence. I love the army but I love our people more than the army. And the army must see the people as our father and our mother. We must serve the people and not oppress the people." I then turned towards the SLORC journalists who were also in the room and said in a loud voice, "I take this sentence with pride. It gives me great dignity to go to prison for my belief in democracy." The room fell silent—then I was quickly escorted to my cell.

<u>AC:</u> What does it take emotionally and psychologically to survive the severity of prison and solitary confinement? Where do you find the courage to face yet another day, month, and year of aloneness?

<u>UTU:</u> Well, it doesn't come easily but remember that I had already spent five years in solitary prior to my imprisonment by the SLORC.

I can't say that you ever get used to prison but it is something that one does adjust to. It depends on the individual. Some break, while others use the isolation and cruel living standards to their favor. As for me, I never felt the slightest bit bored throughout the time I languished in prison. Even though I was very restricted, I had ways to keep my spirit alive. My hut within the prison compound was completely encircled with barbed wire. I was indoors all the time. And the wire was a constant reminder of how precious freedom was. Like in the Buddha's teachings, obstacles can be seen as advantages; the loss of one's freedom can inspire reflection on the preciousness of freedom. This filled me with joy.

Also, I knew from my years as a practicing monk the benefits of *sati*—mindfulness meditation. As you know too, with mindfulness everything you see, hear, taste, think, and smell becomes simply an experience, without anything extra placed upon it. Just phenomena.

So in that way too, the thought of imprisonment, is seen as just a thought. It comes and goes. And without attachment to it there's no problem. It's just a thought. That's all.

I would also regularly recite the Buddha's discourses in Pali as well as study them, which inspired me greatly.

In addition, a small book containing quotations of Jesus was smuggled through to me. I very much liked his attitude of forgiveness and sincerity.

Also, I made it a habit to give *dana* [the offering of something], some eatables brought to me by my wife, to my captors—warders, jailers and even some of the MI personnel. I wanted to overcome any feelings of seeing them as the "enemy" so I tried to make a practice of sharing a little of my food with them. They too had a hard life in prison. This eased my emotional and psychological pain to some extent.

Of course, my wife visited regularly. She never failed to come to the prison fortnightly. She was not only my wife, but also like a mother, an elder sister, a close relative and a very good friend.

I exercised every day. And observed the eight Buddhist precepts[*] by not taking any food after midday. But perhaps most importantly I would reflect on the preciousness of friends in my life. I think friendship is one of the greatest of all gifts. So in moments of difficulty I would envision their faces one by one and talk to them a bit. I would recall the moments of laughter and the joys we shared. It's the love that you feel that keeps your sanity.

AC: So the isolation never got to you?

UTU: I never felt unhappy, really. But one time when I was sick, I became weak, and I felt a bit lonely. I wanted somebody to care for me. I felt sorry that I was away from my family. But I was cured and returned to normal. As I said mindfulness is the key to sanity.

Just do everything you do with mindfulness and there is no room in one's mind for negative thoughts. I approached every day in

---

[*] In addition to the Five Precepts (p. 44): take no solid food after midday, dress in plain white, and abstain from high beds and big beds.

prison as I did as a monk in the monastery, mindfully. I tried to notice everything that occurred in my mind and body. In this way I could keep my mind free of obstructive emotions that might otherwise upset me. This is basic *dhamma*.

AC: There's such irony in asking you this question but how did you as Chairman of the NLD, learn of your party's landslide victory in SLORC's "free and fair elections," while in solitary confinement?

UTU: Ah, yes! Even our jailers voted for us! It happened like this. It was a key moment during my imprisonment, ironically, it relates to the story of my cage. I had been confined to a hut detached from the main cells. After six months, the authorities became paranoid that the Americans would swoop in by helicopter and rescue me. So they went to the trouble of having barbed wire strung around my hut—the sides and over the top—like a cage. This was to be my home for the next five years. In any case, it was the workers, who were also prisoners and constructed the cage, who secretly informed me of the election results. Apparently they had convinced the jailers that they were expert fence-builders. Then as they started work, I peered through a crack in my wall, and one of the men showed me our NLD emblem—a small red badge with a golden fighting peacock on it. I was stunned. As the election results came in he scratched information on bits of thick sandpaper. Each line was a township and an NLD victory. Eventually, it added up to 390 elected MPs from the NLD. My cage was the harbinger of the greatest news I received while in prison, and I was so thankful to those daring workers who freed my spirit, so to speak, while they caged me in (*laughing*).

AC: When did you learn that the SLORC had no intention of honoring the election results?

UTU: The prison became Parliament—it was filling up with increasing numbers of NLD elected representatives. So, it was easy to figure out the real election results. Also, after the elections the authorities gave us newspapers which told the obvious. I did learn that Daw Aung San Suu Kyi, U Kyi Maung and myself had all been expelled from the NLD [SLORC having compelled the remaining

NLD members to do this]. It was only after these arrests that SLORC called for a National Convention to create their constitution. A sham, deplorable—what more can I say? But I did not feel defeated. On the contrary, with this new wave of arrests it strengthened my resolve to persevere with the struggle, freedom had to be won, it was not going to be given—it remained a victory in that sense. You see, there is no way that SLORC can crush us, because oppression only increases our resolve. A strong heart and mind cannot be broken. It might be hurt but it can never be broken.

AC: Does torture exist in Burma's prisons?

UTU: I myself haven't been tortured but I have learned that there have been cases of torture and ill-treatment to other inmates. Of course solitary itself is just one form of torture. Another would be lack of medicine for those who are ill. Think of something as simple as a headache with no medication or a toothache without proper dental treatment. Now think of those with acute amebic dysentery without medicine. Remember that time when we were walking on alms rounds as monks and you ran up to me in pain because of the dysentery you had. You needed medical attention at once. Think of not getting it. These are the most minor forms of torture in prison. It happens all the time. Then of course, during my years in prison rarely a night would go by without the sounds of screaming. Loud cries from men in pain. The type of screaming that comes from only one thing—torture, severe torture.

AC: Perhaps it's a naïve question, but why do the authorities use torture?

UTU: They usually want information or they suspect the prisoner has some information they want. Sometimes they must do it out of sheer boredom. There's a lot of pent-up anger among warders. It's sick...

AC: Could you shed some light on the political prisoner situation?

UTU: So far we have counted more than 600 political prisoners. We are still collecting names of political prisoners. We think it's more than 1,000, maybe as high as 2,000 or perhaps even more. It is difficult to find out. Because very often political prisoners are either kept in total isolation or dispersed to any number of other prisons in the countryside.

Of course, because of the deplorable living conditions, many political prisoners are suffering from various kinds of diseases, especially malnutrition and dysentery. Medicines are very few, if any. Also, we have evidence that SLORC authorities use one syringe for many patients, without sterilization after each use.

The little food that is provided is miserable by all accounts. Families must supplement this, but few families are even allowed to visit. Every one of our NLD members who has been released in recent months said that, "even dogs wouldn't eat the food."

Daw Aung San Suu Kyi's personal secretary, U Win Htein, said that every evening they would serve him, "vegetable soup made up of a little bit of oil, a little bit of onion, plus the vegetable. The whole vegetable. Branch, root, dirt and all. It was literally pulled out of the earth and dished up, as it were." He would have to wash it repeatedly and then eat it with less dirt.

There are no mosquito nets and often political prisoners sleep either on the concrete floor itself or with a thin bamboo mat. Without blankets this is terrible during the winter and the rainy season. The toilet is a small bowl kept in the cell. There is no drinking water inside cells. The sleeping space is small, about $1^1/_2$ feet in breadth and $5^1/_2$ feet in length. In the other cells which are a bit larger they cram them with sometimes five or eight other prisoners. Sometimes our political prisoners are made to stay in the cell where police dogs are kept. This is a punishment cell. For instance, the Chairman of an NLD township was found with a little cash in his possession during a routine monthly check. As punishment he was put in leg chains and sent to the dog cell for two months. He was taken out every day and brutally beaten with a cane, just for having smuggled in the money. There are a few NLD MPs serving terms in dog kennels right now. The leading one is U Win Tin, the Secretary of the NLD. He was a great asset to us and because of this SLORC refuses to release him. This is just the most basic description of the situation of our political prisoners, but I do think it is enough to give you a rough idea.

AC: I know that you were sentenced to "hard labor" in prison. Would you explain what that actually means to an inmate at Insein Prison?

UTU: Well, I was sentenced to hard labor but the authorities didn't force it upon me because of age and ill health. However, hard labor is common among prisoners not only at Insein but at all of SLORC's prisons throughout the country. "Hard labor" means just that. While you are in prison you work hard, extremely hard. Mostly inmates are sent to a rock quarry, or any number of SLORC construction projects such as the building of a road or dam. Such prisoners break rocks all day, from early morning until late into the night. They are not allowed a midday meal, only a small amount of food in the morning and evening, but not always. Some days they are not allowed any food at all. They're all chained around the waist and with steel leg irons. Often such prisoners die from exhaustion, disease, or starvation.

AC: Who is the warden at Insein Prison?

UTU: A major—an intelligence officer—I don't remember his name.

AC: Will this major take his orders directly from the Military Intelligence chief, SLORC Secretary-1 Lt. General Khin Nyunt?

UTU: Yes.

AC: How did you hear of Aung San Suu Kyi being awarded the Nobel Peace Prize and what effect did it have on you?

UTU: My wife informed me during one of her visits to the prison and immediately I felt this great upsurge of joy. I felt really happy for Daw Aung San Suu Kyi, because she really is a remarkable woman.

Each time my wife came to visit me many Military Intelligence personnel would stand in the room and listen to our conversation. They also videoed and taped the meetings. So when she told me about Daw Aung San Suu Kyi receiving the award I really smiled into the camera with a look of victory.

The Peace Prize uplifted my courage for the future struggle for our cause. Obviously, you're quite alone in prison and the prize became a companion. I knew that the world, those who loved freedom, were watching our situation very closely. We had just made new allies.

AC: Sir, would you share the story of your release after nearly six years of imprisonment?

UTU: Well, it came in stages. 14 February 1992 was the day that my original sentence was to be completed. As I was waiting for my release a group of MI personnel and jailers came to my cage and informed me that the higher authorities wanted to see me at once. This escort group who came to my cage were congratulating me on my release. But I didn't feel the least bit happy and told them, "I'm not at all glad for my release, so long as my colleagues are still suffering in prison." So they went silent and took me to see the higher authorities. Along the way I was flanked by long rows of special armed guards standing at attention. Now this was odd, so odd that I realized it was a deceit. When I entered the Martial Law Courtroom it was festooned with large red flags everywhere.

Immediately the prosecution rose up and read out the charges against me; one of the charges was the same as before. The SLORC officer said, "How do you plead?" I said, "Not guilty. Furthermore you can't charge me again for charges for which I have already been sentenced." The officer sternly said, "This is a Martial Law Court and a Martial Law Court has no laws. And this court can hand out any decision that it deems fit." He then said, "You are sentenced to seven additional years of rigorous imprisonment."

Three years later, on 27 March 1995, SLORC released me on the condition that I do nothing to undermine "state security." They took me by truck back to my home and I immediately made plans for the continuation of our democracy struggle. It was just a matter of time before Daw Aung San Suu Kyi would be free. And...here we are again, stronger and more unified than ever.

AC: You've been branded by SLORC as "public enemy number one". But why do the authorities have a special hatred for you in particular, say more so than for your colleagues, Daw Suu and U Kyi Maung?

UTU: Because I was once the Chief of Staff and all these army people consider my behavior as a betrayal. They fail to understand that my commitment is to the people and not to the military. I think I told you before, a good army sees the people as their parents, not their slaves. The military should be the public's friend, not their enemy.

AC: Martin Luther King encouraged his people during their struggle for equality by saying, "Our aim must not be to defeat or humiliate the white man, but to win his friendship and understanding." As a leader of the NLD is it your policy to win the friendship of SLORC, a regime that seems bent on humiliating and destroying you?

UTU: Sometimes one-time enemies can make the best of friends. This is why we consistently ask for dialogue and reconciliation. I do not want to destroy the SLORC. I just want them to stop destroying the lives of our people and to stop destroying our beloved country. It's quite simple. And as a Buddhist I firmly believe in kindness and compassion as the best ways of winning the sympathy of SLORC.

This is one of the reasons why Daw Aung San Suu Kyi has called our movement for democracy a "revolution of the spirit." We must all have a change in spirit, all of us. We must make this spirit grow.

AC: Without a bare minimum level of morality one feels no shame at committing any act of harm to another human being. How does one go about fostering a sense of shame in the mind of their oppressor?

UTU: In all honesty, I think the SLORC generals should lay down all their weapons just for ten days and undertake a period of *vipassana* meditation practice under a competent Sayadaw [senior monk]. If their meditation is developing nicely then I think they should extend their practice indefinitely. I think the whole country would applaud them for this noble behavior. In this way, the meditation practice will automatically reveal to them, by themselves, without anyone's help, their true inner state of being. All Burmese will understand this. They can foster *metta* in this way.

AC: And if they don't?

UTU: Sooner or later I think their attitudes will change through the will and strength of the people. If the people are sufficiently convinced that they want democracy and are willing to achieve that democracy then no power can stop them, be it weapons or repression. The people's pressure and determination will in the end make SLORC realize their shortcomings. Because you can only oppress people for so long before truth sprouts up in the most unsuspected places. It is a bit like trying to remove a bamboo tree by cutting the stalk. The more you cut it, the more it branches out, the more it spreads.

AC: Do you see anything redeemable about the SLORC?

UTU: Nothing…not today anyway. But it may appear tomorrow. They are changing all the time. One day they consider the armed minorities as enemies; the next day they are friends. One day Khun Sa is SLORC's enemy; the next day he is toasting them in celebration. Maybe it will be the same with the NLD. One day, the NLD is a subversive organization they want to crush and annihilate. The next day, the NLD might be considered their friend. Maybe even their best friend.

So it is possible they might change, and then we might be able to see some redeeming qualities in them. But I still think they should meditate first. That may hasten the process. People are suffering.

AC: Do you see a role for SLORC in a democratic government led by the National League for Democracy?

UTU: Yes, but they must genuinely demonstrate, and I emphasize this point, they must show that they have greatly reformed their behavior and attitudes. If this is shown, yes, they do have a place in the future of Burma under a democratic government. But like all democratic systems, the military's position will be honorable and dignified. The military will be `servants' of the people governed by a civilian leadership, and used only as a noble body to safeguard the nation's security.

AC: Is Ne Win the man still in control? Is Ne Win the man who's in control of SLORC?

UTU: Some people think so.

AC: How does an eighty-five-year-old man control from his lakeside mansion twenty-one SLORC generals and their 400,000 armed soldiers?

UTU: We have no solid evidence that he is controlling SLORC. But it is natural that many of them should feel a sense of loyalty towards him. He put them where they are now.

AC: What advantage is it to SLORC to have released Daw Suu, U Kyi Maung and yourself?

UTU: I think it was a miscalculation. They thought they had effectively crushed us by having imprisoned us. I don't think they had any notion that it would strengthen our unity, rather than weaken or crush it.

AC: Sir, you're one of Daw Aung San Suu Kyi's closest colleagues and friends. May I ask you, how it is that you, sir, a sacked general who commanded the entire armed forces for two years under Burma's dictator, Ne Win, whose totalitarian regime mercilessly repressed every form of human rights for over three decades; how is it that you now stand together with Aung San Suu Kyi who has been awarded the Nobel Peace Prize for leading a non-violent struggle for democracy? It seems curious that the right-hand man of a dictator is now the colleague of "Burma's Gandhi." That's one colossal transformation. Would you explain the inner process of how that change occurred?

UTU: When you live for nine years in solitary confinement under the most severe forms of repression, a man has a lot of time to reflect. Since I know the worst in human nature it gives me more confidence to seek the best in people. I've seen both sides. The dark and the light. I've seen it in myself. From observing my mind through the practice of *vipassana* meditation I have come to realize that loving-kindness and compassion can be developed. If I can do it, it gives me great hope that others can do it too. Since I was blinded by a deeply unrecognized level of ignorance, I feel more sympathy when I see others that are so deluded. But it was all those long years in prison and my years as a monk that really made me appreciate *metta*.

AC: A difficult question, but do some people doubt your sincerity?

You stayed with a dictator for years after many good people turned their backs on the old man. And do you feel fully redeemed within yourself? Do you ever doubt?

UTU: No, I never doubt. And it's not so strange that some people may doubt my sincerity, because I stayed with a dictator for years and now I am working with the democratic movement. But there would be no question of doubt, were they to realize my true reasons, which are not visible to outsiders and could hardly be understood by someone in their position. I just explained to you some of my reasons and how those changes occurred. Solitary confinement is not to be underestimated as a potent method of "soul searching" as you might say it.

AC: I'm sorry to press you on this issue but I would like to know how and why you stayed with an authoritarian regime for so many years? You were general of an army that killed its own civilians whenever it was ordered and you were part of the top command.

UTU: I stayed out of a sense of duty. When I was appointed Commander in Chief in 1974, I intended to ask for my release after four years of service. But the government beat me to it, by sending me to prison because I was too popular. I no longer wanted to continue with an administration which whenever there were problems, instead of trying to resolve them by discussion, adopted the policy of arresting, repressing and at times killing, or even massacring its people. As the Defense Chief I was forced to fire on people, gun people down, this was the policy and I followed it blindly.

AC: How did the final break with the regime come about?

UTU: It was around the time of U Thant's funeral in Rangoon and the refusal of the government to treat the occasion in a dignified way. University students took the matter into their own hands and started shouting, "Long Live U Tin U." From then I started falling from favor. In March 1976 I was dismissed on the grounds that my wife accepted bribes.

AC: What was the allegation of bribery towards your wife?

UTU: The charge fabricated against my wife contained a very small grain of truth. I was well-loved by Burmese military attachés posted in various countries. These military attachés would frequently bring gifts to my wife when they visited Burma, but as a matter of policy she never accepted them. However, one time she did accept ten pounds from a military attaché to buy some medicine. You see, we had a child who was born with a congenital heart disease, and when she was in England she accepted this money to buy the medicine because it was impossible to buy it in Rangoon. This incident was the pretext for dismissing me from service. But things got worse. Two weeks later it was announced in front of the National Assembly that I was to be put on trial for this "economic wrongdoing." The entire National Assembly was shocked. I was also shocked when I heard about it. I was put in prison a few months later.

AC: Are you asking the SLORC to go through the same grueling psychological process that you went through. How can this be done?

UTU: I think I said it before, it's one thing to profess Buddhism and it's another thing altogether to practice it. Perhaps the best way to overcome any inner hindrance is to train yourself in *sati*—mindfulness or awareness—it's shining a light on one's darkness.

I had to learn the hard way. I was forced to confront myself while in prison. You can't just run away in solitary, you can certainly try but there is no place to go. If members of SLORC wish to avail themselves of what I have come to see as a shortcoming in myself—blind obedience—then I think they must first want to make that change. It's always better to initiate change than to have it forced upon you. But until they show a real change in their ways, we at the NLD will continue in every way possible to point out democracy.

AC: Many of your friends say that sincerity, kindness, and courage are the qualities they admire the most in you. How does one develop those virtues, especially the quality of sincerity—the ability to be authentic?

UTU: Well, where such qualities originate is not within my grasp of understanding. What is most important to me is that they exist and because of this, the best place to relate to them is in the moment, here and now. This is, as you must know, the basis of our Buddha's teaching; the here and now. *Ehipasiko* is the Buddha's invitation to all, to come and see for oneself the value of investigating truth as it appears, now. So in this way I don't concern myself with the past so much. So my idea about being sincere is quite simple, just be sincere, be as sincere as you can, that's all. Sincerity to me means being candid and open in your relationships and dealings with people. Sincerity also means that you must try to be able to feel for others. If you were to do wrong to somebody, you must consider how you would feel if that wrong were done to you. The less one is concerned with oneself the more sincere one is with others. Simple.

AC: How is it that totalitarianism so often distorts one's identity to the point that insincerity becomes a habit?

UTU: Totalitarianism is a system based on fear, terror and violence. If one lives under such a system long enough one becomes a part of it, often unknowingly. Fear is insidious. And from fear one easily and most often unconsciously adapts oneself to fear as a way of life, as a way of being. As Daw Aung San Suu Kyi has said, "Fear is a habit." Of course, as a practitioner of meditation, I have seen that habits can be broken in any number of ways. Perhaps the most important way to break the habit of insincerity is to be in association with sincere people. If one can't be close to sincere people, one should listen to them from a distance. If you can't listen to them, one should read the words of sincere people. But in order to become sincere one must at least want to be sincere and with this, I think, sincerity will blossom, little by little.

AC: What prompted you to be ordained as a Buddhist monk and enter the monastery at the age of fifty-four?

UTU: During my first period of incarceration from 1976 to 1981, my conditions in prison were harsh—extremely harsh. Sometimes, when I thought over my affairs, I felt full of resentment and outrage.

I was in a terrible state of mind, alone in solitary, and without anyone to discuss things with. I was at times seething, really mad. And I had no ability to control my mind. I knew very little about meditation at that time, nor was my conviction in the *dhamma* very strong. You know, I was trained to be a soldier, I was a combatant.

In solitary confinement I felt like a caged, enraged animal. Furthermore, after my sacking from the army as Chief of Staff, I received a few months' pay and that was it. My pension stopped and my name was struck from the annals of history of the Burma Army. My photographs and speeches during the tenure of my service were all destroyed.

In addition, they issued an order stating that nobody was to address me as "General," only as U Tin U. In fact, if someone were to address me by rank they would be punished. Then the BSPP party published a scathing book portraying me as a notorious criminal. At the same time, I thought about my wife and how difficult it would be to live without an income. The situation as I felt it in prison was like a pressure cooker. I was ready to explode. Suddenly, I came down with severe dysentery. My stomach-pains doubled me over. And my anger made the pains in my stomach worse. The combination of the two forms of suffering, and without any release, was terrible. I sat down on the floor of my cell and felt like I was going to weep. Well, it just so happened that I had brought a small booklet with me by the Mahasi Sayadaw on *vipassana* meditation. I picked up the booklet and started reading his instructions on mindfulness or bare attention. He suggested that one should simply be aware of all experiences as they arise. If it's pain, be aware of pain. If it's joy, well, just be aware of joy, so on and so forth. So I sat cross-legged on the floor and just started to be aware of the pain and the anger. Well, it was like a miracle. After the first ten minutes or so the anger and pain increased. I said, "This is only creating more pain." But I stayed with it and after an hour or so, the pain and anger simply disappeared. So you can imagine how I felt. I now had a friend in prison, myself, my mindfulness. So when I came out of solitary in 1981 I was ordained at the Mahasi monastery and learned meditation under the guidance of a teacher. Of course, this is when we met. So many good things can come from critical moments, if you're mindful.

AC: During your two years in the monastery what would you say that you learned?

UTU: That through attachment one lives a very shallow fearful life, and the value of *metta* or loving-kindness—because we all live to a certain degree with attachment and this *metta* eases the journey.

AC: That's nicely put...perhaps you'd share more of your learning?

UTU: Well, Buddhism is very democratic, isn't it? The idea that the members of the *Sangha* talk to each other and admit their mistakes, particularly in the *Pavarana* ceremony that occurs at the end of the rains retreat, is a very democratic idea. In the army you learn to be obedient to authority, whereas as a monk you learn obedience to the truth. As monks, you talk to each other, admit your mistakes openly, and sort out differences in a very respectful and dignified manner.

AC: How do you feel that the *Sangha* in Burma could play a more active role in supporting the struggle for democracy?

UTU: The *Sangha* have a responsibility for the health and happiness of their lay disciples. Under such circumstances where the people are so poor and so unhappy, where they are undergoing both physical and mental suffering, the *Sangha* have a duty to speak out and to speak up for their disciples. They must not just ignore what is happening. They must speak out for whatever needs to be done in order to bring health and happiness, that is, mental and physical ease. If democracy is to be achieved in Burma it is everyone's duty to help, monks and nuns included. Everyone can do their part. I am not saying that it has to be a big part, but many little parts do make a big difference. That's what we want from the people.

AC: And specifically, as you speak on the weekends to the crowd?

UTU: We speak about the "repression and unhappiness" of the people. The fact that the people are too afraid either to speak out or to do what they want to do, is not according to the teachings of the Buddha. The fact that they are so inhibited by fear is against the teachings of the Buddha. The Buddha taught us to confront our fear. That can be done in many ways. The first way is to say no, I'm not going to be controlled by fear. Then say yes, I will do my part in bringing democracy to my country. Fearlessness must become a habit.

AC: Aung San Suu Kyi has called the democracy struggle a revolution of the spirit, saying that "a people who would build a nation in which strong democratic institutions are firmly established as a guarantee against state-induced power must first learn to liberate their own minds from apathy and fear." I'd like to ask you as a man who has engaged in combat, who has seen death, who has killed and has been wounded on numerous occasions, and you, a man who has been treated inhumanely through imprisonment and harsh living conditions, how does one learn to "liberate their own mind from fear," other than in engaging in the long-term practice of Buddhist meditation?

UTU: You might think this is an over-simplification but my belief is that to overcome fear one acts despite the fear. You just do it and face the consequences, because if you know something is right then you should just do it. Also, the more that one acts courageously, the more it becomes a habit. Like mindfulness in meditation. At first you must try to be mindful. Later on as one goes on trying the mindfulness just occurs naturally, it becomes effortless, it too becomes a habit.

AC: Sir, do you ever feel that you would like to walk away from the volatile world of Burma's politics and return to the calm, peaceful existence of a monk within a monastery? What keeps you struggling?

UTU: I would never walk away. If I did I would feel like a coward. What keeps me struggling? It's my love of freedom. What else is there in life?

AC: You've killed men in battle. You've ordered tens of thousands of men under your command to mercilessly destroy the enemy. Now you espouse non-violence not only as a political tactic in your struggle for democracy but even more fully as a way of life, a way of being. A direct question: how committed are you to non-violence?

UTU: I am not somebody who is cruel or enjoys violence. Although I fought and killed, it was my duty as a soldier. I treated the enemy with respect. As for captives or our enemies in helpless positions we fed them and served them as if they were our own men. I believe that people should show mercy and abhor violence. For me, non-violence is a philosophy and at the root of that philosophy is harmlessness and compassion. What is the point in hurting people when you can achieve your aim peacefully? It might take longer, who can say, but you remain dignified in your life through living harmlessly. Through non-violence one can never be defeated, really. Because as a Buddhist, I firmly believe that oneself is one's enemy or one's friend. This is very Buddhist, that from one's mind the world originates. I want to see democracy before I die, I want to see democracy for my people before they too die, but to achieve democracy through any means other than non-violent ones is not a democracy that I wish to be a part of. When I read a few words of Jesus in prison, I at once thought to myself that this man is very Buddhist. He knew very well that love was the greatest power on earth. I'm not one for that old thinking of an eye for an eye and a tooth for a tooth. That's rather uncivilized, as I see it.

AC: Sir, you're seeking genuine reconciliation with the SLORC, which is tantamount to forgiving them for their atrocities. How does one learn to forgive the oppressor? Isn't some form of justice required in order to genuinely forgive?

UTU: In this matter, I cannot speak for others. I cannot say to the people, "Forgive SLORC or forgive the authorities. Forgive them for their atrocities." I would not be honest at all if I said that. It would be a lie. Because many people in my country have suffered and many more continue to suffer daily. So forgiving the SLORC at this point is not the issue. Compassion is what is needed. The SLORC are the ones who need to feel compassion. If they could feel compassion they might just see that these atrocities are hurting people badly. Now let me say, compassion and forgiveness are quite different. In order to forgive, one must be courageous, one must not seek revenge or harbor thoughts of anger towards one's oppressor. Otherwise that is not forgiveness at all. You cannot forgive someone and want to hurt them at the same time. This is why I'm saying that compassion is more important at this point. Because there are many people in Burma who are angry, who feel hurt and do not like the authorities. Of course, this is understandable. But I can say to the people that if we have compassion for them we will remain blameless in our struggle to continue forward until that time when they see that we genuinely do not wish them harm. But to tell our people to forgive the SLORC would be bypassing an essential step. Compassion is what is needed.

AC: Fear is obviously driving the SLORC at this point. And perhaps it's the fear of retribution by the people if they were to transfer power to the NLD. How can you gain the trust of SLORC to relax this fear that they have? Some of them must be fearing for their lives.

UTU: Well, if some of them are fearing for their lives, that may be a good thing. It may indicate that they can actually feel. It may show them, that is if they choose to see it, that this "fear" they live with is identical to the "fear" they have created among the people.

They may feel how unpleasant this fear is. Fear is unpleasant, now, isn't it? No one likes to live in fear. But it's up to each person to deal with their fear. For SLORC, they can deal with their fear by listening to words that encourage them to lay down their weapons and stop their atrocities. This would make the people very happy. At once their fear would dissipate. Then we would be on the road to forgiveness. The Burmese people are very forgiving, they know that.

But they must act in such a way that we would want to forgive them. It should not and cannot be one-sided. It is not just a matter of us gaining SLORC's trust. They have got to win our trust. They have got to show us, the entire country, that they deserve forgiveness.

AC: So you, sir, as a principal leader of the democracy struggle, are ready to forgive the SLORC authorities, right now? Unconditionally?

UTU: Would I sit down at the table with the authorities and discuss our differences without a precondition, without thoughts of anger, without the demand to assert our view as the absolute one and only way to move our country out of the mess that it is now in? Indeed!

But I can't say that right at this moment I would be able to forgive the SLORC. That will depend on how they demonstrate their sincerity. I just can't sit down and tell myself to achieve enlightenment. Just like I can't sit down and tell myself to forgive them. This is why sincerity is the most important thing right now. I do feel sincere when I tell you, that I do not wish the SLORC harm. But I am not at all ready or able to forgive them, yet! I would like to...but as I said, they must show us something that is forgivable. As it is, I see nothing but belligerence and more and more repression. This is my way of telling you that I'm ordinary. Furthermore, if I said that I was ready to forgive SLORC, they would not believe it. Nor would it be honest. That's all.

AC: Why do you feel that SLORC is unwilling to open dialogue with you and other leaders of the NLD? Secondly, will they, the SLORC, ever open dialogue with the NLD? By all indications they want to crush you.

UTU: It's very simple. When you have something that you don't want to let go of—power—you become desperate to hold on to that power until either you die with that power and therefore lose it upon death, or you see that your power is nothing without honoring the people whom you think you have the power to control. So it all boils down to *moha*—delusion. Real power is rooted in compassion, not in ignorance. *Dhamma* like democracy should have the welfare of human beings as its priority. And of course, fear compromises the feelings of compassion. When SLORC eases their fear a bit they will have dialogue with us. I'm quite sure of that.

As for all their press about "crushing" us. You cannot crush the truth. Nor can they crush the entire population. The people of Burma want democracy, that is clear. Even SLORC say that they want democracy. So all this crushing business isn't very democratic, is it? Talking to each other is democratic. Listening to each other is democratic. Democracy is about learning from each other and from that we all grow, our country flourishes. Crushing is *adhamma*, that is to say, it's completely contrary to the welfare of human beings.

AC: All eighty-three NLD delegates have now walked out of SLORC's much-touted National Convention. May I ask you to clarify why SLORC's convention has been labeled by almost every democratic nation in the world, in such unflattering terms as "bogus, a ludicrous parody of the democratic process, a sham, and a fantastic deceit."

UTU: The labels given to the National Convention by other democratic nations are appropriate, but they don't go far enough to accurately describe the truth. From their words and behavior it can be seen that SLORC is not honest. First of all they failed to keep their promise that after the 1990 election they would hand over power to the legitimately elected assembly. They annulled the results of the elections in which of course, we, as the NLD, won a landslide victory. Instead, they imprisoned the large majority of successful NLD candidates who had won seats. Also some died in prison. Then they issued a notification on the eve of our Conference at the Gandhi Hall where we asked them to abide by their promise and convene the parliamentary assembly. That notification, known as 1/90, stated their change of policy regarding the purpose of the National Convention. SLORC's newly ordained purpose was to render assistance to the elected officials. Obviously no one needed their assistance. It was just their way of holding on to power. Under the threat that the party would be dissolved, the leaders of the NLD were compelled to make a written undertaking that they would accept the terms of Notification 1/90. Some reluctantly chose self-exile abroad. Some of the remaining NLD members were arrested, sentenced under various charges and imprisoned. Again, some were tortured while in prison, while many others remain imprisoned to this day. So as you can see this is the basis from which SLORC's National Convention convened.

AC: It's obviously more than a sham...

UTU: Now the present composition of SLORC's National Convention is absurd, it's ridiculous. This thing they call `national convention' is no national convention at all. It's not even a convention. It's more like their Martial Law Court, just called by a different name. There's one way, SLORC's way. It's lawless and it has nothing to do with democratic principles at all. Out of the 700 or so representatives, only about 100 were duly elected. The rest were all hand-picked by SLORC. The Chairman of the Convention is a SLORC general. The panel that oversees the convention are all SLORC appointees. The majority-winning NLD was only allowed to send over eighty representatives, whereas we had won 392 seats. The members were made to discuss six basic principles which were prearranged, already fixed. Out of these, the most dominant one is that the military will take the leading political role in the nation. This is the most blatant violation of democracy and has been done with the intention of establishing eternal, complete hegemony of "military rule" over the civilian administration. This convention is an attempt to enshrine totalitarianism under the veil of democracy.

<u>AC:</u> But what is all this SLORC rhetoric about where they state *ad nauseam* that they are proceeding magnanimously towards a multiparty democracy, when every action they take is completely contrary to that process? Just who are they appealing to when they say this?

<u>UTU:</u> Your guess is as good as mine. Is it foreign business people who may be wanting to invest in Burma? Is it self-deception? Is it that they know that the people of Burma want democracy while assuming the people are so stupid they won't notice SLORC's lies? Are they so out of touch with reality that they actually think that totalitarianism is in fact democracy? Is it just sheer arrogance? We do not know whether they really believe in multi-party democracy or not. It's impossible to know, really. But what we do know, and as you can see, what they do is not in accordance with what they say. From this observation, one can easily state that this is hypocrisy.

<u>AC:</u> In addition to your many qualifications you are also a lawyer. You head the NLD's Legal Aid Committee which aims to support and counsel individuals who have been arbitrarily arrested, tried and imprisoned by the SLORC authorities. A two-part question: would you provide examples of several recent cases of arbitrary arrests by SLORC; and what rights, if any, do the accused have in a SLORC court?

<u>UTU:</u> That's easy. There are no rights and there are many arbitrary arrests. I've already told you about my trial. That's SLORC's idea of justice. Stand. Pass judgment. Hear your sentence. Off to jail.

<u>AC:</u> And it's the same everywhere, with every person, no matter what?

<u>UTU:</u> It can get worse than that. Straight away to jail without any

mock trial whatsoever. Please do understand this, Burma today under SLORC is lawless. There are no human rights. We are under siege!

People can be arrested at any time, for any reason. And it happens. People have been arrested for placing flowers on the tomb of Daw Aung San Suu Kyi's mother. People have been arrested for watching videotapes of her in their own homes. People are arrested all the time for refusing to slave for SLORC in any number of their "forced labor" round-ups. Others who refuse to slave are often chained and handcuffed and forced to watch those who are slaving. This is why Daw Aung San Suu Kyi repeatedly says, "Let the world know that we are prisoners in our own country." She's not exaggerating, it's a prison within a prison.

AC: But actual cases of arbitrary arrests, would you explain some?

UTU: Fine. I'll give you some cases. One man, U Kyi Sang, read a greeting recently at the anniversary celebration of the Karen New Year's Day, with the consent of the Chairman of the Organization Committee for that event. This greeting simply expressed wishes and best compliments, with the hope for prosperity in the coming year. For reading this greeting, U Kyi Sang was arrested and held for twenty-four hours without being remanded before the magistrate. When his case was filed before the judge, no defending counsel was allowed for his defense. After great pressure from the township NLD Legal Aid Group, a defense counsel was permitted. U Kyi Sang died under detention in May 1996 while awaiting sentence.

In another recent case, a schoolteacher let some friends listen to a Voice of America and BBC broadcast in his home. At his trial no defense counsel was allowed. He was sentenced to two years' rigorous imprisonment. His family has been threatened by the authorities so that they do not dare approach our NLD Legal Aid Group for the possibility of an appeal to a higher SLORC court.

Another case from January 1996 is that of one U Thein Tun and two others. They sent a poem of condolence to the family of the late U Tin Maung Win, who was tortured to death while in prison. Our Legal Aid Group for the Rangoon division has already arranged for lawyers for these men but we can't even locate where they are being held. The authorities simply ignore every request.

In another big case which happened in late November 1995, U Win Tin, an NLD Executive Committee member, and twenty-eight others who are all serving long terms in Insein Prison were accused of sending a letter to the United Nations Human Rights Committee, explaining the deplorable living conditions of all the political prisoners. They have now been given additional prison terms of five to twelve years.

AC: Recently the SLORC did a deal with the Burmese citizen Khun Sa, better known to foreigners as the world's most notorious drug lord; supplying 60 percent of the world's heroin, something like 2,000 tons last year alone and having escalated each year since the SLORC coup in 1988.

Now, for the last month SLORC has publicly broadcast on their TV station such scenes as the generals shaking hands with Khun Sa, sitting down to banquets together, giving his 13,000-man army cash to "return to the legal fold" in SLORC-speak. And just recently, it's been reported that he's moved to Rangoon. Would you please clarify the real story?

UTU: What do you want to know, that isn't already obvious to you?

AC: Well, I have my opinion, but I'd like to hear yours.

UTU: As you said, heroin production has increased annually since the time of the SLORC's takeover in 1988. That increase occurred with SLORC at war with Khun Sa. Now that he's at peace with SLORC we'll have to wait and see how much heroin comes out of those areas that are now "fully under" the SLORC's control. One would think that the heroin trade would be completely eradicated now that Khun Sa has "returned to the legal fold." Perhaps SLORC doesn't want the truth of the Khun Sa affair to come out.

AC: There are human rights abuses the world over and equally there are men and women who courageously confront injustices, some with non-violent methods, others through violence. From your unique position may I ask you for your views and advice to other dissidents around the world in their struggles for decency, dignity and basic freedoms in their own countries?

UTU: I have seen first hand that dictatorial systems are controlled by one man. And when so much power is concentrated in the hands of one person, mistrust becomes both lethal and psychotic. Fear and terror become so pervasive in such societies that people lose their sense of dignity and self-worth. They gradually wither away under the immense pressure of fear. So I can confidently say that any form of authoritarian rule, any form of totalitarian rule, any form of government other than one chosen by the people and for the people is in itself detrimental to the welfare of those societies.

Human rights violations and the loss of basic civil liberties are natural when any individual, any leader, is gripped by madness. So for those who're struggling for justice in their own countries, I would advise them first and foremost to do everything within their power to remain calm, level-headed and work systematically towards their aims. I have come to regard non-violence as the best possible means of working towards our aims in Burma. But I live by the Buddha's way, which is my way, so I can't say others should follow my way...but the way of the Buddha is the way of harmlessness. So I can only say what I believe. Non-violence might be the slower road but I do think that in the long run the results are more solid than if one achieves victory through violent means. In this regard, patience and perseverance go hand-in-hand. Anger is an easy response to all forms of cruelty. I have seen this in myself. But with patience I think one can in time cool one's temper and resume practical work.

Finally, I would say that compassion is something we all need more of in the world. Whether you are a human-rights activist or a despotic leader we can always find ways to be more compassionate.

Through our compassion I feel that the world will be a much better place to raise our next generation, and their children. What all of us are struggling for today is a world that is free of fear. In so doing we must try to free our own hearts from fear. Let us all try.

AC: How can the ordinary, common people of the world assist you and the people of Burma in their struggle to achieve genuine democracy?

UTU: I think if someone wishes to assist our cause they can do so in many ways, small or large doesn't really matter. Perhaps the most essential thing is first to reflect upon how precious freedom is to all living creatures. No one likes to feel insecure. No one likes to suffer. All people wish to live happily. In Burma, we are right now struggling for these qualities. If someone wishes to help us in that struggle they can start by refusing to buy any product produced by any company that does business in Burma. Start there, and as they're doing that and feel they want to do more, I do think that the next step will become self-evident.

AC: Sir, should it be that you are re-arrested and imprisoned, held incommunicado, are there any words you would care to leave behind for those who will continue to carry on the struggle for democracy?

UTU: If I am re-arrested, if Daw Aung San Suu Kyi is re-arrested, or if U Kyi Maung is re-arrested, or any other member of our NLD Executive Council, please do remember that it's "you" that must carry on the struggle for democracy and do not depend on us. We will carry on in our own way from prison, but it is you that must join hands and continue the vision until it's successfully achieved. Please do not give up.

AC: Are there any final words you would like to say to the people of the world? Is there anything that you would like to ask them?

UTU: The Buddha has said that good friendship is one of the greatest gifts of life. In our struggle for democracy in Burma we need more good friends—people who cherish freedom and desire to help us gain ours.

CHRONOLOGY

1942: The Japanese invade Burma with the Burma Independence Army under the command of Aung San.

1943: Aung San is Minister of War in independent but Japanese-occupied Burma.

27 March 1945: The Burmese army rises against the Japanese. The Anti-Fascist People's Freedom League (AFPFL) clashes with the British.

19 July 1947: Aung San is assassinated.

4 January 1948: Declaration of independence. Birth of the Union of Burma. U Nu is Prime Minister until 1962; his government faces Communist opposition and rebellion by the Karens.

2 March 1962: General Ne Win seizes power.

20 March 1964: The Burma Socialist Program Party becomes the country's single party.

1974: A new constitution is adopted. Birth of the Socialist Republic of the Union of Burma.

1975: The various ethnic movements join forces to become the Democratic National Front.

1988: Anti-government demonstrations. Martial law is proclaimed and a period of bloody repression follows.

26 August 1988: Aung San Suu Kyi's speech at the Shwedagon Pagoda.

18 September 1988: The State Law and Order Restoration Council (SLORC) is established.

27 September 1988: The National League for Democracy (NLD) is established.

20 July 1989: Aung San Suu Kyi is put under house arrest where she remains until 15 July 1995.

27th May 1990: The general elections are won by the Opposition.

December 1990: The National Coalition Government of the Union of Burma is formed.

Between 1989 and 1996: The SLORC obtains fifteen ceasefires from the rebel groups (Kachins, Mons, Karens and Shans).

April 1996: A United Nations Commission on Human Rights report reveals the existence of torture and forced labor in Burma.

July 1997: Burma becomes member of the Association of South-East Asian Nations (ASEAN).